The Turnout Myth

Matthew,

Thanks for your friendship + wisdom.

Your Boy,

Daun Shaw

The Turnout Myth

*Voting Rates and Partisan Outcomes
in American National Elections*

DARON R. SHAW AND
JOHN R. PETROCIK

OXFORD
UNIVERSITY PRESS

OXFORD
UNIVERSITY PRESS

Oxford University Press is a department of the University of Oxford. It furthers
the University's objective of excellence in research, scholarship, and education
by publishing worldwide. Oxford is a registered trade mark of Oxford University
Press in the UK and certain other countries.

Published in the United States of America by Oxford University Press
198 Madison Avenue, New York, NY 10016, United States of America.

CIP data is on file at the Library of Congress
ISBN 978-0-19-008946-7 (pbk.)
ISBN 978-0-19-008945-0 (hbk.)

1 3 5 7 9 8 6 4 2

Paperback printed by Marquis, Canada
Hardback printed by Bridgeport National Bindery, Inc., United States of America

Sidney Verba died in March 2019. His legacy includes a rich body of writing on the democratic order and generations of his graduate students who were inspired to make democratic politics a focus for their research and teaching. Petrocik, as Verba's graduate student, and Shaw, who studied with Petrocik, both owe something—and Petrocik a great deal—to Verba's commitment to better understanding the views and behavior of citizens, the processes of mass politics, and the institutions of America's democracy. This book does not have the sweep of Sidney's writing, but we think he would appreciate our examination of a topical question about turnout. It is for that reason that we dedicate this book to Sidney Verba, scholar and intellectual with few peers.

Contents

Preface   ix

Acknowledgments   xi

1. If Only Our People Had Turned Out!   1

2. American Voter Turnout: A History and Portrait   15

3. A Theoretical Exploration of Turnout and Voting   35

4. Turnout and Partisan Vote Choice: Over Time and across States and Districts   59

5. Turnout and Partisan Vote Choice: Over Time and within States and Districts   75

6. Congressional District Results: A Further Look   95

7. Why Is the Conventional Wisdom Wrong?   101

8. If Turnout Isn't Driving Election Swings, What Is?   121

9. Some Final Data and Thoughts on the Link between Turnout and Vote Choice   141

Appendices   157

Notes   169

References   179

Index   185

Preface

THIS BOOK WAS written to demonstrate that the belief that turnout has systematic partisan consequences—an idea that is widely embraced by social scientists (including our fellow political scientists), almost every member of the media, both party apparatuses, and our fellow citizens by virtue of what they hear from the media—has a weak empirical foundation. In fact, we will state our conclusion even more strongly: there is no systematic or consistent partisan bias to turnout.

Having made that statement so unequivocally, we will also acknowledge that turnout can be consequential and has figured in the political strategy of many (most?) issue and candidate campaigns. Both authors know of initiatives and referenda where early strategy discussions dealt with *when* the matter should be put on the ballot because of what surveys indicated about the mood of the electorate. When the surveys indicated that citizens with the highest likelihood of voting supported a proposition—while those who were less likely to vote opposed it—proponents sought to place the proposition on the ballot when turnout figured to be low. Primaries of any kind and local municipal elections were always favorites for special issues (taxes, for example) when (a) opinion was divided between those most likely to vote and the others and (b) the core electorate supported the proposal that some group—party leaders, public officials, an ideological interest group, union, or business sector—wanted to pass into law. On the other hand, on-year presidential elections were favored when those supporting the proposition believed—usually because of survey data—that those least likely to vote were the core constituency for the initiative or referendum proposal. Sometimes the strategy worked, and those behind the proposal and the scheduling celebrated their insight and political savvy. On occasions when the scheduling strategy did not produce the desired outcome, the postelection rumination usually wondered why turnout was higher than expected (when it was) or so low (when it was), or, most commonly, the proponents blamed the poor quality of the strategist's machinations or the relevant pollster's work. (It has been our experience that pollsters are often targeted for a disproportionate amount of recrimination.)

Turnout levels are also common aspects of strategies for partisan general elections, with lots of paid consultants selling ideas about how to register more of their most likely supporters and get them to the polls on Election Day. In an election where one side overwhelms the other with a "get out the vote" effort, turnout can make the difference. Usually, however, one side does not overwhelm the other. The election becomes something of an arms race in which GOTV on one side generates comparable efforts by the other. The result is usually a turnout stalemate. Of course, more generous absentee voting provisions and, even better, mail balloting for many or all increases a campaign's emphasis on strategies for getting their prospective supporters to cast a ballot. Despite the huffing and puffing about turnout strategies, however, most elections with a substantial GOTV dimension produce near-stalemates in turnout effects on the vote (albeit with more voters contributing). The results reported here may actually give rise to some of the new techniques that parties and consultants are exploring and exploiting to get "their" supporters to cast a vote.

However, this book is about the dynamics of the current status quo, setting aside approaches (some new, some causing concern) for registering the eligible, getting out the vote, and collecting ballots. We feel compelled to note that we do not have a partisan interest in this debate. We believe that the norms of citizenship expect citizens to vote, and we believe that every citizen has an obligation to vote. High-turnout elections confer a degree of legitimacy on the outcome of the election and all the resulting policy, a legitimacy that is diminished with a low rate of participation. We doubt that very high turnout, on the order of 90 percent or higher, is likely in this country, although it might be achievable with compulsory or nearly compulsory regulations. In reality, such compulsion is unlikely. In the short term, we encourage both parties to promote secure voting. We do not believe that it will work to the disadvantage of either.

Acknowledgments

AS YOU MIGHT imagine, this project owes a great deal to many individuals. We wish to acknowledge the following people for providing useful feedback and, when appropriate, constructive criticism to the authors at public presentations or in private conversations: Joel Aberbach, Bethany Albertson, Ted Brader, Jim Campbell, Lindsay Dun, James Endersby, E. J. Fagan, Nadine Gibson, Colby Humphrey, Vince Hutchings, Gary Jacobson, Stephen Jessee, Bryan Jones, Karen Kaufmann, Cornelia Lawrence, David Leal, Eric McDaniel, Seth McKee, Mark McKenzie, Yul Min Park, Dennis Patterson, Tasha Philpot, Brian Richter, Brian Roberts, Larry Sabato, Tom Schwartz, John Sides, Bat Sparrow, Jamie Stokes, Sean Theriault, Nick Valentino, and Chris Wlezien. Early versions of the argument underlying this book were presented at meetings of UCLA's Center for American Politics and Public Policy, at department seminars of the University of Missouri and Texas Tech University, the annual meeting of the Midwest Political Science Association, the University of Michigan's Interdisciplinary Workshop for American Politics, and the University of Texas's American Politics Speaker Series; these were tremendous opportunities to develop our thinking on critical aspects of the project, and we appreciate the support of these organizations, their staff, and their members. We also wish to acknowledge our partners at Oxford University Press. Most notably, we thank our editor, David McBride, whose enthusiasm and patience toward the project has been invaluable. In addition, our gratitude extends to Holly Mitchell and Liz Davey, whose assistance with the text, tables, figures, and graphs was critical to helping us realize our final vision for the book. Last but not least, we bow in humble thanks to our respective families; without them, this book would not exist.

I

If Only Our People Had Turned Out!

Why Should We Care about Turnout?

Academics often assume that any literate reader will understand the many aspects of their pet topic that make it interesting and important. In our experience, this assumption is frequently unwarranted. In many cases, it is not obvious why a reasonable citizen should care about what we are presenting because it is not obvious why or how the subject matters much to anything they care about, except in a very general way—so general that it does not elicit much engagement.

Turnout and voting, however, are mostly exempt from this disinterest. More than 80 percent of Americans said they were either "very much interested" or "somewhat interested" in each presidential election campaign since 2000.[1] This rate tops 70 percent for midterm congressional elections.[2] Similar size majorities regularly express their concern about the result and agree that voting is an obligation of our citizenship.[3]

The interest has two sources. The first is the drumbeat of exhortation to which most of us were exposed during our early years. Grade school classrooms conduct mock elections. Class content emphasizes the importance of voting for a democratic order that assures personal freedom, with references to wars fought and lives sacrificed to ensure that the citizenry selects its public officials. This kind of political socialization emphasizes America's history of civil rights struggles and conflict against foreign dictatorships. And, of course, the media and public figures remind us on the eve of every election of every citizen's obligation to "get out and vote." Few challenge the urging; even fewer do so publicly; so voting is assured its status as a norm of citizenship. Second, we acquire a motivation to vote because of the attitudes we develop about candidates and the positions they espouse. On the positive side, we vote

The Turnout Myth. Daron R. Shaw and John R. Petrocik, Oxford University Press (2020). © Oxford University Press.
DOI: 10.1093/oso/9780190089450.001.0001

(and believe we should) because of what candidates represent and promise; on the negative side, we turn up at the polls (and believe we should) because of what candidates represent and promise. That is, many of us are trying to assure some policy outcomes, and many of us are trying to prevent some policy outcomes, and some of us evince a bit of both motivations.

The act of voting is the essential precursor to the *outcome* of elections, about which there is often great concern even if diffidence is occasionally attached to voting itself. If too many fail to vote, should we worry about the representativeness of those who did? There are many arguments, buttressed with a mass of proffered evidence, that nonvoters are not a representative sample of the eligible electorate and that election outcomes and policies reflect this distortion. Recent history is helpful for putting this representativeness concern in context.

Representativeness: A 2008 Case Study

The Democrats were politically dominant after the 2008 elections. They controlled the presidency and both houses of Congress; most of the states' governors were Democrats, and twice as many state legislatures had Democratic as opposed to Republican majorities. This commanding control of government after 2008—as President Barack Obama is reported to have said in postinauguration meetings with Republicans—had "consequences," perhaps the most notable being passage of the Affordable Care Act.

One prominent explanation of this Democratic success was that typically abstaining citizens showed up at the polls in unusually large numbers in the 2008 elections (turnout exceeded 62 percent) and expressed the latent predispositions assumed to be common among abstainers by voting overwhelmingly for Democrats.

Why the surge? Excitement about Obama's candidacy is one cause, according to many. Another centerpiece of the 2008 election's turnout story is the Obama campaign's sophisticated get-out-the-vote efforts, which relied heavily on innovative technologies targeting individuals from low-turnout groups (Latinos, younger voters, Asian Americans, and blacks are commonly mentioned) thought to strongly prefer Democrats. The result of the 62 percent turnout—a participation rate exceeded in recent years only by the 64 percent registered in the Kennedy-Nixon contest of 1960—was a Democratic sweep.

The next election (see Table 1.1) seemed to confirm this turnout-driven account. In November 2010, the first election after the 2008 sweep, turnout

Table 1.1 Election Outcomes: 2000–2018

	2000	2002	2004	2006	2008	2010	2012	2014	2016	2018
National turnout rate (percentage)	55.3	40.5	60.7	41.3	62.2	41.7	58.6	36.4	60.0	50.3
Presidency	R	R	R	R	D	D	D	D	R	R
Democrats in the House	213	205	201	233	257	193	201	188	193	235
Senate	50	48	44	51*	59*	53*	54*	46*	49*	47*
Democratic governors	19	23	22	28	28	20	20	19	15	23
State legislatures controlled by										
Democrats	16	16	19	22	27	16	17	11	14	18
Republicans	18	21	20	15	14	25	27	30	32	30
Split control	15	12	10	12	8	8	5	8	3	1

Notes: The Senate totals include two independents who caucused with the Democrats prior to the 2012 election (Lieberman-CT and Sanders-VT) and two who caucused with the Democrats after the 2012 election (Sanders and King-ME). The national turnout rate is calculated by dividing the total number of ballots counted by the number of age-eligible citizens.

declined to less than 42 percent of the eligible electorate and the result was disastrous for the Democrats. The party lost sixty-four House seats and thereby control of Congress. Their Senate majority was reduced and might have been lost except for the particular seats that were contested that year. Republicans took over most of the governorships and most of the state legislatures. Overall, Democrats were almost as much a minority after 2010 as Republicans were after 2008.

How much of this Republican ascendance was driven by a 20-percentage point decline in turnout? A straight pairwise comparison of 2008 with 2010 by anyone looking for evidence that turnout greatly shaped both outcomes might elicit a cry of "Eureka!" A fuller examination of Table 1.1, however, would temper that satisfaction.

Compare 2006 with 2010. Both are off-year elections. Turnout was virtually equal, but a Democratic sweep in 2006 became a Democratic rout in 2010. Throw in the 2014 election and the pattern yields muddiness. Two low-turnout elections produced Republican sweeps; one resulted in a massive

Democratic triumph. The presidential elections of 2012 and 2016, both with high turnout, did nothing to help the Democrats; Republican majorities in Congress and the states actually increased. If we look at election outcomes before 1990—specifically, the years since 1950—Republican presidential candidates have won in relatively high turnout elections (1952), lost in other high-turnout years (1960), and lost in low-turnout years (1976). Moreover the Democrats won control of Congress in every presidential and midterm election from 1954 through 1992 whether turnout was below 40 percent in the midterm year or in the 60-percent range in the presidential election year.

Contrasting particular elections does not improve the credibility of the notion that lower turnout rates necessarily make the outcome unrepresentative of Americans' preferences. Consider the 2000 through 2004 presidential elections. Neither election, each with relatively high turnout (especially in 2004), eroded the Republican majorities that preceded them. In fact, the 2004 contest, which brought out more voters than in 2000, yielded bigger Republican congressional majorities, more GOP governors, and more Republican-controlled state legislatures. The 2018 election produced unusually high turnout (over 50 percent) for a midterm election. It was well below the 60 percent that voted in 2016, however, and while the 2016 contest gave the GOP a 235-seat majority, the 2018 election produced a 235-seat majority for the Democrats. The indisputable fact from these simple data is that there is no axiomatic connection between the turnout rate and the partisan outcome of the election, although large majorities of scholars, media commentators, and average citizens believe otherwise.

This book is about the conventional wisdom that there is a correlation between turnout rates and election outcomes. Figure 1.1 summarizes this belief. It connects the lower turnout rates among those with Democratic inclinations to Democratic losses, especially in midterms and off-years. It also connects lower turnout rates to results that are unrepresentative of citizen preferences but reflect the demography of the party coalitions, electoral structure, and institutions.[4]

The following analysis establishes the underpinnings of the results presented in Table 1.1 and that the conventional expectation in Figure 1.1 is wrong by documenting the absence of a predictable bias associated with turnout and offering a different explanation of elections that is well supported by the data.

Turnout did not have much to do with the ups and downs of Democratic Party success summarized in Table 1.1 or, for that matter, with the Democratic Party's uninterrupted control of Congress from 1954 until 1994. Democratic

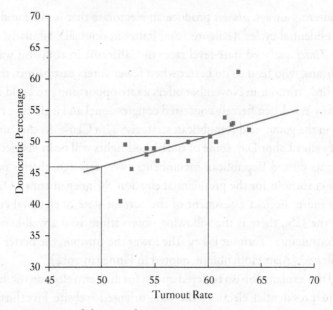

FIGURE 1.1 Turnout and the vote: the expectation.
Source: Simulated data.

presidential candidates, gubernatorial candidates, congressional candidates—indeed Democratic candidates from the top to the bottom of the ballot—have won in high- and low-turnout elections since the end of World War II. There is no observable partisan bias to turnout during the past seventy years. The bottom line seems obvious: although many knowledgeable commentators emphasize what we know about the kinds of people who vote—and do not vote—to assert a connection between turnout rates and election outcomes, the results from Table 1.1 thoroughly undercut such a connection and provide no empirical support for Figure 1.1.

The Turnout Bias

If there is any question about how strongly a turnout bias is assumed among those who follow politics, consider the following response to the "drubbing" (in President Obama's words) of the Democrats in the 2014 elections.[5] One *Washington Monthly* reporter argued, "The biggest single under-discussed aspect of contemporary national politics is the *consistent* disparity in turnout patterns between presidential and non-presidential elections, which now happen to align almost perfectly with party preferences. By that I mean that midterms always, *always* produce an electorate that is older and whiter than presidential cycles" (Kilgore 2012; italics in original). Similarly, the *Los Angeles Times* analyzed state-level races in California in 2014 this way: "For Republicans, who tend to do better when fewer voters cast ballots, the prospect of little turnout in November offers a rare opportunity to build an edge in as many as a dozen fiercely contested congressional and legislative races. 'It puts us in the game,' said Republican strategist Tim Clark. As the campaigns intensify after Labor Day, some of the biggest fights will be in districts where Democrats ousted Republican incumbents two years ago, thanks partly to high voter turnout for the presidential election" (Finnegan 2014). Or, if you prefer a more succinct assessment of the current state of electoral competition in the U.S., there is the following observation from a well-known political consultant: "Turnout is key. The lower the turnout, the better it is for Republicans" (Alan Hoffenblum, quoted in Finnegan 2014).

And this explanation isn't offered up just for midterm election results. After the 2016 presidential election, the data-oriented website FiveThirtyEight. com ran an article entitled "Registered Voters Who Stayed Home Probably Cost Clinton the Election." Analyst Harry Enten, relying on a national poll conducted by SurveyMonkey, offered data like that in Table 1.2 showing that registered voters who did not vote were less Republican-leaning. Enten (2017) wrote:

> Given how closely party identification tracks with vote choice, the disparity in turnout probably cost Clinton the election. SurveyMonkey did not ask non-voters whom they would have voted for, but we do know that more than 90 percent of self-identified Democrats who cast a ballot voted for Clinton and more than 90 percent of Republicans voted for Trump. Moreover, voters who didn't identify with or lean

Table 1.2 Partisan Bias and Turnout in 2016

	Party share among			
	Registered Voters	Those Who Voted	Those Who Did Not Vote	Difference
Democrats	44%	44%	35%	+9
Republicans	43	46	32	+14
Neither	13	10	33	−23

towards either party were slightly more likely to prefer Clinton to Trump. That means that had the non-voters cast a ballot in accordance with their party identification, Clinton's advantage over Trump nationally would have expanded by about 2 to 3 percentage points. That almost certainly would have been enough to flip enough states for her to win the Electoral College.

The intuitive appeal of this argument is perhaps even more obvious if we take the spirit of Enten's analysis and apply it to more groups and more elections. Table 1.3 presents turnout data by party identification, ideology, income, and race for presidential elections from 2004 to 2012 and compares them to turnout data averaged across elections from 1976 through 1992.

Table 1.3 Unequal Turnout and Compositional Effects, in Percentages

	"Baseline"			2000			2004			2008			2012		
	A	B	C	A	B	C	A	B	C	A	B	C	A	B	C
Democrat	50	73	50	47	85	46	52	78	52	49	77	49	47	79	49
Independent	14	52	9	9	50	6	9	54	6	10	43	6	14	48	9
Republican	37	79	41	44	93	48	39	86	42	42	82	45	40	82	43
Liberal	26	78	25	25	76	25	34	80	36	27	80	27	37	80	37
Moderate	32	75	31	32	71	29	14	66	11	31	72	28	14	70	13
Conservative	42	82	44	43	80	46	52	79	53	42	85	45	49	80	50
Lowest 1/3 income	32	59	27	35	63	28	32	68	28	35	62	28	31	63	26
Middle 1/3 income	34	73	34	31	82	33	31	78	31	31	80	33	33	77	34
Top 1/3 income	34	84	39	34	90	39	36	86	40	34	88	40	36	86	40
White	81	74	84	75	80	79	72	79	73	71	78	73	70	79	72
African American	11	65	10	12	71	11	12	79	12	12	82	13	11	77	11
Latino	6	61	5	8	61	6	12	67	10	11	62	8	12	65	10
Other	3	65	2	5	66	4	4	66	5	6	60	5	8	67	7

A: The total size of the group in the category.

B: The self-reported turnout rate for the group.

C: The group's share of the electorate, with turnout factored in.

These "baseline" elections are offered as a comparison point because much of the conventional wisdom about turnout developed during this time.

Consider just the first three columns, "The Baseline." Column A reports the relative size of the groups in the voter-eligible population during these years; column B reports their turnout rate; column C reports the contribution of each group to the voting electorate. Stated differently, column B adjusts column A for the turnout rate of the group, which results in column C—the electorate. The result? While Democrats outnumbered Republicans by 50 to 37 percent, their differential turnout (79 percent for Republicans and 73 percent for Democrats) reduced the Democratic advantage in these baseline elections by 4 percentage points. There is a similar effect for conservatives compared to liberals, upper-income compared to lower-income voters, and whites compared to other racial/ethnic groups. The bottom line is that differential turnout rates reduced the share of voters who are Democrats, liberals, lower income, and ethnic minorities while increasing the share of the electorate that is Republican, upper income, conservative, and white.

Similarly, the turnout *differences* among these groups seem to have increased the electoral advantage of Republicans, conservatives, upper-income groups, and whites in in the later elections (2004 through 2012 in the table)—even though overall turnout increased. The central finding is that the higher turnout rates of upscale, white, conservative, and Republican citizens tend to magnify, albeit slightly, their share of the electorate compared to their share of the population. The question, then, is whether this lends merit to two of the commentariat's beliefs. The first is that higher turnout will compensate for the persisting Republican advantage of turnout differences among the groups, bringing into the polling places enough left-leaning marginal voters to tip elections to the Democrats. The second belief, rarely explicitly stated, is that the link between demographic traits and political orientation is so strong that increases in the share of voters from demographic groups associated with support for the Democrats produce proportionate increases in Democratic support. The first belief is not well supported even by the data presented thus far. The second belief ignores the fact that marginal voters—those who do not vote regularly—are particular susceptible to the short-term forces in the election. This responsiveness to issues and personalities makes them more likely than the median voter to shift between the parties, supporting Republican candidates much more than our stereotypes of voters have them doing.

But partisan loyalty in the polling place—defection rates from the other perspective—are considered less than turnout. For example, in 2010 and 2014 (especially in 2014, simply because turnout was so low that year) the turnout bias was commonly cited as the reason for midterm losses for the Democrats. A few quotes exemplify the pervasiveness of this interpretation. In April 2014, President Obama weighed in on the looming midterm elections: "Our voters are younger, more unmarried women, more African-American and Latino voters. They get excited about general elections; they don't get as excited about midterm elections. We have this congenital disease, which is in midterm elections we don't vote at the same rates" (quoted in Blake 2014). The evening after the November 5 loss, U.S. House Minority Leader Nancy Pelosi (D-CA) focused her attention on turnout during a seventy-five-minute conference call with fellow Democratic caucus members: "Next year [2015] has to be the year to expand the universe of people who vote. I'm concerned that eligible voters did not vote in the election this year" (quoted in Lillis 2014).

The "we didn't get our voters to the polls" excuse is bipartisan, uttered by losing Democratic *and* Republican campaigns. Rare is the losing political candidate who does not offer this time-honored chestnut as a postelection snack. Indeed both Mitt Romney and John McCain mentioned lackluster turnout of conservative voters in postmortems of their failed presidential bids. But in the wake of Obama's victories in 2008 and 2012 and the Democratic Party's losses in 2010 and 2014, many have accepted the idea that turnout bias *explains* variation in election outcomes: Democrats win when turnout is higher but lose when it is lower. Such conclusions overlook elections like 2006, when the conventionally low midterm turnout did not stop a Democratic sweep.

Of course, it isn't just journalists and candidates who have promulgated the turnout bias thesis. Social scientists have contributed to the conventional wisdom that there is a turnout bias in contemporary U.S. (and other countries') elections. As we discuss in greater detail in the coming chapters, researchers such as Piven and Cloward (1988), Lijphart (1997), Hansford and Gomez (2010), and Fraga (2018) have written extensively and argued forcefully that our intuition with respect to increased turnout benefiting the Democrats is, in essence, correct. In the abstract to their 2010 article in the *American Political Science Review*, Hansford and Gomez write, "The effect of variation in turnout on electoral outcomes is quite meaningful. . . . Variation in turnout significantly affects vote shares at the county, national, and Electoral College levels" (268).

Despite the prominence of those backing the conventional wisdom, not everyone has embraced this argument. In addition to several important academic studies—which we discuss in chapter 3—some journalists have pushed back. Notably, Nate Cohn, a political reporter for the *New York Times*, questioned the axiomatic relationship between turnout and partisan outcomes after the

2014 election: "Low Democratic voter turnout has been blamed for the decisive Republican victory in Tuesday's midterm elections. It has quickly become the scapegoat, even though the Democrats invested millions of dollars in an expansive effort to persuade young and nonwhite voters who do not usually participate in midterm election to head to the polls. . . . But Democrats also lost in states where turnout surpassed 2010" (Cohn 2014).

Cohn made this same argument after the 2016 elections. Relying on an analysis of Upshot/Siena polling data and voter file data from Florida, North Carolina, and Pennsylvania, he wrote:

> In the aftermath of the 2016 presidential election, many analysts suggested that Hillary Clinton lost to Donald J. Trump because of poor Democratic turnout. Months later, it is clear that the turnout was only modestly better for Mr. Trump than expected. To the extent Democratic turnout was weak, it was mainly among black voters. Even there, the scale of Democratic weakness has been exaggerated. Instead, it's clear that large numbers of white, working-class voters shifted from the Democrats to Mr. Trump. Over all, almost one in four of President Obama's 2012 white working-class supporters defected from the Democrats in 2016, either supporting Mr. Trump or voting for a third-party candidate. (Cohn 2017)

Cohn's analysis shows that the 2016 electorate wasn't all that different from what he and others had forecast and that Trump's surprising showing was largely a function of doing better than expected with voters who showed up at the polls. Loyalty among Republican identifiers and defection among Democrats shaped the 2016 outcome. Cohn emphasizes the fluctuations in vote choice among certain groups—especially working-class whites whose partisanship is tilted Democratic—as an explanation for Trump's victory in 2016. The specific observation about the Democrats doing poorly among white working-class voters has been echoed by others, and not just about 2016. For example, after the 2014 midterm elections John Judis (2014) of the *New Republic* pointed out that the Democrats' inability to win over white, working-class voters in recent midterms is at least as important as lower turnout among core Democratic constituencies when it comes to explaining their losses. Michael Barone has also made this point repeatedly in the bi-annual volume *The Almanac of American Politics*. And, as we detail later, a number of political scientists have added to the debate by calling into question the broader connection between turnout and partisan vote choice. But these defection analyses have been eclipsed by a story of elections emphasizing turnout, even as the turnout explanations rely mostly on supposition.

What we see, then, is *some* evidence and a great deal of speculation that increased turnout in a specific election might have helped the Democrats. But there is also skepticism (which, again, we get to in the coming chapters) from those who have systematically assessed the relationship and its significance as an explanation for election *outcomes*. Many things do not add up to an easy confirmation of the widespread beliefs that turnout is biased and that low turnout hurts the Democrats. It is true that Republicans vote more heavily, that conservatives vote more heavily, that upscale voters vote more heavily, and that whites vote more heavily. But in modern U.S. elections these differences almost never tip the balance in favor of the GOP. As we see in Table 1.3, from 1976 through 2016 Democratic-identified voters were more numerous than Republican identifiers in every election except 2004. Despite this, many scholars and even more commentators and journalists continue to believe that there is a strong relationship between turnout and election outcomes and that higher turnout improves the prospects for a Democratic victory.

Our goal in this project is to clarify, theoretically and empirically, the relationship between turnout and election results. We are interested in the extent to which variation in turnout explains who wins national and statewide elections in the U.S. Personally we believe that high turnout is a desirable goal in a democratic political order because it enhances the legitimacy of all governmental activity. However, our analysis of the data has led us to the conclusion that, at least within the range of turnout variation that we experience in this country, there is no systematic link between election outcomes and turnout levels. Moreover, we think almost six decades of research on voting and voters has laid a foundation for understanding why the two are disconnected.

The Plan for the Book

As political scientists, our goal is to present and test explanations of important political phenomena. Toward this end, we begin by exploring what we know (and don't know) about turnout and voting in the U.S. In chapter 2 we describe some of the basic features of turnout in the U.S., discussing historical patterns and trends as well as offering some comparative data. The goal is to provide up-to-date, baseline information about voting so that our readers can understand and assess our subsequent comments and analyses. Cliché though it may be, we think that a common, agreed-upon base of knowledge is an essential aspect of scholarship.

In chapter 3 we present an overview of the literature on both electoral outcomes and turnout; the research on each is voluminous, but neither has been well-connected to the other. Even though the two halves of the act of voting are usually separated for analysis, there have been several studies that examine the partisan implications of turnout variation. These analyses have produced no consensus; some recent academic studies featuring different modeling techniques suggest there may be a connection between lower turnout and Democratic electoral losses, while others find little or no relationship. Against the backdrop of this scholarly ambiguity, the ascendance of the Obama coalition—with its emphasis on undermobilized groups such as young people, Latinos, and Asians—has lent credence to the more impressionistic assumptions of journalists and practitioners about a turnout bias.

In chapter 4 we examine the simple aggregate relationship between turnout and partisan vote choice across a time series. Referencing state- and district-level election data over the span of five decades, we look at the relationship between turnout and vote choice in presidential, U.S. Senate, U.S. House, and gubernatorial elections. The data suggest a mostly random relationship between turnout and partisan vote share.

Chapter 5 takes an even more granular look at the connection between turnout and vote choice, focusing on how turnout influences partisan vote choice *within* election units over time, controlling for other factors that might conceivably drive the vote. Responding to recent studies suggesting a partisan bias to turnout based on local voting results, we present evidence from county elections going back to the 1940s. Our data not only call into question the existence of a pro-Democratic bias to turnout; they suggest a small but consistent bias in the opposite direction. To corroborate this result, we examine district-level results from U.S. House races across the past two decades. Once again we find little evidence of any systematic relationship between increased turnout and greater Democratic vote share.

In chapter 6 we offer another examination of the relationship between turnout and partisan vote choice in congressional elections. This time, however, we focus on the most recent elections (from 2000 to 2016) and consider more particularly other factors that vary at the congressional district level, such as race, ethnicity, and geographic location (urban vs. rural). We do all this within the context of testing the "surge and decline" theory of presidential and midterm elections. Results from regression analyses indicate that the magnitude of the partisan vote shift from the previous election is quite independent of the size of the attendant turnout surge or decline.

With our aggregate data showing little relationship between turnout and partisan vote choice, in chapter 7 we offer a theoretical understanding of voting that emphasizes the role of interest and engagement on turnout. Drawing on the seminal work of scholars such as Angus Campbell and Donald Stokes, we posit that "peripheral" voters (those who show up for some elections but miss many others) are less engaged, less interested, and less involved in politics and that they are disproportionately likely to respond to extant circumstances when thinking about or acting in politics. As such, they are less latent partisans than they are bandwagon fans; they blow with the political wind, padding the margins of candidates advantaged by current conditions, which we refer to as "short-term forces." We therefore expect that turnout rates matter, but that higher turnout will help whichever side benefits from what is going on, that is, by the direction of the short-term forces.

Building on the theoretical perspective offered in chapter 7, in chapter 8 we explore our alternative explanations for election outcomes. If turnout doesn't explain Democratic losses in recent midterm elections, what does? During this exploration, we present and test aggregate-level theories of voting, relying on cross-time data from states and districts. We estimate the impact of incumbent approval, economic performance, and campaign spending on aggregate vote choice, along with turnout, to demonstrate the relative power of these variables for explaining the vote. The results show that turnout is minimally correlated with vote choice compared to other variables that capture political context or electoral differences.

Chapter 9 concludes this volume, offering an in-depth look at aspects of the relationship between turnout and vote choice that we think deserve a little more scrutiny. We consider the potential effect of party identification distributions and statewide electoral competitiveness on the turnout–vote choice relationship, the causal relationship between turnout and voting, and how polarization plays into all this. We then venture some predictions about the next few elections, using our theories of surge and decline to inform what we might expect in upcoming midterm and presidential contests. Finally, bearing in mind our results, we question the ferocity with which the Republicans and Democrats contest every proposed change in the laws and regulations regarding eligibility, registration, and turnout. There may be very good reasons to argue over these matters, but partisan advantage is not one of them.

These chapters—and the data and arguments they hold—seek to address an important aspect of democratic functioning in the U.S. The overall goal of this book is to answer a single question: How does turnout affect electoral outcomes? The implications of our answer, however, promise to be much broader and more consequential. In the first two decades of the new millennium, U.S. election results have varied considerably despite partisan polarization. Yet political scientists have not offered much instruction to the news media or the public about *why* this has happened. By examining the role of turnout in shaping partisan election outcomes, we seek to improve our understanding of what makes the American voter tick. In so doing, we just might improve the content and quality of U.S. campaigns.

2

American Voter Turnout

A HISTORY AND PORTRAIT

THE UNITED STATES is the world's first nation that selected its political leadership based on the preferences of ordinary citizens. The size of this electorate has produced discussion, debate, and sometimes bitter argument since the nation's founding. The architects of the Articles of Confederation and the Constitution left the decision about who was eligible to vote to the governments of the individual states, resulting in considerable variability in the definition of eligibility. Moreover, there were different perspectives about who and what should be represented in the state and national legislatures: voters, or places and groups of people. The Constitutional Convention of 1787 was even conflicted over whether voters in the nation or voters within the states needed to be the frame of reference. Who could vote and how they would do so were straightforward for office seekers within the states but convoluted at the national level. The Constitution provided for congressional districts that tallied voters (albeit within state-based districts). The Senate was elected by state legislators, in a compromise that acknowledged that many thought of the nation as a union of states—the United States—that required representation and a voice. Finally, the design created an Electoral College that aggregated votes within states to produce an intermediate-level "electorate" to cast the votes that elected the president, a decision that has produced presidents (in the elections of 1824, 1876, 1888, 2000, and 2016) with less than a plurality of the popular vote.

Concerns too numerous to list or tally shaped this, but suffice it to say that although "the people" were uniformly seen as the source of legitimacy in the design of the nation's political order, there was also no small concern about the threat of "mobocracy" to the country. The *Federalist Papers*, which told

The Turnout Myth. Daron R. Shaw and John R. Petrocik, Oxford University Press (2020). © Oxford University Press.
DOI: 10.1093/oso/9780190089450.001.0001

readers what to think about the proposed Constitution and why it deserved ratification, deal with this concern from several perspectives. State-imposed limitations of the franchise to men who held property taxed at a specified amount was the first formula to guard against perceived dangers to democracy embedded within the franchise. The limitation to men reflected cultural norms that did not consider women appropriate participants. Of course, neither blacks nor Native Americans, the first people to arrive on the continent, were usually included among potentially eligible voters. Briefly, the vote was trusted to white male property holders at the founding, yielding a relatively small potential electorate. Eligibility restrictions have been under challenge ever since.

The first restriction to fall was the property requirement, usually expressed as an amount of tax paid on one's land and possessions. The tax requirements were reduced and finally repealed almost everywhere as popular opinion embraced the idea of universal white male suffrage. The notion that every white man deserved the right to vote developed quickly, and the populism embedded in Jacksonian Democracy and the Second American Party System accelerated the change. Indeed, while Jackson's "everyman" politics certainly reflected and contributed to increased electoral participation, the Second Party System was probably the bigger contributor.

Second Party System politics is a study in mutual causation. Electorally oriented party organizations, articulated down to the grassroots, developed to mobilize and deliver newly eligible voters. As more voters were created, a more electorally oriented party structure was necessary, which then (of course) worked ever harder to get potential voters to the polls. The electoral focus was so consuming that it helped to set the character of American party politics. The system became and has largely remained an electoral party system, focused on winning elections rather than providing ideology for voters or programmatic alternatives in government.

U.S. Turnout Rates: The Long View

Between 1824, when Andrew Jackson was defeated, despite winning a plurality of the popular vote, and 1828 turnout surged from an estimated 24 percent of the eligible electorate to almost 60 percent (Figure 2.1). It plateaued in the 55 to 60 percent range for the next couple of elections, before surging to almost 80 percent in 1844, and then oscillating in the 75 to 80 percent range for the remainder of the nineteenth century. As Figure 2.1 indicates, and as

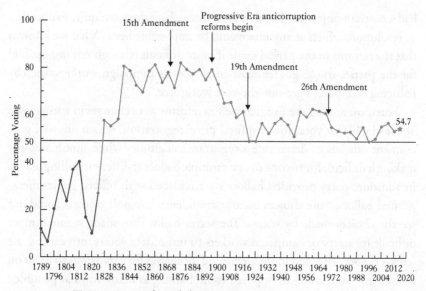

FIGURE 2.1 Turnout in presidential elections, 1824–2016.

we explore in this chapter, one perplexing historical irony is that major electoral reforms since the Second Party System have generally had the effect of decreasing turnout in U.S. elections.

Consider, for example, the constitutional amendments passed in the aftermath of the Civil War. The immediate aggregate effect of the Fifteenth Amendment was a decline in turnout for the 1872 election, an increase for the 1876 election, and then a steeper decline thereafter. The post-1876 drop should not occasion too much surprise since the amendment increased the number of eligible voters—millions of freed slaves—but provided no sustained mechanism to ensure they were able to vote. Black turnout was virtually nil throughout the South—the Fifteenth Amendment notwithstanding—because states controlled electoral eligibility and southern states found many ways to disqualify blacks (poll taxes, literacy tests, and more than a little physical intimidation) after the end of Reconstruction in 1876.

Other institutions and practices similarly failed to compensate for well-intended changes in the law. A quick review of the data demonstrates that turnout actually declined (though somewhat irregularly) through the elections of the late nineteenth century despite the vaunted mobilization efforts of the parties. After 1900 it dropped even more dramatically as the Progressive Era reforms took hold throughout the country. There is disagreement among political scientists about whether the Progressive Era reforms had a partisan objective. The details of that debate do not require explication or resolution, which at any rate would be impossible here. What we know is that the reforms of the period made it more difficult (though not impossible) for the parties to use government employees as campaign workers, thereby reducing each party's get-out-the-vote workforce.

Foremost among the Progressive Era reforms were changes in voting laws. To be eligible to vote now required prior registration, which allowed government officials to determine a registrant's eligibility while simultaneously making it difficult for anyone to cast multiple ballots at different polling places. In addition, party-provided ballots were replaced with official government-printed ballots. Vote choices became confidential, so poll workers could not see the choices made by voters. The secret ballot thus made it much more difficult for party or campaign workers to intimidate voters into casting the "correct" vote. This development created incentives for campaigns to focus on mobilizing "sure" votes as opposed to mobilizing as many votes as possible.[1] Collectively these changes played some role in the decline in the turnout rate.

Additional constitutional changes also had a negative impact on the overall turnout rate (if not on the number of voters). The Nineteenth Amendment extended the franchise to women, and the Twenty-Sixth reduced the voting age to eighteen years. Both initially depressed the turnout rate. The Nineteenth Amendment became effective just prior to the 1920 election, but while it enfranchised all women, only a minority showed up at the polls. Many believe this was because a significant fraction of these newly eligible women embraced traditional gender roles that did not include voting. Middle-class and upscale women quickly availed themselves of the opportunity to vote, but first- and even second-generation immigrant women and others in subcultures that were more traditional took some time to embrace this new option. The result, as was the case with the Fifteenth Amendment, was to increase the denominator (the pool of eligible voters) without commensurately increasing the numerator (people casting ballots); thus the turnout *rate* declined.

The Twenty-Sixth Amendment was passed in 1970 and had a similar effect on the national turnout rate. Prior to the amendment, voters between twenty-one and thirty years of age voted at rates about 20 percentage points below the overall turnout rate and nearly 40 points below the turnout of those over sixty years old. Adding eighteen- through twenty-year-olds to the young cohort increased the fraction of the electorate with the lowest probability of voting, which resulted in an overall turnout rate decline. This cohort, barely

3 percent of the eligible electorate, is estimated to have contributed more than 50 percent of the decline in turnout between 1968 and 1972.

The More Recent Past

The number of voters has increased almost monotonically over the past seventy years, as Figure 2.2 shows, largely through population growth but also due to a more facilitating political and legal environment (more on this later). The turnout rate, however, has gone up and down, as the number of voters has only somewhat kept pace with the increased number of eligible voters. More specifically, turnout rates increased in the late 1940s, then continued to hover around the 60 percent range from 1952 through 1960. (The 1960 election produced the highest turnout in the past seventy years.) The rate then declined (unevenly) from 1960 until 1996, with a notable spike for the 1992 election, which featured a spirited three-way presidential race. Beginning in 2000, turnout rates increased through the 2008 contest, after which they declined slightly in 2012 and then rose again slightly in 2016. Overall, however, elections since 1996 produced a high turnout plateau, one roughly equal to that of the 1950s.

Note that Figure 2.2 graphs two estimates of the turnout rate from 1948 through 2016. The first is based on the voting-age population (VAP), which relies on the total number of individuals who are at least eighteen years of age as the denominator (twenty-one prior to 1972). The second is based on

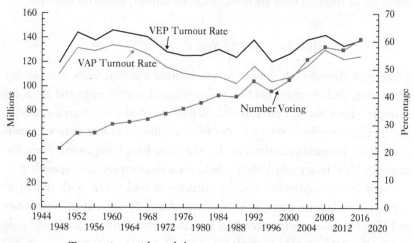

FIGURE 2.2 Turnout in presidential elections, 1948–2016.

the voter-eligible population (VEP), which uses as the denominator the total number of citizens who are eighteen and older (again, age twenty-one prior to 1972) and not institutionalized.[2] Put another way, the VEP adjusts the age-eligible population by subtracting (a) the number of noncitizens, (b) the number who are institutionalized, and (c) the number who are ineligible according to each state's criminal laws.

Comparing this adjusted potential electorate to the number who vote in the election produces the VEP's turnout rate: the rate among eligible voters. The VEP provides a more sensible estimate of turnout than the VAP, which regards anyone over the defined minimum age as a potential voter even though many cannot vote.[3] Turnout based on the VEP, as Figure 2.2 demonstrates, has hovered around 60 percent since 2000; it was a little above in 2008 and a little below in 2012. The VEP turnout rate is between 2 to 5 points higher than that associated with the VAP, with the largest difference occurring for elections later in the figure (i.e., 1980 and after), a difference mostly reflecting the increasing fraction of the population who are noncitizen immigrants and unable to vote.

Although the VEP provides the best estimate of how many eligible voters turned out, the VAP is often used to study turnout over an extended period (Figure 2.1 is based on the VAP, for example) because it is frequently not possible to determine the number of eligible citizens among all those who were of the minimum voting age. Turnout rates based on the VEP, however, are preferable because they are based on an accurate count of who was really a potential voter under the law. The resulting comparisons among countries, among elections, or through time are therefore more sensibly based on the VEP.

The On-Year/Off-Year Cycle of Turnout

Turnout is considerably higher in presidential election years than at any other time, and elections held in odd-numbered years—2017 and 2019, for example—have the lowest turnout. When the odd-year elections are for city or country offices, turnout rates often decline to as low as 10 to 15 percent.[4] Even statewide elections in the odd years have low turnout rates. For example, New Jersey and Virginia hold their election for state-specific government offices—governor and legislature—in odd years; both did so in 2017. Statewide VEP turnout in 2016 was about 66 percent in New Jersey and Virginia, but in 2017 fewer than 36 percent voted in New Jersey and only 43 percent cast ballots in Virginia.

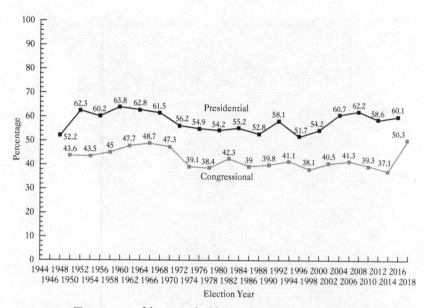

FIGURE 2.3 Turnout rate of the voter-eligible population, national elections, 1948–2018.

Turnout for national midterm elections (the even-numbered years between presidential elections) runs between 15 and 20 percentage points below presidential election turnout (see Figure 2.3). The major influence that shapes the difference is a lower level of voter interest. Presidential elections involve billion-dollar campaigns that produce traditional television commercials and yard signs and frequent (some might say constant) social media and email messages about the campaign, the candidates, and the issues. News coverage and the commentariat amplify everything, giving an additional impulse to the median voter's interest and a motivation to vote among individuals who are generally only mildly attentive to politics and government. Presidential contests strike Americans as consequential; they pay more attention to them, and they are more motivated to vote in them.

All this activity declines greatly in the off-years, so that what you get is a perfect storm—less media attention, lower voter interest, and less effort by the campaigns—of events that do little to stimulate voter interest in the election, resulting in lower turnout. Moreover, Senate and House incumbents are usually odds-on favorites to win, which has the effect of reducing efforts by the challenging candidates and party to mobilize voters for what they see as a nearly hopeless effort.

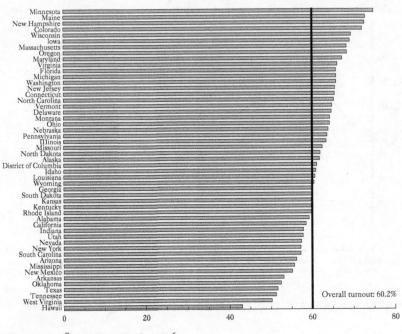

FIGURE 2.4 State turnout rates, 2016.

Turnout among the States

Turnout does not simply vary by the on-year/off-year cycle. There is also variance among the states with respect to turnout in presidential, congressional, and gubernatorial elections (see Figure 2.4). Minnesota was at the top of the turnout rankings in 2016, closely followed by Maine, New Hampshire, and Colorado. Hawaii was noticeably the lowest. The rank order of the states by turnout changes a bit from election to election, but the order in one election is very similar to the ones before and after it. Some states seem to have a tradition of high turnout; other states less so. And those participation norms that arise from those traditions do not appreciably change over short periods. Also, the legal environment of the states regarding registration, absentee voting, early voting, the acceptance of provisional ballots, and mail balloting is quite stable. In addition, voter mobilization efforts and techniques tend to persist at whatever level is typical for a given state. Collectively these factors induce stability in the turnout rates. We can be confident that most of the ten states at the top of the turnout ranking in 2016 will also be in (or near) the top ten for the next several election cycles, while those at the bottom in 2016 will also be among the low turnout states in 2020 and beyond. Drastic short-term changes in the institutions, practices, and orientations of the electorate of a state are possible, but unlikely.

Regional Variation in Turnout

A traditional observation about American elections is that turnout is (and has been, historically) much lower in the southern states. Figures 2.5A and 2.5B document this gap, focusing on turnout differentials in presidential and congressional elections. North-south differences were considerable at the outset of the time series, in the 1940s. They diminished noticeably during the 1960s, however, and may have declined even further in the past few election cycles. Two simultaneous changes are the probable cause.

The first influence was the effective enfranchisement of African Americans because of the civil rights movement during the 1960s. Voting rights and equal treatment in public accommodations were the centerpieces of protest, and the passage of laws that invalidated discrimination against blacks in both areas produced dramatically higher levels of black turnout and, therefore, turnout overall.

Coinciding with the civil rights movement was the realignment of party allegiance throughout the old Confederacy. Democrats had outnumbered Republicans everywhere and without interruption in the South since the end of Reconstruction in 1876. Democrats won almost all gubernatorial, congressional, and state legislative races, while Democratic presidential candidates swept the "Solid South" in election after election. There were, to be sure, occasional bumps in the road for unusual candidates, such as Al Smith in 1928 and Adlai Stevenson in 1952. But from 1876 until 1964 a solid wall of Democratic dominance continued to the lowest level of every southern state's political order. Democrats were often the only political party providing members to city and county councils, mayor's offices, and official legal positions (prosecuting and municipal attorneys, as well as sheriffs). General election results were foregone conclusions; the Democrat always won, so there was not a lot of motivation to vote once the candidates were nominated. (Oftentimes no GOP nominee even appeared on the ballot.) Rather, the general election result was determined by the Democratic primary, where turnout frequently exceeded general election turnout.

The civil rights movement, the politics of the counterculture in the late 1960s, and divisions over the Vietnam War undid the Solid South. Inexorably, white southerners began to take the side of the national Republicans on these and related issues. By the start of the 1980s, white southerners were equally divided in their party preference, general elections had become decisive, and different parties, candidates, and interest groups (most notably African Americans) had a reason to get their supporters in southern states to the polls. Turnout began to increase and has since come close to turnout rates in the North.

Today the remaining north-south gap in turnout is mostly a reflection of general turnout influences. Lower education levels in the region and a higher

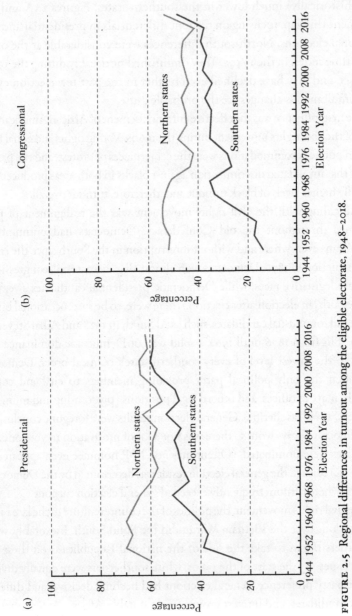

FIGURE 2.5 Regional differences in turnout among the eligible electorate, 1948–2018.

(a) Presidential

(b) Congressional

Northern states

Southern states

Percentage

Election Year

1944 1952 1960 1968 1976 1984 1992 2000 2008 2016

rate of habitual nonvoting may be in play here. The ethnic/racial composition of the population may play some role as well. Black Americans are a larger share of the South's population and have lower education levels that are associated with less political participation (see Figures 2.6 and 2.7).[5] Collectively these predispositions and demographic differences between the regions may be supporting the regional turnout gap that persists to this day. Overall, however, the regional difference in turnout rates is vastly smaller than it was in the past.

Who Votes?

Attitudes and predispositions are the proximate influences motivating turnout, and its strongest correlates. For example, an individual who is a strong party identifier is the most likely to vote; independents are the least likely. Those with strong opinions on public issues are more likely to vote than their counterparts with weakly held issue preferences. However, there are also persistent and consistent demographic predictors of turnout. Specifically, women are slightly more likely to vote, and government employees have higher than average turnout rates, as do members of unions or trade associations. Married people are relatively more likely to vote, the explanation being their stake in the community—owning a home, having kids in the public schools, and so forth— which fosters participatory skills and encourages voting.

The religiously observant are also more consistent voters than those who are not religiously observant, and turnout differences persist among religious denominations. Jews have the highest turnout rate, well ahead of Catholics, who, in turn, lead Protestants (except among Hispanics). Interestingly, black Americans who report no religious affiliation are notably more likely to vote than church-going African Americans, despite a conventional wisdom about the role of the black church in promoting black political activity.[6]

The effect of religious observance on voting has been attributed to the generalized civic skills and orientations that emerge through involvement in church, synagogue, or temple activity (Verba, Schlozman, and Brady 1995). Some such effect is possible, but it is also likely that the moral worldview of the religiously observant promotes norms of good citizenship that in turn motivate participation in elections, which our political culture also defines as an essential activity for citizens. Resolving these competing explanations requires further research, but survey data clearly demonstrate that the sense of duty and obligation associated with church attendance is related to the sense of duty and obligation associated with voting.[7]

The consensus among political scientists is that there are few important turnout differences stemming from sexual orientation, occupation, veteran status, or residential location (urban, suburban, ex-urban, and rural).[8] It seems that the more distant these characteristics are from other aspects of civic participation, the less they matter for turnout.

Among all the different demographic characteristics, three stand out for having the most powerful and consistent influence on getting Americans to the polls:

- Race/ethnicity. Whites have the highest turnout rate; black turnout trails white turnout by a couple of percentage points; Hispanics and other ethnic groups (Asians, most prominently) have the lowest turnout rates.
- Education. Those with more years of formal education turn out at higher rates than those with fewer years of schooling.
- Age. Younger voters are the least likely to turn out for any given election. Those at or older than middle age have the highest turnout rates.

Race/Ethnicity

Figure 2.6 profiles racial and ethnic differences in turnout from 1988 through 2016.[9] The stratification of voting rates by race/ethnicity is familiar: whites

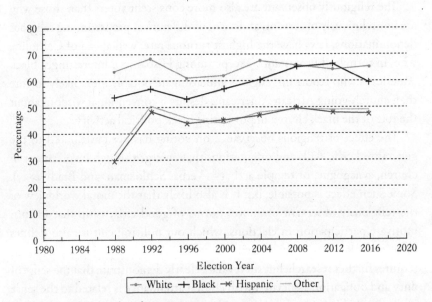

FIGURE 2.6 Turnout by ethnicity, 1988–2016.

have the highest turnout, followed by blacks, with all other ethnic groups showing a markedly lower likelihood of voting. The differences are consistent over the thirty years graphed in the figure, although there is some interesting variation in recent elections. Black turnout surged in 2008 and again in 2012; white turnout sagged in 2012; and black turnout dropped significantly in 2016—all movements that demonstrate the influence of social identities and political context on voters (more on this later). In general, however, the figure displays an important set of facts about ethnic differences in turnout that are largely independent of education, age, employment, gender, or religiosity.

Education

The number of years of a citizen's formal schooling is consistently one of the more effective predictors of political behavior in the American electorate. Political participation and especially voting is one of those consistently predicted behaviors, independent of virtually everything else. Figure 2.7 plots the zero-order relationship between years in school and voting participation for elections from 1988 through 2016.

The gap in turnout between the four education levels in the figure is a stable 10 to 15 percentage points, with the smallest gap separating the two highest educational strata (college-educated versus postgraduates), and the

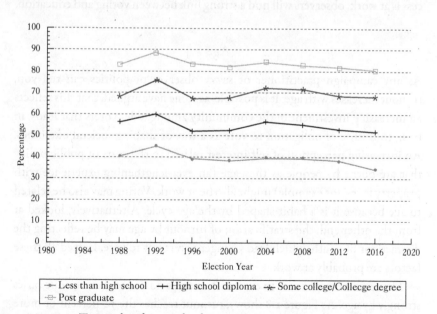

FIGURE 2.7 Turnout by education level, 1988–2016.

largest gaps between those with some college education and those who have completed high school, and those who have completed high school compared to those who did not.

A couple of social processes explain this strong and persistent educational effect.[10] One is simple political socialization: the more time one spends in an educational environment, the more one is exposed to the society's norms. In the U.S. one of those norms is the obligation to vote (which most Americans do view as an obligation; see chapter 1). We teach it with mock elections in the primary grades and reinforce it through a variety of mechanisms all the way through university, where campuses are brimming with political groups who try to mobilize the student vote at election time. There may also be a selection effect behind some of the education difference; that is, while postsecondary education is widely available to virtually every segment of the society, those from the middle class, who are likely to have well-educated parents, are raised in an environment in which voting is taught as a desirable behavior. If this linkage exists, education may simply reinforce social class norms about voting that precede educational attainment. In other words, education may be an intermediate variable that is as much an expression of social class as it is of institutional socialization.

It is difficult to resolve the causal dilemma of how much educational attainment promotes voting participation. At the end of the day, whatever process is at work, observers will find a strong link between voting and education.

Age

As any campaign practitioner or savvy observer of politics can tell you, turnout increases with age. It is possible, as some have argued, that this reflects an increasing investment in the community among older voters that leads, in turn, to a sense of obligation to vote as a way of shaping societal outcomes. An increasing perception of self-interest related to the costs of public policy that are borne by people as they age (an ever-lengthening experience with property taxes, for example) might also be at work. Voting may also be related to age because it is a habit shaped by the age cycle. Alternatively, looked at from the other end, the stratification of turnout by age may be reflecting the distractions of youth, which lead younger voters not to vote. Indeed all these factors are probably at work.

However we might care to explain it, there is no doubt that turnout varies strongly by age. As Figure 2.8 shows, turnout reaches the 70 percent or more level by the time individuals reach their midforties and largely remains at that

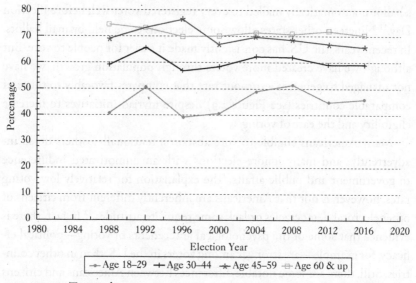

FIGURE 2.8 Turnout by age, 1988–2016.

level throughout one's life. It is about 10 percentage points lower for those age thirty to forty-four, while fewer than half of those younger than thirty vote in presidential elections. The very young, age eighteen to twenty-five, have particularly low turnout rates. In off-year elections participation drops even lower, especially among the young.

American Turnout in Perspective

The immediate result of repeated extensions of the franchise was not always an increase in the turnout rate, as Figure 2.1 documented, and recent efforts in the second half of the twentieth century to make voting easier have not produced turnout rates near those observed in the second half of the nineteenth century. This last point merits deeper consideration: while institutions, rules, and laws often affect turnout, the removal of unnecessary hurdles in recent years has not had a significant effect on the voting rate in the U.S.

Over the past fifty years, registration has become easier and registration deadlines have been moved ever nearer Election Day, when election excitement provokes the less interested to register and vote. Many states now permit registration at the polling place, which is immediately followed by casting a vote. Absentee and early voting is simple and available in most states. Three states—Oregon, Washington, and Colorado—conduct all elections by mail;

a ballot is automatically mailed to every registered voter well before Election Day.[11] Nineteen other states allow some elections to be held by mail ballots. In recent years, the U.S. has consistently made it easier for people to vote. But although we have created more voters through population growth, we have not managed to generate a turnout rate that compares favorably to those of comparable countries (see Figure 2.9) despite myriad initiatives to increase eligibility and the ease of voting.

Many Americans eligible to vote abstain intentionally; others do so inadvertently; and many ignore elections with an unmotivated indifference to government and public affairs. The explanation for relatively low voting rates, however, is not that Americans are inherently different from citizens of other electoral democracies or lack some requisite attitudes.[12] In fact, there is evidence that some of the psychological antecedents of voting—political efficacy, for example—are stronger among voters in the U.S. than in other countries. Still, there are some notable differences between Americans and citizens of other democracies that make the turnout dynamic in the U.S. distinct.

For example, one famous multination study of participation examined various kinds of political activity (voting, campaign involvement, attention to politics, political opinion, contacting government officials about general

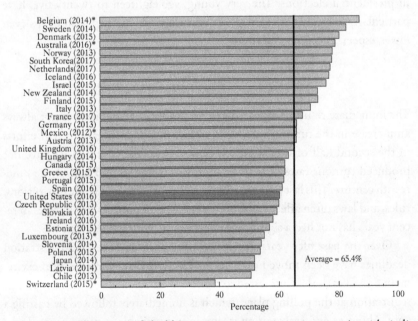

FIGURE 2.9 U.S. turnout of eligible voters in comparative perspective. Asterisks indicate countries with compulsory voting.

political matters and personal issues) and their correlates (Verba, Nie, and Kim, 1978). The U.S. was unique in that the variables that distinguished social status and a habituated interest in politics predicted all the types of political activity—voting, campaign activism, attempts to influence government officials, and so forth. In the other countries, voting participation was essentially uncorrelated with such status markers as education, although education and related status measures predicted all the other types of political activity.

Verba, Nie, and Kim (1978) did not proffer a definitive explanation for this American distinctiveness, but they did examine some interesting party system differences that might matter. One they emphasized is the extent to which countries differ in the homogeneity of their party coalitions. Countries such as Belgium, the Netherlands, and Austria had at the time of their research and, by comparison with the U.S., continue to have, parties that represent constituencies that are overwhelmingly of a particular religious denomination, class, occupational group, or linguistic group. Elections in such countries are occasions in which people are not only asked to display their policy preferences but also to affirm their social identity as a member of the working class, a religious Catholic, or a Flemish speaker. Concerns with public policy mediated by intellectual skills are less influential in highly aligned party systems when the election is framed as an opportunity to support people like yourself—a party representing religious Catholics or French speakers—rather than others. Social identities, to put it simply, are formidable motivators. By contrast, the Democrats and Republicans are and always have been heterogeneous coalitions that bargain over internal disputes to achieve a majority vote.[13] Appeals to groups are muted and, if too obvious, become divisive within the party, with accompanied denunciations in the wider society.

Social identity dynamics operate in the U.S. in muted ways. Consider that turnout among blacks lags that for whites in every election for which we have been able to collect the data, except in 2008 and, especially, 2012. There is little doubt that blacks were individually—and through group and social dynamics—attracted to Barack Obama in the 2008 and 2012 elections because he was black, and they voted in unusually heavy numbers for the candidate who shared their racial identity. The nomination of two white candidates—Hillary Clinton and Donald Trump—resulted in a drop in black turnout (to a rate lower than that observed for whites) in 2016, a racial difference that has existed for as long as we have collected national survey data.

Ethnic identity appeals and effects have always existed in the U.S. because we are a nation populated with voters of different national origins and religious preferences. However, the Democrats and Republicans do not emphasize social identity appeals because neither party commands the exclusive loyalties of most groups, and, as indicated, the legitimacy of narrow subgroup appeals is neither widely nor fully accepted in the country. As a result, turnout is influenced more by citizenship norms associated with education, such that voting rates vary by education and other social position markers.

There are other differences between the U.S. and the countries in Figure 2.9. Mandatory voting explains some of the high-turnout countries (these are noted by an asterisk in Figure 2.2). Many have repealed their mandatory voting laws, but the residuals of those laws may still have an effect. Historically, countries with compulsory voting reported an average turnout rate 7 percentage points higher than other countries. Other things that matter include making Election Day a national holiday. Similarly, a few countries hold elections on weekends, which seems to increase turnout. Nations with a proportional representation electoral system typically also have higher turnout rates than those, like the U.S., that elect by districts. Uncompetitive districts diminish voter enthusiasm and keep many away from the polling place, while they also diminish efforts by the parties to get out the vote. After all, if few voters show up but your candidate wins handily, does it matter?

At the end of the day, no one factor is responsible for America's relatively low turnout. We might manage higher turnout by doing what the Dutch did after repealing their mandatory voting law in 1967: they required voters to sign in at the polling station. Dutch citizens were not required to vote, but they were expected to show up and affirmatively refuse to vote by signing in and then leaving. Consequently the Dutch continue to have high turnout rates. More dramatically, the U.S. could cut the Gordian knot by mandating turnout. Penalties could include nominal fines or a notation that might jeopardize opportunities for public employment. (Some countries use that tactic to punish nonvoters.)

It seems to us, however, that imaginative penalties are a waste of imagination. As much as we want people to vote, public opinion is soundly against compulsory voting. The American electorate lacks the divisions that have allowed parties to infuse elections with strong social identity incentives, and the electoral system is unlikely to be changed to a form, such as proportional representation, that would vastly increase party incentives to get their voters to the polls. Until those incentives can be ratcheted up, every individual American's decision to vote will reflect their partisanship, issue concerns, and sense of obligation to vote. We have made the institutional environment as permissive as possible, or nearly so. The puzzle is how we might make the political culture more inclined to motivate turnout. It is worth noting, though, that some doubt that we would like the consequences of doing so.

This assessment of historical trends and basic correlations also suggests that very little of what we know about turnout in the U.S. hinges upon the partisan preferences of voters. This fact is at the core of chapter 3, in which we examine more specifically how political science research has conceptualized turnout and the relationship between turnout and partisan vote choice.

3

A *Theoretical Exploration of Turnout and Voting*

CHAPTER 2 FOCUSED ON some of the basic facts and characteristics of turnout in the United States. Such a baseline is necessary to explore fruitfully the complex relationship between turnout and partisan vote choice. This chapter addresses why people vote in elections: What affects their calculus? How much do these motivations create the unequal turnout rates observed among different social and political groups? This discussion in turn informs our initial pass at how the decision to vote might (or might not) be related to partisan vote choice.

More specifically, our review of the academic scholarship on turnout has two distinct components. The first part traces the evolution of turnout studies, from classic rational choice studies through the raft of theoretically rich empirical studies relying on aggregate election results and survey data. This review of the turnout literature is somewhat perilous from our perspective; notable in its absence is the role of partisan vote choice in driving turnout, which can make the effort seem discursive. But that, of course, is the point: there is an impressive amount of scholarship about turnout, yet few of our predictive models feature the partisan candidate preferences of voters as a key variable. By tracing the theoretical ideas that animate our understanding of turnout we attempt to show why the absence of partisan vote choice might make sense.

The second half of the chapter observes that the academic literature does not specifically show that turnout and partisan vote choice are unlinked. Instead we find that the river of scholarship on turnout simply flows in another direction, such that it is not entirely clear from our most famous studies whether (or how) vote choice might affect turnout. Put another way, there

The Turnout Myth. Daron R. Shaw and John R. Petrocik, Oxford University Press (2020). © Oxford University Press.
DOI: 10.1093/oso/9780190089450.001.0001

is a gap in our knowledge. This gap has most often been filled by intuition, or if you prefer, deductions from solid empirical facts to certain conclusions about how turnout rates and election outcomes must the linked. These can be summarized as follows:

1. Members of racial and ethnic minority groups, the young, and the less well-educated vote at lower rates than whites, older people, and better-educated people.
2. Members of racial and ethnic minority groups, the young, and the less well-educated are more supportive of Democratic issue positions, and thus of Democratic candidates, than Republican issue positions and Republican candidates.
3. Increases in turnout, or greater turnout overall, will disproportionately bring into the voting pool people who are relatively more likely to support Democratic candidates. Thus, given the empirical facts in points 1 and 2, increased turnout leads to increased Democratic vote share.

Beginning in the 1980s, however, a few political scientists began to question the intuition producing the conventional wisdom that Democratic candidates benefit from higher turnout. We therefore trace the attendant flow of empirically derived claims and counterclaims, which we argue has not produced a consensus and has mostly left the conventional wisdom of biased turnout—the turnout myth—in a solid embrace by many academics, almost all political commentators and reporters, and the majority of average citizens.

In the final section of the chapter, we offer a critique of the scholarly literature supporting the conventional wisdom, planting our flag firmly on the side of those who see little correlation between turnout and partisan vote choice. One specific criticism warrants particular attention: a problem in the literature we refer to as the "cross-sectional inference fallacy" or, more simply, the "aggregation fallacy," which underlies the three points specified earlier. The broader critique includes both empirical and theoretical aspects, though, and serves as an important companion to the empirical analyses of subsequent chapters.

Theorizing about Turnout and Vote Choice

We are prepared to offer as a rebuttable proposition that voting is the most studied facet of American democracy. Perhaps we are only confirming our understanding, but it is at least as likely that we are displaying a preoccupation with an activity that almost everybody views as fundamental to the American political order, so it should elicit no surprise that we have studied it, and continue to study it, intensively. Although we think we understand it well, we continue to examine its features: how many turned up at the polls, what groups voted for whom, and why voters chose a specific candidate.

The core of our understanding is that voters will choose candidates who will pursue policies and otherwise run the government according to the values and principles embraced by most voters. Anthony Downs (1957), building expansively on the innovative work of Harold Hotelling (1929), formalized this notion under the rubric of an "economic theory of democracy." Sensible voters, like sensible consumers, behave rationally by casting a vote that reflects the benefits they want from government. In the language of Downs's formulation, everyone calculates the benefits from electing each of the candidates, and each votes for the candidate who provides the greatest net benefit to him or her, where the benefit could be anything but usually refers to preferred policy outcomes. The calculation is a "proximity model," in which the distance between one's issue position and those of each candidate is calculated, and the candidate whose position is closest to the voter's on all or perhaps only the most important issues receives his or her vote.[1] These calculations can be complex. Scholars have examined these distances or proximities or benefits, sometimes weighting the result by the salience of the issue to the voter (Enelow and Hinich 1984). Their findings show that the proximity model works whether one concern or many shape the voter's choice.

Within this framework, the decision about whether to turn out for the election also involves a calculation of the costs of voting to the individual prospective voter. More formally:

$$V = (P^*B) - C,$$
where:
V = the probability of voting in the election
P = the probability of one's vote determining the winner
B = the perceived benefit from electing the preferred candidate
C = the cost of voting.

The calculation has two key aspects. One is whether the benefits of voting are greater than the costs of voting (normally thought of as the effort required to register, paying enough attention to be informed, and getting to the polls or mailing an early vote). Put another way, the question is whether the benefit a voter expects from electing a preferred candidate exceeds the cost of learning enough to make a decision. When the cost of choosing a candidate and getting to the polls seems greater than any likely benefit from the outcome, the formula expects the voter to abstain. The second aspect is a discount to the candidate benefit term that is equal to *the probability that the individual's vote will determine the outcome*. A large expected benefit if a preferred candidate wins will not be sufficient to bestir a rational voter who also realizes that his or her vote has no probability of tipping the election.

Curiously, while proximity models of vote choice generate highly accurate predictions about whom a voter will support (see, e.g., Joesten and Stone 2014), this stark and stylized abstraction about citizen decisions to turnout generates less accurate predictions of whether an individual will vote. This is probably because there is considerable disagreement on what constitutes a cost and, perhaps more important, how costs might be measured on a metric equivalent to the benefits produced by the first part of the calculation. How, for example, is a unit of cost to be measured so that it bears some relationship to each unit of benefit obtained by comparing the candidates' policies and qualities? Typically researchers have maneuvered around this difficulty by using an equation in which the costs and benefits are entered as separate variables and their influences are assessed by the resultant coefficients. This approach substantiates the existence of both influences. It calculates that some voters face prohibitive costs, which results in a lower probability of turning up on Election Day. It also calculates high benefits for others and documents a strong likelihood of voting. Overall the approach demonstrates that both choosing to vote and choosing among candidates parallels the account economists and marketers proffer about purchase decisions.

The most notable slip in the turnout calculation occurs when someone notices that a person's vote generally has a trivial to no influence on the outcome of the election. A calculation of benefit from buying a pickup truck rather than a sedan is straightforward. The purchaser will receive that benefit upon the purchase if the costs are in order. It is not the case that an individual's decision to vote will produce the calculated benefit because the probability that one's vote—the vote of that single individual—will determine the election outcome in the U.S. is almost always effectively zero (although we often enjoy reporting examples where elections are decided by a single vote). *Any cost*, therefore, should cause a rational voter to stay away from the polls because no rational individual is likely to spin a scenario in which the election at hand will be a tie without his or her vote.

The heuristic value of the utility theory is considerable, though, even as we must remind ourselves not to accept it as a factually perfect descriptive statement about how voters go about deciding whether (and for whom) to vote. Utility theory forces (1) an inventory of the attitudes, beliefs, and perceptions that lead to a candidate preference and (2) a determination of whether there are obstacles to voter turnout despite that preference.

Notice also that the interplay between partisan vote choice and turnout assumed here is somewhat indirect: it is the *intensity* of partisan preference—rather than its *direction*—that may affect turnout. This is a critical theoretical point, one that explains why the turnout literature tends not to focus on partisan vote choice as a key explanatory variable. As we move forward in this chapter, we draw heavily on utility theories of turnout, as these are obviously relevant to understanding both the individual's likelihood of voting in any election and the aggregate level of turnout. Utility theories are similarly important for our theoretical understanding of partisan vote choice, which we consider in the next section.

The Candidate Preference Calculus

If voters are indeed rational actors seeking to maximize their benefits from the election, what does this tell us about partisan vote choice? For starters, it tells us that voters should vote for the candidate whom they believe shares their preferences. It also tells us that the relative utility of voting increases as the perceived benefit of electing a given candidate over the other(s) increases. Finally, it tells us that voters ought to acquire—as cheaply as they can—the requisite information to make a beneficial decision. Given all these, we are often at a loss to explain the public's persistent low level of interest in and knowledge of public affairs (Campbell et al. 1960; Delli Carpini and Keeter 1996). How is it that people construct a candidate preference given that they probably do not know much about the substantive policy differences that animate political debates?

The most prominent explanation is the theory of party identification, which contends that most Americans develop a psychological attachment to a political party, much the same way we develop other attitudes (Campbell et al. 1960; Niemi and Jennings 1991). Thus we come to think of ourselves as Democrats or Republicans, and this attachment informs our positions on issues, our response to political candidates, and our vote choice. Party identification tends to strengthen as we age, which leads us to turn out more consistently, announce our partisanship more comfortably, and rarely deviate from that party preference when we vote.[2] Recently some researchers have argued that political judgments are increasingly based on party identification because of issue polarization (Abramowitz 2012). They posit that as the parties have become more programmatically coherent in the wake of racial and social conflicts, ideologues on both sides have increasingly sorted themselves into the "correct" parties: conservatives with the Republicans and liberals with the Democrats. As a result, partisan polarization has increased. Partisans on one side do not share many (or even any) issue positions with those on the other side of the aisle. This leads to a reflexive rejection of people and ideas associated with the opposite party. In this universe, turnout and candidate preference are mostly determined by the activation of one's partisanship, which is always sufficient to identify greater benefits from one candidate and therefore a reason to turn out.

A different view—one that is comfortable with citizenry's low involvement and interest in politics—focuses on voters' retrospective evaluations of national conditions such as the manifest honesty of officials, peaceful foreign relations, and, especially, economic conditions (Key 1966; Fiorina 1981; Kinder and Kiewiet 1981; Hart 2017). Voters in this framework do not require a lot of policy and governance detail to notice that things are going well or poorly. These positive or negative assessments of current conditions in the country are easily made and then used as the basis for judgments about whether to renew or terminate the employment of public officials. This theory has produced a robust set of results that has even allowed us to compare assessments based on personal circumstances (self-interest) with those that reflect a broader perspective, such as the state of the economy overall (sociotropic voting), regardless of how well-off individuals believe they are.[3]

Still another theory of vote choice focuses on social dynamics. The original formulation proposes the existence of opinion leaders for many different segments of the society, who provide information and a rationale for backing a candidate or viewpoint. Opinion leaders come in many guises—organization leaders, social notables, religious figures, prominent ethnic personalities—but their role and effect are the same: they guide those who trust them to judgments and choices that will be good for people like themselves (Berelson, Lazarsfeld, and McPhee 1954). These group dynamics now occur through social media platforms and provide a fresh example of this classic theory of opinion formation and leadership. The major difference between the social media version and the notion of leadership in the initial formulation is that social media usually does not depend on any specific person. Its power arises from the homogeneity promoted by the information networks on which so many of us rely. In the contemporary social media environment, people subscribe to sources that provide congenial information and interpretations. The mass media and to an even greater extent social media do not broadcast. They "narrowcast" to a homogeneous audience looking for information that is consistent with their preexisting beliefs and preferences.

Broadly speaking, theories focusing on social dynamics assume that social groups are important because political information flows from elites (who are informed and knowledgeable about politics) to nonelites (who are not) within racial, ethnic, religious, occupational, and other group contexts. This guidance can be factual and nuanced or based on emotions and affective judgments. Although this is not a deeply explored area, the role of emotional reactions such as anger, fear, and anxiety on opinion has attracted scholarly attention recently, and evidence has emerged supporting the idea that candidate preferences can be powerfully shaped by the mood of voters in response to complex external events (for an overview, see Brader 2006).[4]

Once again, however, note the common point of origin for vote choice theories: almost all assume that voters do not have much information about the policy debates in an election and must instead rely on something else to arrive at a vote choice. The plausibility of this perspective is strengthened by recent theorizing and empirical research suggesting that human judgment and decision-making relies on unconscious orientations that are based as much on biological as mental orientations (see Haidt 2013).

Given all this, what are we to make of the theoretical connection between turnout and partisan vote choice? The main point of connection is the prominence of social group cues for partisan vote choice, especially for the less engaged. The stronger identification occurs within and between groups, the stronger the political effects of information and suggestions from other members of their group. If these groups are also systematically less interested, engaged, and involved politically, there might be a turnout gap and (potentially) a partisan bias to turnout. Some scholars (e.g., Fraga 2018; Lijphart 1997; Piven and Cloward 1988) contend that members of left-leaning groups are, in fact, systematically less interested and engaged due to either their lack of resources (Lijphart 1997; Piven and Cloward 1988) or their belief that the political system is unresponsive to their input (Fraga 2018). This logic gives rise to—or is at last consistent with—the three premises articulated earlier. Despite the intriguing nature of this line of reasoning, however, attempts to test empirically the effects of higher turnout on Democratic vote share are almost nonexistent in classic studies of vote choice.

What Affects Turnout?

As suggested earlier, turnout may be the single most written-about subject in the field of political science, reflecting the centrality of voting for our conception of what is required by democracy. While there are other forms of political participation, voting is the foremost democratic act. Partly, however, the prevalence of turnout studies reflects the availability of data; while we enjoy entertaining hunches and intuitions about many political phenomena, empirical evidence is the coin of the realm and analyses of turnout can be used in myriad ways to inform our understanding of democratic functioning. As we noted throughout our empirical overview of U.S. turnout in chapter 2, much of what we know from these studies suggests that the decision to vote is influenced by institutional arrangements, demographic factors, and a few key attitudinal variables.

Institutional Arrangements

At least until recently, political science has emphasized that many people do not vote because it requires a nontrivial degree of psychological involvement (and modern American society offers many other, immediately rewarding attractions and activities), information, and physical effort to surmount the barriers the electoral system places before individuals. In chapter 2, for example, we pointed out that voters in the U.S. must register to vote, often well in advance of the election date, although the nature of the registration requirement varies considerably from state to state. In addition to registration requirements, U.S. elections are most often held during working hours on a single work day. Having the polls open from 7:00 a.m. until 7:00 p.m. on a Tuesday is not conducive to high turnout, especially when compared to countries with extended voting hours or two- or three-day voting holidays. Furthermore, because of the federal nature of the U.S. political system, Americans tend to have multiple elections spread out over the calendar year. There are party primary elections (and perhaps even run-offs) as well as general elections for school districts, municipal districts, cities, counties, and states. These could be consolidated and held on a single date, but for the most part, in most states, they produce many separate elections. However rewarding the variety was a century ago, when distractions in daily life were few, the multiplicity of elections in this era leads to less enthusiasm for voting, especially when the election seems less important (see, e.g., Sigelman and Jewell 1986).

Of course, institutional arrangements can affect cost-benefit calculations in a way that increases turnout. In chapter 2 we also mentioned that nations that require citizens to vote have high turnout rates for almost all elections, even when, as in the United States, separate elections are held for municipal and provincial governments.[5] Strong political parties can also help voters overcome the impediments to voting by registering them and providing information and suggestions about the voting process and the candidates. So too can interest groups and social movements, whether operating in conjunction with or separate from the parties.

Although the link between institutional arrangements and turnout makes intuitive sense and is evident in some of the comparative turnout figures offered in chapter 2, the precise contribution of the environment to turnout has not produced solid estimates of effects. Indeed, while we acknowledge the overall connection, several aggregate patterns make some of the arguments about more permissive institutional arrangements and higher turnout less than compelling. For instance, we know that turnout has not uniformly increased with the loosening of registration requirements. Most notably, same-day registration regimens and increasingly accommodating registration timelines have not produced the surge in turnout that many expected. California, for example, has made registration and provisional voting extraordinarily easy, but turnout has been flat or declining. What is happening? The increasing control of the state by one party, the Democrats, may be making voting less attractive because election outcomes are virtually preordained, as they were in the days of the Solid South. Truthfully, a clear and certain answer has eluded us. The question is complicated by the fact that so many government-level procedures and regulations have changed at the same time.

Still, some interesting explanations for the limited impact of weakening institutional requirements on turnout merit consideration. One intriguing observation is that interest groups have lobbied the government to restrict the purging of the eligibility rolls, a fact that could explain why the number of eligible voters (by registration) often grows faster than the number who show up to vote. Another explanation is that institutional changes have not been successful in increasing turnout because the American political parties focus more on raising money to pay for television ads than on face-to-face contacting to mobilize voters, a possibility suggested by the effect of mobilization on turnout identified by Rosenstone and Hansen (1993). Indeed some studies

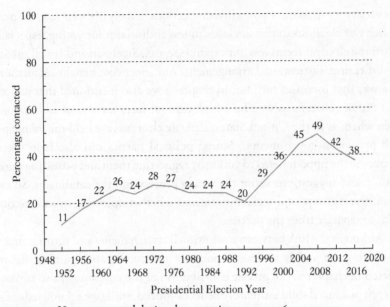

FIGURE 3.1 Voters contacted during the campaign, 1952–2016.
Source: ANES surveys of the indicated year.

contend that the comparative weakness of the American party system as a mobilizing force is a major reason—along with registration requirements—for our "turnout deficit" (Powell 1986). However, while appealing on its face, this notion cannot explain the lack of a correlation between other institutional arrangements and turnout because the parties have contacted far more voters since the early 1990s than they did in previous decades (see Figure 3.1).

The takeaway point here is that differences across the states and across countries strongly suggest that institutional arrangements can have a powerful effect on turnout. Yet voting rules are not everything. Rules for voting in the U.S. have changed dramatically to make voting much easier.[6] The permissive changes, however, have not obviously contributed to more turnout, certainly not as much as reform proponents suggested they would. Conversely, there is some evidence that more stringent voter identification requirements do not depress voting (Ansolabehere 2009; Hood and Bullock 2012).

Demographic Factors

We know that institutional arrangements are not the entire story when it comes to turnout. Given that voting requires information and motivation, it is not surprising that those who can most easily overcome the costs of voting are the most likely to cast a ballot. For example, as noted in chapter 2, the better educated can surmount any difficulties to becoming informed; we have long been aware of the relationship between education and turnout. As Verba, Schlozman, and Brady (1995) propose, turnout may reflect the effect of "civic skills" on political participation. That is, access to formal education and having a certain income makes it more likely that people will participate in voluntary organizations, which is where they develop a store of information from which they draw when faced with opportunities to participate in politics. Of course, civic skills are not derived solely from education and income. People who develop civic skills often come from families and communities that are supportive of volunteerism. Certain churches and workplaces actively promote and help foster this volunteerism. Whatever its provenance, people who have engaged in other forms of civic activity are less likely to be deterred by registration deadlines or not knowing where the polling place is on Election Day; they know how to overcome these obstacles. Political participation is a particularized sort of volunteerism, and the motivations and opportunities that determine who volunteers also determine who votes.

In a similar vein, researchers contend that voting is akin to a habit. Once a person overcomes the costs associated with voting and casts a ballot, that person has (1) acquired the skills necessary to more easily repeat the action in the future and (2) derived a pleasurable satisfaction from the act. After two or three elections, the person reflexively participates without necessarily making a conscious decision (Plutzer 2002; Gerber, Green, and Shachar 2003). Conversely, those who have not voted tend to be sporadic voters, at best, not easily moved to show up at the next election.

It should come as no surprise that demographics related to socioeconomic status and civic skills are powerful correlates of voting. In chapter 2 we noted the strong correlation between turnout and age, between turnout and race/ethnicity, and between turnout and education. Other demographic relationships are less powerful, but they are persistent predictors of turnout.

Attitudes, Beliefs, and Perceptions (The Proximate Influences on Turnout)

Of course, politics is not simply demographics. In almost all situations, demographics are the antecedent to what people think and feel, and the later are the proximate influences on political activity. Demographic traits matter because they indicate the social environments within which people live and interact. They develop beliefs and preferences through contact with and exposure to others who are demographically similar or different. Thus while demographic characteristics are correlated with turnout and other forms of political participation, attitudes, beliefs, and perceptions are more consequential.

Which beliefs and attitudes matter most? Interest and engagement in politics are the attitudes most significantly correlated with voting in U.S. elections. They are, in fact, the most proximate causes of voting. But what attitudes drive interest and engagement? In piecing together the turnout puzzle, we would highlight three other attitudinal factors: civic duty, political efficacy, and partisanship. Voting is widely considered a civic obligation. Rational choice models of turnout suggest that a potential benefit of voting is the satisfaction of performing one's civic duty (Downs 1957; Riker and Ordeshook 1968; Aldrich 1993; Blais 2000). As pointed out earlier, without such psychic benefits, utility models of the sort developed by Downs (1957) suggest that no one would vote (Ledyard 1984; Palfrey and Rosenthal 1985). One hypothesis about why millions of citizens nonetheless vote is that they are willing to pay the usually trivial costs in time and effort to avoid the feeling of shame associated with not voting or, conversely, to enjoy the satisfaction of voting.

Put differently, as noted earlier, voting is regarded by many as a moral obligation and the fundamental duty of every citizen. Most Americans believe they should vote, even when they report sitting out the election. Survey research has measured the sense of civic duty by asking questions about volunteering, serving on a jury, reporting a crime, learning English, keeping informed about news and public issues, as well as voting. Unsurprisingly, those who score highest on these items are much more likely to vote in elections.

A second key attitude is political efficacy. Internal efficacy refers to the belief that one is capable of understanding politics. External efficacy refers to the belief that the political system and the federal government are responsive to your input.[7] When analyzing turnout data, we find that people who are very efficacious are also very likely to vote.

Then there is partisanship. Individuals who strongly identify as Republicans or Democrats are much more likely to vote than independents or those whose partisanship is weak. The underlying logic is simple: those who are most powerfully committed to their side of the political debate are most likely to make the effort to register and show up on Election Day. Those who are less strongly attached are less likely to do so. Feeling committed to one side increases the sense of a benefit, within the Downsian perspective. One's specific party preference also has some effect on turnout. Republicans, for any level of intensity of their party identification, are slightly more likely to vote (and participate in other ways), but the larger effect is the intensity of the identification.[8]

Finally, there is evidence that emotion (which we touched on briefly with respect to vote choice) is also an important driver of turnout. The proposition, with some evidence, is that emotions—anger, fear, anxiety, hope, and so on—might induce someone to bear the costs of voting. While the influence of emotion on turnout is controversial, anticipated future emotions—such as anger and enthusiasm—have been shown to have strong effects on turnout (Valentino et al. 2011). In an era of heightened and polarized partisan conflict, the notion is plausible; as of now, however, it has not been well-connected to the existing literature or understanding of turnout factors.

The upshot is that many factors—institutional, sociodemographic, psychological, and emotional—appear to influence the decision to vote. However, very few studies focus on the effect of voting (turnout) on partisan choice (the actual division of the vote). In fact no one we know of thinks that partisan vote choice is among the most powerful correlates of turnout. This observation stands in marked contrast to the conventional wisdom deriving from the three premises advanced earlier in this chapter. Strangely, only in the late 1970s and early 1980s did research take note of this conundrum and directly engaged the critical question: Is there any relationship at all between partisan vote choice and turnout?

Partisan Vote Choice and Turnout

If the literature examining turnout is voluminous, we would describe the literature examining the relationship between partisan vote choice and turnout as limited but lively. To better understand the totality of these projects, it is useful to sort studies of the effect of vote choice on turnout into two broad categories. In the first, we would place analyses that ask whether election results would be different if everyone voted. These deal with a hypothetical world in which turnout is 100 percent. In the second, we would place studies of whether the Democratic share of the two-party vote increases as turnout rises. These deal with a real world in which both turnout and partisan vote total vary considerably. Our interest is primarily in this second category, but studies of both are concerned with the size of groups in the electorate and what preferences and beliefs command majority support.

The Partisan Effects of Universal Turnout

Largely, studies seeking to estimate the election outcome effect of universal turnout assume that candidates and parties on the political left would be the beneficiaries. The underlying logic draws on premises 1 and 2 offered at the outset of the chapter, which reflect the data presented in chapter 2: individuals with characteristics that correlate with a Democratic vote have lower turnout rates. Its narrative asserts that universal turnout would reveal that most voters are supportive of the kinds of distributive and redistributive policies associated with the political left (premise 3). This majority is created by downscale and socially subordinate groups who look to government for remedies that are characteristic of left-of-center parties but whose influence on government is attenuated by their low participation rates. The effects would be realized even if such voters did not support left parties under circumstances where turnout is less than 100 percent because, the argument further assumes, in a reasonably brief time the act of voting would become educative. That is, regular voting would increase awareness of the effects of policies, who benefits from them, and which party or parties promote the policies that benefit these relatively disadvantaged (but more numerous) groups with low participation rates (see, in particular, Lijphart 1997).

A subordinate argument in this framework is the proposition that 100 percent turnout would create pressure for all parties to be attentive to the expectations of the new median voter in a 100 percent electorate; thus even moderately conservative parties would alter their policies to compete in the expanded electorate. The result is a more democratic political order in which the preferences of all voters are registered with a vote. Piven and Cloward (1988) and Lijphart (1997) offer two prominent examples of this view.

A more limited formulation about the effects of turnout accepts many of the assumptions about nonvoters and how they might behave if they voted and proposes to test them within the range of turnout variation in U.S. elections. That is, how do Democratic Party fortunes fare when turnout moves from the low end (40 percent) to the high end (65 percent) of American electoral contests? This limited formulation expects the Democratic Party to benefit as turnout reaches the upper range, and Republicans to prosper as it declines. This expectation observes that, specific to the American case, nonvoters tend to be younger, from socially subordinate ethnic and racial groups, less religiously attentive, and more likely to be single rather than married. Put differently, voters with lower (and sometimes the lowest) turnout rates have the demographic profile of Democrats, not Republicans, and are more likely to express a preference for the Democratic Party and its candidates. Sound familiar? Empirical assessments of the argument typically impute to nonvoters the candidate preferences of people who look like them demographically but did vote; these analyses then often conclude that most of the nonvoters would have supported Democrats had they voted (see Althaus 1998; Bartels 2002; Citrin, Schickler, and Sides 2003).

These arguments and data deserve careful assessment since our political order assumes elections translate preferences into government programs and policies. Unfortunately some of them are immune to examination. We cannot directly test the merit of the notion, associated with Piven-Cloward (1988) and Lijphart (1997), that the process of going to the polls would inspire individuals of lower socioeconomic status to realize their affinity for left-leaning parties. We think it instructive, though, that elections in countries with mandatory voting laws (which usually produce near 100 percent turnout) have not consistently favored left-of-center parties. More particularly, if we narrow our focus to the small set of countries with mandatory voting that most would describe as democracies, the Piven-Cloward thesis fares poorly since the governments resulting from elections have been conservative as often as not (Australia) or representative of regional, linguistic, and religious divisions (Belgium and the Netherlands).[9] The empirical historical record therefore is most compatible with the hypothesis that elections are occasions to reallocate political power along the lines of whatever divisions are salient to the citizenry, and these are often something other than the economic issues the Piven-Cloward thesis focuses on.

But if we assume, just to simplify, that nonvoters would have the same preferences as voters who look like them, what would greater turnout do to elections? One recent study used exit poll results to model candidate preferences for U.S. Senate races in 1994, 1996, and 1998 and impute vote choices for nonvoters. It found that full turnout would have increased the Democratic vote share but would only rarely have reversed the results of the Senate races they studied (Citrin, Schickler, and Sides 2003). Another prominent study examined the preferences of abstainers to see what varying levels of participation would have done to five presidential elections between 1960 and 2000. It found that the Democrats would have been advantaged by higher turnout in 1960 and 1964, but that by 2000 this effect was all but gone. The authors attribute the change to the erosion of party attachments and the concomitant rise of "peripheral" voters in the electorate (Martinez and Gill 2005).[10] Comparable research points in a similar direction: limited and contextually dependent effects, with the Democrats gaining only slightly or not at all with full turnout (Wolfinger, Rosenstone, and McIntosh 1978; Wolfinger and Rosenstone 1980; Teixeira 1987; Calvert and Gilchrist 1991; Gant and Lyons 1993). These results notwithstanding, critiques have insisted that such imputations are speculative and error-prone and that left-leaning candidates and policy preferences remain substantially underrepresented due to systematic turnout biases (for an overview, see Fraga 2018).

Engaging this debate is the purpose of this book and requires comprehensive and multifaceted empirical analyses, which we present in subsequent chapters. Nevertheless, in response to the question of how nonvoters' preferences compare to those of voters, we cannot resist offering a cursory glance at the pattern over the past sixty years. Figure 3.2 compares the support of voters for the winning candidate with the expressed preferences of nonvoters for the winning candidate in presidential elections from 1952 through 2016. Most of the time nonvoters followed preferences of those who did vote. In some elections they preferred the winner by an even wider spread, proportionally magnifying the winner's margin. The party of the winner was not a factor. A big GOP win among voters was reflected in even more support for Eisenhower among the nonvoters in 1956; yet nonvoters oversupported Johnson and the Democrats in 1964. In only a couple of instances did nonvoters favor the losing candidate, and in most of those

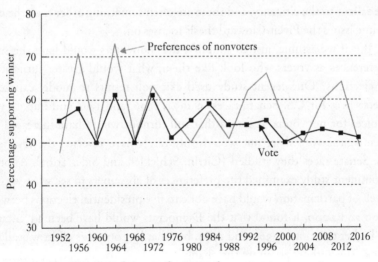

FIGURE 3.2 Presidential preferences of voters and nonvoters, 1952–2016.
The 1980, 1992, and 1996 preferences of nonvoters is calculated only for those interviewed during October in order to account for a clear shift in preference in the last half of the September–October campaign period.

instances—specifically, 1980, 1992, and 1996—there was a dramatic shift in the preferences of voters over the campaign such that by October nonvoters preferred the winner in these elections as well. Put differently, nonvoters went with the tide, and sometimes they would have produced an even greater wave.

These data dovetail with a more detailed study of the self-reported preferences of nonvoters in U.S. elections from 1952 through 1984 (Petrocik 1987). This analysis found that nonvoters mimic the preferences of voters, with the exceptions of 1952 and 1980. Importantly, 1980 may not be an exception; events in the last month of that race changed the choices of voters, but a lack of late-October data on nonvoters leave us unable to get a comparable fix on their (possible) preference dynamics (Petrocik 1987). This brief data-driven interlude is not meant as a definitive comment on the debate concerning the effects of full turnout; it is far too limited an examination to conclusively answer anything, but it effectively reinforces our skepticism that peripheral voters are defined by their latent commitment to a particular political party. We will return to this crucial point in later chapters.

The Partisan Effects of Actual Turnout Variation

There is often a strongly normative, even tendentious bent to analyses of U.S. elections positing universal turnout. A few presume that by limiting the franchise or by creating obstacles to full participation, American elections intentionally misrepresent the will of the people. One or two go even further, suggesting that the system is structured to keep the party of the lower classes (i.e., the Democratic Party) from winning its fair share of elections (Piven and Cloward 1988). We think this is a difficult argument to sustain. The Democrats controlled both houses of Congress almost without interruption from 1932 until 1994 as well as a large share of state governments, providing repeated and multiple opportunities to undo the conspiracy. So we will pass on this claim after registering a dissent and concentrate on whether there is evidence in recent American history that outcomes vary with turnout. That is, among presidential, Senate, House, or gubernatorial races during the past several decades, does higher turnout produce Democratic victories?

The first contemporary examination of this question was conducted by DeNardo (1980), who challenged the notion that higher turnout benefited the Democrats. DeNardo distinguished between "core" and "peripheral" voters[11] and pointed out that increased turnout among peripheral voters, not core voters, is the hallmark of higher stimulus elections. Consequently high turnout creates a natural advantage for whichever party benefits from short-term forces in a race. DeNardo explicitly predicts that minority parties would have the edge in higher stimulus elections, as they give that party a chance to mobilize citizens who vote infrequently and have weak political interest. This presumably reduces the majority party's advantage among core voters.

There have been several efforts to validate or extend DeNardo's (1980) claims, and the results are mixed. Tucker, Vedlitz, and DeNardo (1986) critique DeNardo's conclusion, pointing out that his cross-sectional analysis may not be the best way to test a district-based (i.e., longitudinal) theory. However, their analysis is also cross-sectional—although the units of analysis are states rather than districts—and results in inconclusive findings. Radcliff (1994) examines the presidential vote in districts to test the relationship between turnout and the vote, and he finds that Democrats are advantaged by higher turnout. Again, though, the analysis is cross-sectional and does not examine whether turnout changes within a constituency influence the vote.

This flaw prompts Erikson's (1995) critique, which points out that Radcliff's (1994) findings are driven by the compositional effects produced by regional differences. Erikson observes no relationship between increased turnout and Democratic vote share outside of states affected by the Voting Rights Act of 1965. Nagel and McNulty (1996, 2000) also find that the relationship between turnout and vote share is contingent upon other factors; specifically, they find that defection rates for peripheral voters depend on the partisan composition of the district and the strength of short-term forces (a blending, if you will, of the insights of Michels 1962 and Campbell 1960).

Understanding the relationship between turnout and partisan vote choice is further complicated by theoretical and empirical challenges noted in several recent projects. For instance, Hansford and Gomez (2010) contend that the decision to vote is endogenous to party preference and thus requires a more complex, sophisticated estimation strategy. They develop an instrumental variable for turnout based on county-level weather and use this to isolate the unique effects of turnout on county-level vote choice in a two-stage model. They report a significant pro-Democratic effect associated with higher turnout.[12] Fowler (2015) reanalyzes the Hansford and Gomez county-level data, seeking to identify "marginal" voters and to estimate their partisan preferences. He finds that higher turnout has a massive pro-Democratic effect.

This clutch of studies leaves us with the understanding that there is no consensus with respect to the relationship between turnout and partisan vote choice. The iconoclastic work of DeNardo (1980) continues to be controversial, with some methodological detractors and some defenders. Political science neither embraces nor rejects the popular notion that low turnout dooms Democrats; opinions vary, and where one comes down on the issue tends to hinge on one's view of complex methodological and data-analytical questions. Conventional opinion among academics and the commentariat, however, tends to come down on the side of a bias in favor of the Democrats as turnout increases from one election to the next. Absent a powerful and consistent rejoinder from the academic community, the intuitive power of the three premises remains considerable.

A Critique of the Turnout Bias Literature

Contrary findings and analyses that emphasize methodological critiques have kept the turnout bias notion viable. Therefore, before turning to our analysis, which demonstrates that there is no consistent relationship between turnout and partisan vote choice, we think it appropriate to elaborate on our own initial reservations about the research arguing in favor of the conventional wisdom. Our critique of academic work supporting the conventional wisdom is two-pronged: one-part theoretical and one-part empirical.

The Theoretical Critique: Why Assume Endogeneity?

The theoretical prong to our critique was hinted at earlier and is relatively straightforward. Several contemporary studies asserting a turnout bias begin by assuming, as a theoretical matter, that turnout is endogenous to candidate preference (e.g., Hansford and Gomez 2010). That is, who you support influences your likelihood of voting. Appropriate statistical techniques—especially the use of instrumental variables—are therefore necessary. The subsequent analyses often reveal a relationship between turnout and the Democratic vote share.

We are dubious about this formulation as well as the statistical assessment. Proponents of the endogeneity argument draw heavily on rational choice models of voting; most notably, they refer to Downs's (1957) well-known assertion that the turnout decision is a balance between the cost of voting versus the intensity of a voter's preference for a given candidate and the voter's perception that his or her vote will be decisive (recall $V = (P^*B) - C$). As noted earlier, however, Downs does not claim that the *direction* of partisan preference affects the turnout decision, only its *intensity*. Put another way, why would preferring a Democrat (or a Republican) make someone less or more likely to vote? One might assume that Democrats are generally less intense in their preferences, based on various demographic differences between Democratic and Republican identifiers. We concede that difference is possible, and some data might support it. However, that partisan asymmetry might also explain the documented probability of low-engagement voters to swing sharply between elections, a behavior that, as we show later, is as likely to provide support for a popular Republican as for a popular Democrat.

We are also disinclined to accept the argument that voters preferring the losing side in an election are more easily discouraged and less likely to vote next time. This notion has been floated after recent elections, such as 2010 and 2014 but goes back at least to the close elections of 1960 (after some were persuaded that fraud in Illinois by the Cook County Democratic machine made an Electoral College victory impossible for Nixon) and 1980 (when Carter's concession before California polls closed was held responsible for Democratic losses in California and other western states). If anything, the evidence seems to show that those motivated to vote at all are carried along by norms about voting, causing them to be disheartened voters rather than abstaining voters.

In general, why would the presumed win by one party lead to biased turnout? If one side appears certain to win an election, *no one* has an incentive to participate. Obama was the presumptive winner in 2012; turnout dropped almost 4 percentage points below the 2008 high, and he was reelected. Does this mean that supporters of the likely loser, Romney, stayed home? The survey data do not suggest a demoralized, stay-at-home bias against the underdog for any election. Supporters of the candidate expected to lose still vote, but with less enthusiasm.[13]

Another problem with the endogeneity claim from a rational-choice perspective is that even if the direction of one's vote choice influences the calculation of perceived benefit, this remains theoretically irrelevant to turnout because the probability that one's vote will determine the winner is practically zero. The decision to vote seems to be expressive of a moral perspective (I should vote to be a good citizen), along with issue or partisan intensity. And even if information on the closeness of the race drives turnout, people are notoriously poor at judging the likely outcome of elections, with a tendency to see things more favorable to their side.[14]

The bottom line is that it is unclear why one would assume that preferring one party over the other has any influence on the decision about whether to vote. Our thinking is that while there may be a relationship between having a particular candidate preference and the decision to cast a vote, it is unlikely to consistently or systematically favor one party.

The Empirical Critique: The Cross-Sectional Inference Fallacy

We are also skeptical about the empirical case linking turnout and partisan vote choice, for several reasons. First and most important, we are concerned with what we refer to as the "cross-sectional inference fallacy." Social scientists are well-acquainted with the pitfalls of ecological inference—that is, assuming individual-level relationships from aggregate-level associations (see Robinson 1950). They are less sensitive to the opposite problem, which we think is an issue here: assuming aggregate-level relationships from individual-level associations. Let us put it this way: if Democratic-leaning individuals have, *ceteris paribus*, a lower probability of turning out in an election than Republican-leaning individuals, does it follow that higher turnout will result in a higher Democratic vote share? The answer: not necessarily. In a lower-turnout country like the U.S., there is plenty of room for higher turnout even among groups with already high (on average) turnout. In high-turnout elections, therefore, turnout can readily increase across the board with little or no impact on the partisan vote.

Less grandiosely, a second empirical problem rests in the fact that much of the evidence for the turnout bias comes from recent studies that rely on two-stage, fixed-effects models of county-level voting data. As detailed earlier, the theoretical rationale offered by these studies for two-stage models is straight-forward: they assume that vote choice and turnout are endogenous to one another, such that simple tests of association or regression models can produce biased estimates of the underlying relationship. They go on to offer two-stage models, with the modeled turnout variable being significantly correlated with Democratic vote share. The empirical results are curious, though. Both in these studies and elsewhere, simple, one-stage models show no systematic relationship between turnout and partisan vote choice. Typically (though not always), endogenous relationships result in an *exaggerated* relationship between two variables. The explanatory variable is credited with affecting the dependent variable, when the causal arrow points in both directions. Here the argument is that the relationship between turnout and Democratic vote share is not observed but *becomes* significant once one controls for other factors that affect first partisan vote choice and then turnout. No one, however, has explained the absence of a bivariate relationship, which is fundamental to those who believe turnout shifts have partisan consequences. Put more argumentatively, this strikes us as an assertion that while nothing seems to be going on in the data, a complicated statistical model with many hyperplanes of effects can find something significant at some level of probability.

A third reason for our skepticism involves the treatment of cross sections. Cross sections (or cross-sectional units) are counties, districts, or states where elections occur. Because these often have different rules and unique political contexts, some analysts believe that it is essential to include fixed-effect variables—dummy variables for each cross section—in statistical models. In fact most recent analyses of county-level turnout and vote choice have featured fixed-effects models. As a practical matter, these variables tend to correct (reduce) the magnitude of coefficients associated with other, non-cross-sectional explanatory factors; variance attributable to cross-sectional effects is thus not inadvertently credited to other predictors.

But there are problems with this approach. Fixed-effects models assume there is no change within cross sections across the time series; Colorado elections are Colorado elections, for example, whether they occur in 1966, 1976, or 2016, and they are distinct from elections in California, New York, or Texas. Except that both the rules and the electorate have changed appreciably in Colorado over time; you can register to vote on Election Day now, mail-in voting is the norm, and an influx of Hispanics has created a much more diverse (and Democratic-leaning) voting public. This creates an interpretation problem. In recent elections you see higher turnout (due to greatly liberalized voting rules) and a higher Democratic vote percentage (due to a more Democratic population). But a fixed-effects model would simply estimate the positive relationship because it assumes a static environment at the cross-sectional level. In other words, even though a fixed-effects model is supposed to ameliorate omitted variable biases, such biases remain a major issue for cross-sectional, time-series election data in the U.S.

Another problem is that fixed-effects models tend to produce biased results when there are not many observations at the cross-sectional level. The models examine variance in the relationship between turnout and partisan vote choice over a series of elections in different cross-sectional units, and their estimates of this relationship are not accurate when you do not have many elections. Unfortunately most analyses focus on a relative handful of elections—maybe ten, maybe twenty, but certainly not as many as one needs to be confident in the estimations of the fixed-effects models.

Note that our objections to some of the data analysis linking higher turnout with increased vote share for Democratic candidates are *not* based on a prejudice against complex or innovative modeling. Rather these objections are based on what we regard as a lack of proper attention to (and an understanding of) the more basic patterns and relationships between the variables of interest. Equally fundamental, these approaches—especially cross-sectional estimations—are manipulating data that do not correspond to the substantive nature of the relationship. The turnout bias thesis expects change in the Democratic share of the vote from one election to the next to correspond to change in turnout. Any analysis must examine turnout and vote share *within* the electoral unit to test the bias thesis, as Tucker, Vedlitz, and DeNardo (1986) have stated. All of this informs our efforts in the following chapters to estimate and thoroughly explore whether there is a fundamental, empirical association between the decision to vote and partisan vote choice.

4

Turnout and Partisan Vote Choice

OVER TIME AND ACROSS STATES AND DISTRICTS

IN THIS CHAPTER we directly assess the expectation of the bias thesis: that an increase in turnout from one election to the next produces a larger vote share for the Democratic candidate, while a decline in turnout reduces it. We rely on straightforward data to analyze changes *through time* for each of the following:

- Presidential elections from 1948 through 2016, overall and within the states.
- Senate elections overall, and for all one hundred seats from 1966 through 2016.
- Gubernatorial elections overall, and for all fifty states from 1966 through 2016.
- Congressional elections overall, and for all 435 districts from 1972 through 2010.

In short, this chapter explores the historical record of the relationship between turnout and election outcomes over the past half-century. Our focus, as suggested earlier, is on aggregate patterns. But in the course of this study, we examine a wide range of aggregate data, relying on the grossest (national presidential results) as well as the most granular (county- and district-wide) results.

The Turnout Myth. Daron R. Shaw and John R. Petrocik, Oxford University Press (2020). © Oxford University Press.
DOI: 10.1093/oso/9780190089450.001.0001

National Results: Presidential and House Elections

We begin at the most obvious starting point. Figure 4.1 plots turnout and the Democratic vote for presidential elections from 1948 through 2016; the joint distribution is essentially a cloud of points, with no indication of a higher Democratic vote with greater turnout. The figure seems to show a slight correlation (the slope of the line estimating the relationship is 0.23) if one includes the 1964 election, where turnout was high and the Republican vote was exceptionally low. However, the 1964 election is clearly an outlier. The slope without the 1964 data point is indistinguishable from zero. Even if the 1964 point is treated as probative and left in the analysis, the data do not lend much support to the bias thesis. With or without the 1964 election, the spread around the slope is so great that the ability to predict the vote share with turnout is effectively zero (the correlation is 0.11). The deletion of the 1964 election flattens the slope and generates a correlation of 0.07 between turnout and the Democratic presidential vote. The finding is clear with or without 1964: turnout and the vote share are substantially independent. Democratic candidates won elections with a turnout rate in the low 50s, and won and lost elections with turnout in the 60s.

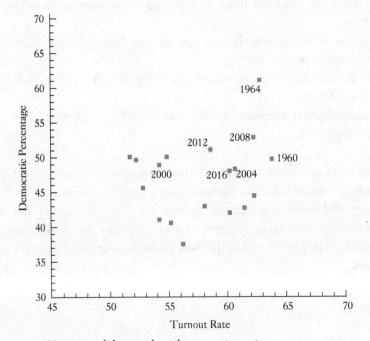

FIGURE 4.1 Turnout and the presidential vote, 1948–2016.

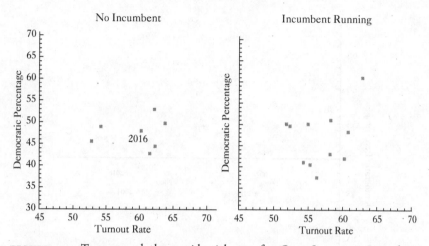

FIGURE 4.2 Turnout and the presidential vote for Open-Seat verus Incumbent Elections, 1948–2016.

Figure 4.2 sorts presidential elections into those when an incumbent was seeking reelection in contrast to elections when the race was open. The figure makes the distinction because it is possible that an incumbent president's reelection prospects are known to voters (seventeen of twenty-four incumbent presidents have been reelected since the Civil War), resulting in a lower turnout rate since the incumbent's near certainty of success may marginally reduce enthusiasm about the election and therefore turnout.[1] The historical success of reelection bids might also have depressed get-out-the-vote efforts by the campaigns; candidates regarded as certain to win (or lose) may have produced less intense GOTV activity. However, as the two data panels demonstrate, the evidence does not support an incumbent effect on the relationship: turnout and the vote are uncorrelated in incumbent and open elections (1964 is the outlier in the "Incumbent Running" panel).

Members of Congress

Is it possible that the presidency is somehow distinct? Might a more consistent relationship emerge if we examine the congressional vote? The short answer is no. The plot of election results for the House of Representative in Figure 4.3 echoes the pattern in Figures 4.1 and 4.2. It shows no relationship between turnout and the Democratic vote for members of Congress in off-years or presidential years. The overall coefficient is 0.03, which is insignificant; slopes for the separated off-year elections and the on-year elections are

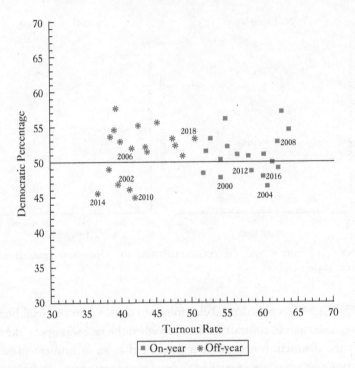

FIGURE 4.3 Turnout and the congressional vote, 1948–2018.

comparable. We would add that House elections seem particularly instructive since the Democrats were the almost uninterrupted majority party from 1948 through 1994 (losing the House only in 1952), with turnout ranging from a low of 38 percent to a high of 64.

Turnout in the off-years (the left-side of the figure) is uncorrelated with the election outcome; turnout in presidential years is similarly uncorrelated with the partisan result. Paired-case comparisons between elections provide supporting detail. For example, turnout in the 1994 midterm election was slightly higher (at about 41 percent) than turnout for the several off-year elections that preceded and followed it, but that did not keep the Republicans from taking the House majority for the first time in an off-year election since 1946. The succeeding (1996) higher turnout presidential election did not eliminate that GOP majority, which survived three high-turnout presidential elections, only to be lost in the typically low-turnout 2006 midterm election. Other paired comparisons tell the same story. For example, turnout increased about 5 points between 2002 and 2006, with the Democrats taking the House in the latter election. This might be an example of the bias at work except that between 2006 and 2010 turnout increased again, yet the Democrats were swept into the minority. Pairwise comparisons for the presidential years also confound the bias thesis. To name just one example, an increase in turnout between 2000 and 2004 reinforced the GOP's House majority.[2]

Statewide Results: Gubernatorial and Senatorial Elections

Figures 4.1–4.3 are the basic test of the turnout–vote choice hypothesis at the national level. They examine a single electoral unit (the country as a whole) through time, which—despite the vagaries of the Electoral College and the specific political dynamics of the states—should have exhibited a turnout effect rather than the null correlations represented in the figures. Figures 4.4 and 4.5 report the Democratic vote as a function of state-level turnout. More specifically, the figures plot turnout and the Democratic vote for governor and U.S. senator in presidential years and off-years. The election cycle is split because off-year turnout is typically about 20 percentage points below that of

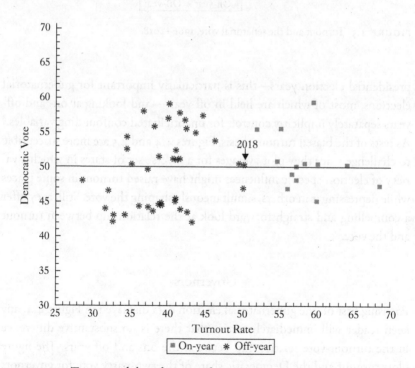

FIGURE 4.4 Turnout and the gubernatorial vote, 1948–2018.

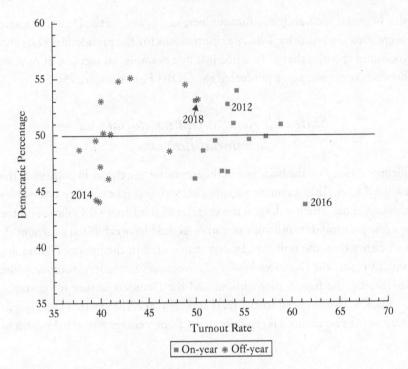

FIGURE 4.5 Turnout and the senatorial vote, 1966–2018.

presidential election years—this is particularly important for gubernatorial elections, most of which are held in off-years—and looking at on- and off-years separately implicitly controls for unanticipated confounding variables.[3] As tests of the biased turnout thesis, Figures 4.4 and 4.5 are more susceptible to challenge since they plot averages for a diverse set of states in which a variety of election-specific influences might have raised turnout in some places while depressing it in others, simultaneously shaping the vote. Still, they offer a compelling and straightforward look at the relationship between turnout and the vote.

Governors

Focusing first on the gubernatorial election data displayed in Figure 4.4, any keen reader will immediately notice that there is no substantive difference in the turnout-vote relationship between the on- and off-years. The figure plots turnout and the Democratic share of the two-party vote for governors from 1966 through 2018, both overall and with on- and off-years separated.

The overall relationship is flat, as are the separate relationships for on- and off-year election cycles. In fact the close similarity of gubernatorial results with those for presidential elections is striking. No matter how one looks at them, the plots in Figure 4.4 echo the first three figures: turnout and vote do not covary. Vote share is apparently independent of the aggregate outcome of gubernatorial elections. In some years turnout was quite low, in others it was very high, but the participation rate did not systematically produce more—or fewer—Democratic governors.

Senators

Figure 4.5 plots turnout and the Democratic share of the two-party vote for U.S. senators from 1966 through 2018, with on- and off-years again separated. The pattern in the figure repeats the earlier data.[4] The overall slope from the regression is 0.06, which is statistically insignificant. A confirmatory mindset might see a relationship between the Senate Democratic vote and turnout in the off-years; however, the very steepness of the off-year slope makes this implausible, and a close examination of the elections that create the off-year pattern suggests another cause. Specifically, all four of the elections that yielded an unusual spike in Democratic support—1970, 1974, 1982, and 2006—occurred when the incumbent Republican president was unpopular (sometimes extremely so, as in 1974 and 2006), producing Democratic sweeps despite typical turnout rates in three of the four elections. In contrast, the high-turnout 1966 election produced significant Democratic losses in the Senate.

The results are clear and compelling: lower-turnout elections do not consistently elect more Republicans; off-year elections that have lower than average turnout do not reliably elect more Republicans; presidential years with higher turnout do not consistently elect more Democrats. Proponents of the turnout bias hypothesis might find some supporting evidence by picking out an anomalous result (recall the effect of 1964 in Figure 4.1), but these anomalous results are usually exactly that: bits of errant data. The overall pattern of the relationship between turnout and vote is a circular cloud in which turnout variation provides no reliable prediction of the vote outcome.

Confounding Influences

The persistence and pervasiveness of the conventional wisdom, as well as unmistakable evidence that Democrats are more likely than Republicans to abstain from voting, make it reasonable to further extend our tests with an additional analytic approach. Consider the following skeptical conjecture: What if national or statewide elections are too aggregated? What if a strong, consistent effect of turnout on vote choice is masked by factors that offset when aggregated up to the state? Methodologically, this possibility constitutes a reversed version of the ecological regression fallacy. Indeed, as suggested earlier, we think of it as something of an aggregation fallacy; relationships that exist at the individual level are sometimes suppressed when cases are aggregated to a higher level (Robinson 1950). Substantively, this is implicit in the work of Hansford and Gomez (2010), who contend that instrumental variables and fixed-effects models are necessary to reveal the true aggregate-level relationship between turnout and Democratic vote choice.

In response to this possibility, we continue to examine aggregate-level data, but our eyes shift to a more granular level and our explanatory focus expands. What exactly are we looking for? First, some have argued that race or ethnicity masks the relationship between turnout and partisan vote choice. For example, if heavily Latino counties or districts turn out at relatively low rates but vote overwhelmingly for the Democratic candidates, could that make it seem like low turnout helps the Democrats and create a misleading aggregate-level relationship? The hypothetical scenario is represented in Figure 4.6, where a fitted regression line accounting for all the data suggests a negative relationship between turnout and Democratic vote share. A closer look, however, reveals that there are two distinct clusters of districts, each of which (on its own) displays a positive relationship between turnout and support for the Democratic candidate. It is the combination of the two that creates the erroneous negative association. Could this account for the null findings in the previous figures?

Similarly, urban-rural cultural differences (other than race or ethnicity) might complicate the aggregate-level pattern. The notion here is that turnout in the cities tends to be lower yet also more Democratic; as with the previous example, this might make it seem as if low turnout helps the Democrats when, within each subset of rural and urban counties or districts, the relationship is the opposite. Rural counties and districts further complicate the story because they tend to have lower turnout rates but are quite heterogeneous with respect to how they vote (consider a lower-socioeconomic-status county in West Virginia compared to one in Mississippi).

The preceding examples demonstrate the need for sensitivity and nuance when estimating aggregate-level relationships between turnout and vote choice. To do so, we look at county-level results from presidential elections as

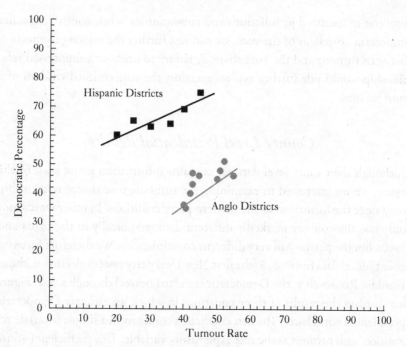

FIGURE 4.6 Confounding effects on vote choice.
Source: Simulated data.

well as revisit U.S. House district results to explore the possibility that a core relationship exists between turnout and vote choice but is obscured by other factors when one telescopes out to the state level.

With respect to county-level data, we rely on detailed political, economic, and social information compiled for every presidential election from 1948 through 2004 by Peter Nardulli at the University of Illinois, Champaign-Urbana. Nardulli's data set encompasses forty-six elections across 3,007 counties, with variables gauging population, registration, turnout, presidential vote choice, partisanship of officeholders and representatives, electoral competitiveness, economic conditions, crime rates, race, ethnicity, age, income, and education (see Nardulli 2007).

We developed a data set of similar depth and versatility for every House of Representatives election from the 2000s (2002–2010) and the 2010s (2012–2016). House districts, of course, are somewhat difficult to examine given that most change their boundaries every ten years after the Census. Still, the possibility of examining the turnout–partisan vote choice relationship with appropriate controls and at a relatively granular aggregate level in the most recent elections makes such an analysis imperative.[5] By looking at the entire universe of localized jurisdictions and communities, while controlling other important correlates of the vote, we can test further the missing connection between turnout and the vote share. A failure to uncover a suppressed relationship would pile further evidence against the conventional wisdom of a turnout bias.

County-Level Presidential Results

Although the county-level data set contains information going back to the 1920s, we are interested in examining the turnout–vote choice relationship only since the formation of the modern party coalitions. In other words, not only was the country markedly different demographically in the 1920s and 1930s, but the parties had very different constituencies. We therefore focus on county-level data from 1948 (the first New Deal party system election without Franklin Roosevelt as the Democratic standard-bearer) through 2004. Figure 4.7 displays the results of three equations in which we estimate Democratic presidential vote share.[6] The first coefficient comes from a simple bivariate regression with turnout as the sole explanatory variable. This coefficient (−0.16, represented by a dot in the figure with lines showing 95 percent confidence

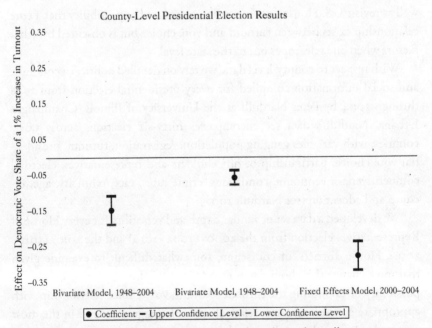

FIGURE 4.7 Turnout effect on Democratic presidential vote share, all counties.

intervals) indicates that turnout is negatively correlated with Democratic vote share; that is, increased turnout coincides with a lower Democratic vote. The result is significant, although this is mostly because the substantial number of cases (counties) makes almost any effect statistically significant.

But what if we control for factors that might affect both turnout and Democratic vote share? The result of the second equation (displayed in Figure 4.7) indicates that the negative effect of turnout on the Democratic presidential vote persists when we introduce a fixed-effects model that controls for the impact of individual states, election years, electoral competitiveness of the county, southern and rural counties, and the county-wide incidence of black and foreign-born voters.[7]

While we are not concerned with the effects of other variables estimated by our models, it is worth noting that they have the expected influence on Democratic vote share. For example, a higher percentage of foreign-born residents in a county correlates with increased Democratic support, as does a higher percentage of African American residents. These effects are more substantial than those associated with residential location or region or, tellingly, turnout. Rural counties are mostly associated with increased Democratic support, although this effect is substantively small and reverses in the equation for more recent elections. Conversely, southern counties tend to produce lower levels of Democratic support, even when one controls for state-by-state effects. Then there is a curious result: electorally competitive counties, on average, tend to be associated with increased Democratic vote share. We admit that our primary motivation for including this variable was to ensure that our estimate of the turnout effect was not biased by neglecting the fact that turnout tends to be higher in competitive races. The attendant curious relationship is substantively quite small and does not interact with or confound the main effect of turnout tested by the equation.

Considering the minimal relationship between turnout and presidential vote choice observed at the county level, some might object to the scope of the time series. That is, examining the relationship between turnout and partisan vote choice over seventy years might obscure a connection that emerges in the latter years of the time series, as the post–New Deal party coalitions finally stabilized. The results of the final equation presented in Figure 4.7 consider this possibility by focusing on county-level data from 2000 and 2004, the last years of our data set. We re-estimate the full model and find that the regression coefficient for turnout is even more negative and significant (−0.27) than for the entire time series. This indicates that the tendency of peripheral voters to look even more like Democrats (in their demographic characteristics) in recent years has not meant that increased turnout produces higher Democratic vote shares.

The analysis was extended to explore further different elements of the turnout–vote choice relationship. For example, it is possible that the lack of a general correlation between turnout and vote choice does not preclude the possibility of such a relationship in particular areas of the country. However plausible the suggestion, it is not observed in the data. Figure 4.8 shows the results when we isolate rural and urban counties and then re-estimate the equations for the Democratic vote share. The hypothesis we are testing here is that there may be a relationship between turnout and vote choice in these places but that it is obscured when examining data from all counties. More specifically, we think that many of these Democratic-leaning locations have lower turnout, and we want to see if relatively higher turnout in these counties might produce even more lopsided results for the Democrats. Once again, however plausible the possibility, the data do not support it. For rural counties, the turnout coefficient is negatively signed and statistically significant (−0.10). For urban counties, the relationship is positive (0.15) but is not statistically distinct from zero. It is important that, statistical significance aside, the relationships are small.

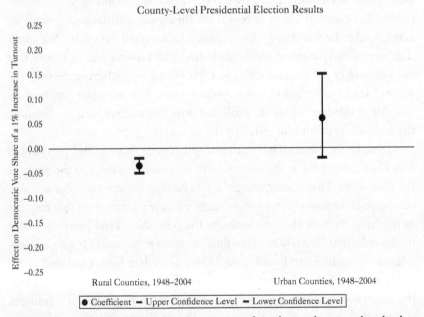

FIGURE 4.8 Turnout effect on Democratic presidential vote share, rural and urban counties.

Other results from the rural and urban county equations lead us to believe the preceding statistical models are sound. As expected, higher percentages of African American voters in a county correlate with improved Democratic electoral performance. Rural counties in southern states also produced lower Democratic presidential vote percentages, though this effect is much smaller and driven by the results of more recent presidential elections. Finally, there were not enough urban counties in the southern states to reliably estimate the impact of region on Democratic voting in the cities.

As compelling as these controlled analyses of granular, county-level data are, they still rely on a handful of demographic and political variables. Ideally we would like to extend the nature of the controls to encompass political and economic conditions. Recall from chapter 3 that many theories of vote choice assume that Americans reward and punish the incumbent party based on judgments about the political, economic, and social environment of the election—and what they indicate about the incumbent's stewardship. We would like to control for these judgments here (or at least use measures of the conditions on which they are based) as we gauge the independent effect of turnout. Practically this means that we need to conduct two separate analyses. The first is to assess how a range of factors affect support for the Democratic presidential candidate when the Republicans are the incumbent party. Presumably, favorable economic data will *decrease* support for the Democratic candidate in these elections.

Figure 4.9 shows the results from such an analysis in the first two dot-and-line plots (which display regression coefficients for turnout, along with their 95 percent confidence intervals). These turnout coefficients come from two equations: the first equation estimates county-level Democratic presidential vote share for elections with a Republican incumbent, based on an array of demographic and political control variables, including an estimate of real gross domestic product (GDP);[8] the second equation concentrates solely on the same types of elections but only in the modern era (1972–2004). Conversely, the two dot-and-line plots on the right-hand side of Figure 4.9 display the results for turnout based on elections when the Democrats are the incumbent party and where we presume that favorable economic data will *increase* support for the Democratic presidential candidate. Once again, the first of these turnout coefficients is based on a fully specified model covering relevant presidential elections from 1948 through 2004; the second turnout coefficient concentrates on the modern era and includes the Democratic incumbent elections of 1980, 1996, and 2000.

County-Level Presidential Results

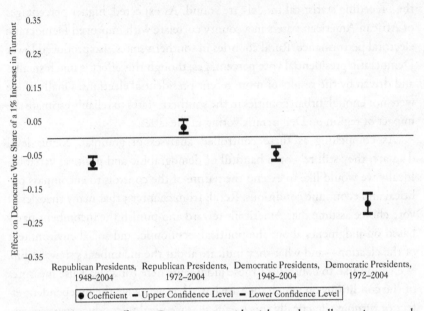

FIGURE 4.9 Turnout effect on Democratic presidential vote share, all counties, controlling for economic performance.

Focusing first on the elections in which the GOP controlled the White House, the results document the electoral rewards for positive economic conditions: the nonincumbent (Democratic) party vote share decreases. The effect is consistent across both equations. More important for our purposes, adding economic conditions to the mix does not create (or reveal) a consistent association between turnout and Democratic vote share. For 1948 through 2004, presidential elections with a Republican incumbent produce a turnout coefficient that is negatively signed and statistically significant. But in presidential elections from 1972 through 2004, the estimated impact of turnout on Democratic vote share is positively signed and statistically significant. However, in neither equation does the estimated effect of turnout merit attention. The regression coefficients of −0.04 and 0.07, respectively, document a trivial effect and are significant only because the very large number of observations depresses the standard error of the estimate.

This story of minimal turnout effects is mostly the same when we focus on elections in which the Democrats control the White House, although there are some twists. For example, from 1948 through 2004 the data indicate that economic growth *negatively* correlates with the Democratic vote share. This apparent anomaly disappears in more recent presidential elections, suggesting that it may have been an artifact of unpopular wars in the earlier years of the time series (Korea in 1952 and Vietnam in 1968). However, these nuances and details should not obscure the main finding: higher turnout is *not* associated with increased Democratic vote share. In purely statistical terms, a negative relationship exists, mostly because of the thousands of counties underlying the analysis. Substantively, however, there seems to be little meaningful association between turnout and partisan vote choice at the county level, as there was not at the level of national aggregation.

5

Turnout and Partisan Vote Choice

OVER TIME AND WITHIN STATES AND DISTRICTS

THE PREVIOUS CHAPTER presented analyses of the vote as a function of turnout among elections at the national level (the presidential contests) and by states (senators and governors), congressional districts (House contests), and counties (House and presidential), finding no consistent relationship between turnout and the Democratic vote. But while these analyses offer scant evidence of a turnout bias, the data can be explored from an additional perspective. Our goal in this chapter is to address some of the limits of previous analyses (both ours and others') and to directly examine the association between turnout and vote choice without introducing confounding statistical effects.

The design in this chapter explores the link between turnout and the vote across an extended series of elections *within* each state and *within* electoral districts. The strength of this design is that it conforms exactly to the ordinary language that analysts and commentators use to assert a connection. That is, the proponents of a turnout bias argue that increased turnout in a forthcoming election should increase the Democrat's share of the vote compared to the previous election, while a turnout drop will erode that share. We build straightforward data into a specific analysis of changes *through time* for presidential elections from 1948 through 2016, for each Senate seat from 1966 through 2016, for each state's gubernatorial contests from 1966 through 2016, and for all 435 congressional districts from 1972 through 2010.

This design controls for endemic and long-term turnout and vote share differences among states and districts. This approach permits us to examine how turnout influences vote choice in a low-turnout Republican state (such as Oklahoma, where turnout was only 49 percent in 2012) or a high-turnout

The Turnout Myth. Daron R. Shaw and John R. Petrocik, Oxford University Press (2020). © Oxford University Press.
DOI: 10.1093/oso/9780190089450.001.0001

Democratic state (such as Massachusetts, where turnout was 66 percent in 2012), without the *typical* turnout or party division confounding the correlation between turnout and vote share.

This approach directly addresses a pervasive problem in the literature. A fundamental flaw of most studies of the partisan effects of turnout is that they are cross-sectional, with data pooled from several elections. They do not test what the turnout bias thesis expects: changes in the vote share as a product of changes in turnout. They generally examine only whether there is a relationship between turnout and the vote, which is not what the bias thesis proposes. These analyses often purport to be assessing turnout effects because their equations attempt to control for differences among the units of analysis (usually states, sometimes counties) with fixed-effects dummy variables. We think that approach is flawed, as we noted in chapters 3 and 4, because the fixed-effects models cannot handle unobservable factors that vary with time, such as a state's (or county's) demography or voting laws. Our own equations estimating the impact of turnout on vote choice in chapter 4, while more attentive to these issues than previous analyses, are subject to the same limitations. Equally troubling is that although the pooling of data from states and across elections provides sufficient cases for estimation, the number of fixed-effect controls (fifty states, for example) often exceed the number of elections, a factor that confounds the estimates.

While potentially instructive, cross-sectional correlations of turnout and the vote do not adequately test the turnout bias argument.[1] The bias hypothesis expects correlated *changes* in turnout and the vote, from one election to the next, within a constant electorate. Political practitioners and journalists look for an increase in turnout compared to the preceding election to benefit Democratic candidates because, as we documented earlier, voters with a profile associated with Democratic sympathies are disproportionately less likely to vote (see Table 1.1 in chapter 1), and when turnout increases, they are disproportionate contributors to the increase. According to the commentariat, an increase in turnout from one election to the next, for any city, county, district, or state, compared to the preceding election, should increase the participation of voters with a Democratic profile simply because the most consistent participants across several elections are disproportionately oriented to the GOP.

A Test for Turnout Bias

The most direct way to observe the bias effect is to examine whether the Democratic vote varies with the turnout from election to election for each office or district. Our data set therefore includes every gubernatorial and senatorial election from the mid-1960s through 2018, and we analyze the turnout–vote share relationship for every Senate seat and gubernatorial contest across this time span. Congressional districts, because they are stable for only a ten-year/five-election period following the redistricting, provide a shorter analytical period. However, whatever is lost by the five-election limit is compensated for by the replication of four redistricting eras: 1972–1980, 1982–1990, 1992–2000, and 2002–2010.

The test for bias calculates a slope for the regression of turnout on the vote share for every Senate and gubernatorial election held in the fifty states from the mid-1960s through 2016, and for all 435 congressional districts from 1972 through 2010.[2] For any given Senate seat, governor's chair, or congressional district, the regression will produce a positive slope when increased turnout generates more Democratic support, flat slopes when turnout and the vote share are independent, and negative slopes when the Republicans benefit from increased turnout in the state or district. Some House districts, Senate seats, or gubernatorial elections may deviate from the turnout bias expectation of a positive slope and yield flat or negative results, but the deviations should be few and the average of the slopes should be positive if the conventional bias expectation exists. Put differently, a histogram plot of the distribution of the calculated slopes for the fifty gubernatorial chairs, one hundred Senate seats, and 435 House seats in four redistricting regimes should result in a positive average value. A distribution with many negative values or values relatively close to zero—whether large or not—constitute evidence *against* the assumption that increases in turnout help Democratic candidates. It does not prove that GOTV efforts or spontaneous mobilization in some election cannot produce a victory where defeat was otherwise likely. However, it does establish that turnout variation in typical partisan elections is not a systematic influence on national election outcomes. More to the point, it refutes the conventional proposition that high turnout is a Democratic asset while low turnout advantages Republicans.

How the Analysis Is Done

Figure 5.1 provides hypothetical examples of the analysis that follows. The numbers 1, 2, or 3 on each data point in the graphs report the order of the elections: election 1 was the first election, and election 3 was the third. The order of the elections is not germane. Elections 1 and 2 might have low turnouts and be followed by a high-turnout Election 3 (see panel 1). What

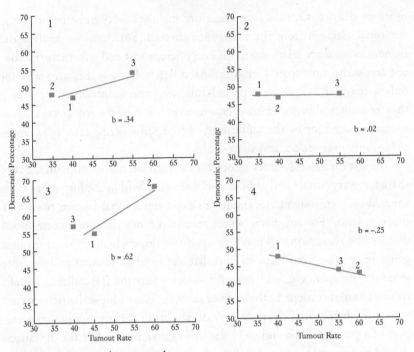

FIGURE 5.1 Turnout bias: examples.
Source: Simulated data.

matters is whether the vote share varies with turnout, whether the Democratic vote is greater with high turnout and smaller with lower turnout. Panel 1 in Figure 5.1 shows the conventionally expected bias. In elections with a turnout of less than about 40 percent, the Democrat can expect to lose. By contrast, the 55 percent turnout election in panel 1 results in a Democratic win. This is slightly different from what we see in panel 3, which shows Democratic victories at low- and high-turnout levels. There is still a turnout bias, though, because the Democratic vote surges with turnout. Panel 2 shows no evidence of a turnout bias: the slope is near zero. Panel 4 does indicate a bias, but one in which higher turnout favors the Republicans. The average regression slope across the four districts is 0.18; in this hypothetical universe, increasing turnout is linked to increased Democratic support. The story is more complicated, however, as the spread of outcomes among the four districts is evidence against a systematic effect. The positive slope average is created by the relatively extreme value of the district in panel 3.

Figure 5.2 further illustrates the point with turnout and vote share data from three districts selected at random: Ohio CD 5 during the 1980s, Iowa

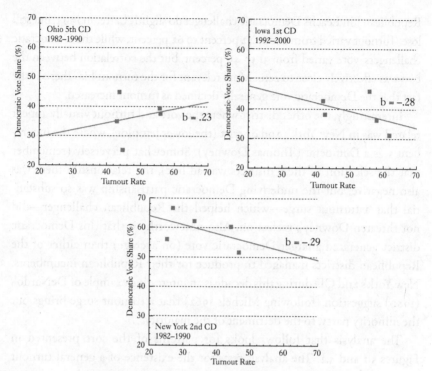

FIGURE 5.2 Turnout and the Democratic House vote, three cases.

CD 1 during the 1990s, and New York CD 2 during the 1980s. Ohio's 5th district, in the upper left corner, was represented by Republicans throughout the decade of the 1980s. Del Latta held the seat through 1988 and was succeeded by Republican Paul Gilmour. One of Latta's victories occurred in a presidential year (1984), while the other two occurred in off-years (1982 and 1986). Gilmore was elected in the 1988 presidential election year and then reelected in the off-year of 1990. A Democratic challenger did best against Latta in 1982 (a lower turnout, off-year election), receiving 44.8 percent of the vote with a turnout just below 44 percent. The weakest Democratic opponent received a bit more than 25 percent support when turnout was marginally greater (just under 45 percent). Both presidential elections produced 55 percent turnout rates and Democratic challengers who managed 37 and 39 percent. There is no meaningful turnout influence to observe in the graph, despite a seemingly large regression coefficient.[3]

The scatterplot for Iowa's 1st district is almost a mirror image of the pattern for Ohio's 5th. The highest turnout (in 1992) yielded the lowest Democratic support. The nearly 20-point turnout decline between 1992 and 1994 saw incumbent

Republican Jim Leach's Democratic challenger do slightly better in 1994, but still lose. Turnout varied from about 42 percent to 62 percent, while the Democratic challengers' vote varied from 31 to 46 percent, but the correlation between the two was effectively close to zero. More relevant for the turnout bias thesis is the fact that the Democratic vote generally declined as turnout increased.

Interestingly, the other district where the vote and turnout visually appear related was in New York's 2nd district (the lower left plot), where the incumbent was a Democrat (Thomas Downey). Somewhat perversely (remember that the selection of these districts was ad hoc), the relationship there was also negative, but the underlying Democratic partisanship was so substantial that a turnout surge—which helped the Republican challenger—did not threaten Downey's reelection. Also noteworthy is that this Democratic district generated a larger Democratic vote (on average) than either of the Republican districts managed to produce for their Republican incumbents. New York's 2nd CD during this decade is an interesting example of DeNardo's (1980) suggestion (following Michels 1962) that a turnout surge brings out the minority party, to the detriment of the majority.

The analysis that follows looks for patterns of the sort presented in Figures 5.1 and 5.2. The analysis tests for the existence of a general turnout bias by examining the distribution of slope coefficients from the regression of turnout on the Democratic vote for one hundred Senate seats, 435 congressional districts, and gubernatorial contests in the fifty states—where the Senate seats, congressional districts, and (for the governors) the states are the units of analysis. There are several possible shapes to this resulting distribution of regression coefficients, but whether they are normal, peaked, flat, or multimodal, the key tests for the bias thesis is the central tendency and the attendant distribution. A distribution that is (on average) positive with most of the coefficients being positive indicates that the Democratic share of the vote (on average) increases with turnout. In contrast, a distribution of coefficients with a negative average indicates that Republicans are more likely to prosper from a turnout increase between elections. Finally, a distribution that is approximately symmetrical (or perhaps multimodal) around a mean at or near zero indicates that there is no consistent pattern. That is, the distribution shows that the vote for Democratic candidates for these offices sometimes increases with turnout, sometimes declines, but overall favors neither party.

Analyzing Senate and gubernatorial elections is difficult because of (a) the length of terms for senators (six years, excepting special elections) and (b) the variable terms for governors across the different states (two years in some states, four in others).[4] The time necessary to produce sufficient Senate or gubernatorial elections that will support an analysis (let us say five or six cycles, representing twenty or thirty-six years) will include confounding candidate effects (since different candidates are likely to be involved), possibly substantial changes in voting and registration laws, and shifts in the underlying demographic characteristics of the population. However, all of these are factors that cause turnout and the vote to vary, presenting an important real environment for ascertaining the influence of turnout. Further, most of the changes that have occurred in recent decades are more likely to create (rather than confound) a turnout bias.

As mentioned in chapter 4, Colorado comes to mind as an illustrative example. Turnout in the Rocky Mountain State has increased in recent elections, and the formerly Republican bastion has trended Democratic. Turnout was relatively high in the 2012 and 2016 elections, and both elections were won by the Democrat, Obama and Clinton. This is consistent with the turnout bias hypothesis, although other factors complicate this simple interpretation. For instance, the state has consistently liberalized its voting laws since 2000, culminating with the adoption of same-day registration and mail-in voting in 2013. Easier voting laws should increase turnout, at least modestly, so we should expect to see the Democrats benefit if the old laws were disproportionately keeping Democratically inclined voters from the polls (as many suggest). Meanwhile, the statewide Hispanic population has grown significantly over the past couple of decades. This adds a pro-Democratic group to the electorate. These simultaneous legal and population changes might make it difficult to estimate how much turnout or Hispanic population growth uniquely contributed to a new Democratic vote equilibrium. This analysis, however, is not estimating these change components. Our interest is singularly in whether turnout variation—from whatever source—correlates with the Democratic share of the vote. Moreover we assume that examining the relationship for Senate seats, governorships, and House districts over a fifty-year period most likely removes the confounding effects of some of these unknowable peculiarities.

To further illustrate the method, consider Figures 5.3 and 5.4, which report turnout and the Democratic vote for Senate elections from California (Figure 5.3) and Texas (Figure 5.4).[5] The data in the figures are scatterplots and line graphs of the turnout rate and the Democratic vote for every election from 1966 through 2018 for the seats currently held by Kamala Harris and Diane Feinstein in California and John Cornyn and Ted Cruz in Texas. The figures display the regression line estimating turnout's effect on the Democratic vote for these elections. Inserted within each figure is a year-by-year line graph of

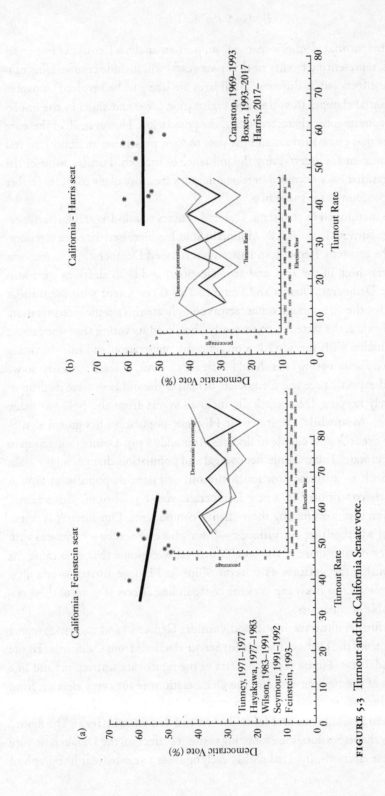

FIGURE 5.3 Turnout and the California Senate vote.

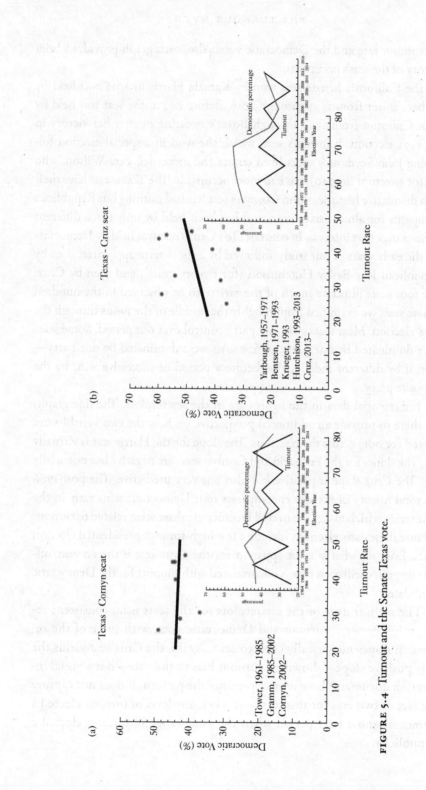

FIGURE 5.4 Turnout and the Senate Texas vote.

the turnout rate and the Democratic vote. Also, each graph provides a brief history of the seat's occupants.

The California Senate seat won by Kamala Harris in 2016 was held by Barbara Boxer from 1993 through 2016. Before Boxer, the seat was held by Alan Cranston from 1969 through Boxer's swearing in after her victory in the 1992 election. Feinstein's seat, which she won in a special election following John Seymour's short-lived tenure (he succeeded Pete Wilson, who ran for governor in 1990), has had more occupants. The Texas seats have their own distinctive histories. John Cornyn's seat has had nothing but Republican occupants for almost sixty years and has been held by only three different persons over that interval. In contrast, Ted Cruz's seat was held by Democrats for the early years of our study, followed by a short-term appointee, then by Republican Kay Bailey Hutchinson (for twenty years), and then by Cruz. The four seats illustrate much of the variety to be observed in the hundred Senate seats we examined from roughly the middle of the 1960s through the 2018 election. Most seats switched party control over our period. Some seats were dominated by one party. A few seats were dominated by one party—even if by different individuals—before a period of successive wins by the opposite party.

The essential data in the figures are in the scatterplots. The line graphs are there to provide an additional perspective on how the two variables are related (or not) across the elections. The slope for the Harris seat is virtually flat. The slopes for the Feinstein and Cornyn seats are negative but essentially flat. The Cruz slope is positive but also not very predictive. The post-1966 electoral history of his seat encompasses four Democratic wins early in the time series, which makes the overall Democratic share seem related to turnout because these early elections include a few high-turnout presidential election years. Even so, what is most apparent for the Cruz seat is the on-year/off-year turnout oscillation that is uncorrelated with support for the Democratic candidate.

The main feature of the scatterplots for the seats is no consistent relationship between turnout and Democratic vote, with three of the regression slopes numerically close to zero. Again, the Cruz seat yields the only positive slope—showing a turnout bias to the vote—but a visual inspection documents how it misrepresents the pattern. It does not capture the fact of two eras for this seat: one when any level of turnout elected a Democrat and a later period when the same range in turnout elected a Republican.

Looking for a Turnout Vote Relationship: The Presidency

Presidential elections, like gubernatorial and senatorial elections, occur at the state level. Therefore the relationship between turnout and the Democratic vote can be examined in the same way in which the correspondence of turnout and the vote share is assessed for gubernatorial and Senate elections. That is, we can look at the distribution of slope coefficients for turnout and the presidential vote for each of the fifty states over the period from 1948 to 2016. As before, the key question is straightforward: Can the Democratic presidential candidate expect his or her vote share in the state to rise as turnout rises?

The answer is no, as Figure 5.5 demonstrates, an answer we expected given the overall relationship between turnout and the presidential vote scatterplots in Figures 4.1 and 4.2. On average, there is an overall slight turnout bias in favor of the Democratic presidential candidates. The tilt, represented by the average of the slopes, is not large (0.17 is the mean of the slopes), but it indicates that Democratic presidential candidates have tended, on average, to get a higher share of the vote among the fifty states with increases in turnout. There are many states, though not a majority, where turnout increases have

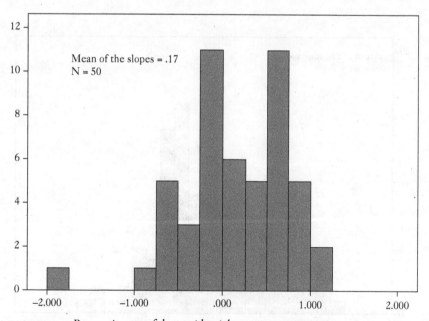

FIGURE 5.5 Responsiveness of the presidential vote to turnout, 1948–2016.

typically reduced the Democratic vote, as the cases on the left side of the histogram document. Still, the visible tendency is the average reported for Figure 5.5, and in most states increases in turnout have been a benefit for Democratic presidential candidates. This finding, however, is similar to the results for the Senate in Figures 5.3 and 5.4. While there are more states with positive slopes, there is considerable spread around many of them, so the tendency for turnout to be a Democratic asset in presidential elections is weak and cannot be predicted with any great confidence.

Senate Elections

Figure 5.6 summarizes the turnout–vote share slopes calculated for ninety-nine Senate seats for the 1966 through 2018 period.[6] The average of the slopes is virtually zero. There are as many Senate seats where turnout increases helped the Republican candidate (the negative values) as there are Senate seats where rising turnout aided the Democratic candidate (the positive values). Equally important, as is the case for the presidential slopes, many of the positive and negative values are statistically meaningless—as the Cruz seat in Figure 5.3 illustrates—because the spread around the slope limits the utility of turnout to predict the Democratic vote.

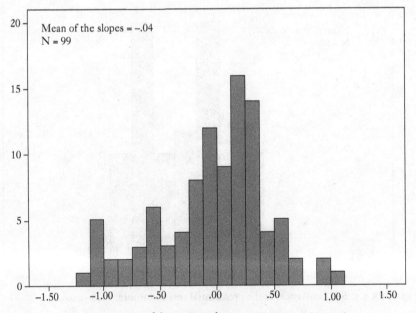

FIGURE 5.6 Responsiveness of the senatorial vote to turnout, 1966–2018.

The data for Senate seats are thus quite variable: there are, in fact, some states where turnout oscillation is systematically consequential for the vote and where turnout increases the Democratic candidate's vote. However, that is not the general case. There is not a consistent influence of turnout on the two-party vote for Senate elections. Indeed turnout for Senate elections appears to vary with no predictable benefit to either party overall.

Gubernatorial Elections

Paralleling the results for the Senate, Figure 5.7 demonstrates that neither Democratic nor Republican gubernatorial candidates seem to be systematically helped by turnout. This distribution of slope coefficients for gubernatorial elections is much more peaked than it was for presidential and Senate elections, and most of the positive value of the mean is provided by a batch of coefficients that are only slightly above zero, with standard errors too large to support confident predictions about what will result from turnout increases. The essential point is that turnout has a very weak correlation with the magnitude of the Democratic candidates' vote shares for the 1966 through 2018 era. That limitation noted, there are a few more states where higher turnout helped the Democrats, and the average slope value reported in the figure indicates that fact.

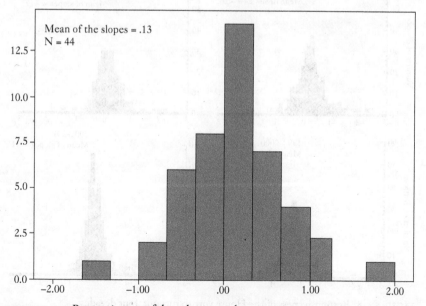

FIGURE 5.7 Responsiveness of the gubernatorial vote to turnout, 1966–2018.

The House of Representatives

The pattern for the House of Representatives repeats the data presented earlier. The only wrinkle in the analysis of House elections is the need to conduct the turnout–vote share assessment within decades when the districts are stable. Figure 5.8 summarizes the slopes for congressional districts for each of the four redistricting decades from 1972 through 2010, showing the same pattern we observed for presidential, senatorial, and gubernatorial elections. There are districts on both sides of the zero point, indicating that turnout increases produced more Democratic votes in some districts, during some periods, and more Republican votes in other districts and at other times. In some cases, the relationship was reasonably strong and predictive, but for most districts the Democratic vote rises and falls without much regard for the variation in turnout. If the data set is pooled, the average is negative—although this is a statistically insignificant result, as the visible spread around the mean of the slopes makes clear.

Foreshadowing results reported later, the shifting shape of the distributions and their positive means in some decades indicate how consequential presidential tides are for down-ballot elections.

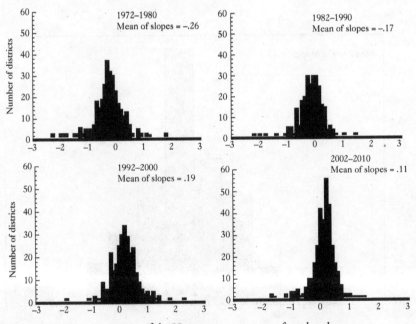

FIGURE 5.8 Responsiveness of the House vote to turnout, four decades.

Presidential Election Effects on House Elections

The presidential race dominates elections for all other offices contested in a presidential year. It creates the spike in political interest, consumes a huge portion of all campaign funds, and generates most of the political news. We are aware of these effects. Up until now, we have been less attentive to the extent to which the presidential campaign moderates the relationship between turnout and the vote choice for offices farther down the ballot. Presidential candidates have coattails or, perhaps more accurately, winning presidential candidates have coattails, which moderate key influences on the vote for lower-level offices. Partisanship is affected by presidential wins with coattails but so also is the connection between the vote share and turnout. The presidential effect on this connection is particularly apparent among House elections. We will analyze coattail effects more fully in chapters 7 and 8, but its influence on the turnout-vote slope for House districts is the focus here.

The basic effect is straightforward: winning presidential candidates boost the vote share of their party's candidates as a function of the magnitude of the win. The result is more wins down-ballot when the presidential candidate does well (e.g., 2008) and fewer wins—or even losses—when the candidate does not do well (e.g., Trump's minority vote in 2016 did not help the GOP).[7] A related effect is that the winning presidential candidate moderates the relationship between turnout and the vote share. For instance, a winning GOP presidential candidate creates a relationship between turnout and the vote share that makes turnout a Republican asset, while a winning Democrat makes turnout look like it is contributing to the Democrat's vote. The effect occurs because, as noted in chapter 2, the turnout rate for presidential elections surges 20 or more percentage points over turnout in off-year elections. The coattails of the winning presidential candidate thus make Republicans the apparent beneficiaries of the turnout change in decades when the Republican presidential candidate wins most of the presidential elections (the 1980s) and benefit Democrats in decades when the Democratic presidential candidate succeeds (the 1990s). Put differently, turnout is epiphenomenal; the causal agent is the coattail, which contributes to votes down-ballot creating a misleading linkage between the turnout rate during the period and the vote share.

Refer back to Figure 5.8. It reports a distribution of slopes for the 1970s and 1980s that is shifted to the left, representing a tendency for increased turnout to generate more Republican votes. The average slope value is −0.26 for the 1970s and −0.17 for the 1980s. The third and fourth histograms, for the 1990s and 2000s, have positive averages, indicating that greater turnout produced more Democratic support. The difference between the 1970s and 1980s versus the last two decades is not a change in political dynamics but a change in party success at the presidential level.

Richard Nixon won by a large margin over George McGovern in 1972, and the overall GOP congressional vote (and, of course, the vote for most individual Republican congressional candidates) surged in that year (though not enough to take control of Congress from the Democrats). The Democratic sweep in 1974, coinciding with low turnout in the 1974 off-year election, and the tight race in 1976 fell into the middle of the distribution at a point that made turnout look like a Republican asset during the decade. Something very similar happened in the 1980s with the election of Ronald Reagan in 1980 and his reelection in 1984. Reagan's wins produced larger than normal votes for Republican House candidates in both years. Neither surge was sufficient to undo the Democratic majority in the House (although it gave the GOP a Senate majority in 1981), but the overall congressional Democratic vote declined in both presidential years as Reagan's coattails narrowed the typical party division compared to the off-years of the decade. This coincident positive upsurge in turnout and Republican votes created a relationship between high turnout and GOP voting when low Republican support coincided with the low-turnout off-year elections of 1982, 1986, and 1990. In the 1980s, briefly, low-turnout elections produced Democratic wins while high-turnout presidential years accompanied Republican success.

The 1990s and 2000s were essentially a mirror image of the 1970s and 1980s. The political environment of the 1990s gave Bill Clinton wins in 1992 and 1996 and helped Democrats down the ballot. Republican majorities in the low-turnout off-year elections of 1994 and 1998 produced the average positive value of the slope coefficients for congressional districts for the 1990s. The 2000 presidential election—which was part of the 1992–2000 redistricting for the 1990s—filled in the center of the distribution with a middle-of-the-distribution presidential turnout rate (much like the 1976 election did in the 1970s), with a virtual tie in the presidential vote and no swing in the congressional status quo of a Republican majority.

Turnout was not a *cause* of the congressional vote choices in the 1970s, 1980s, and 1990s or after the 2001 redistricting. Turnout varied because of the on-year/off-year cycle; voter choices reflected the short-term forces of the elections of each decade. Two of the decades had winning Republicans, while the 1990s produced a Democratic president. The takeaway: turnout variance within each decade had nothing to do with the vote outcomes, which reflected the short-term forces at play in the presidential elections.

A Closer Look at Presidential Election Effects: The
Post-2000 Data

Dissatisfaction with George W. Bush's presidency became a Democratic surge in the 2006 election, an off-year election with a typical off-year turnout of 41 percent. The dissatisfaction with Bush and the Republicans, and not turnout, opened the way for Democrats to take control of the House and Senate and win most governor's offices and state legislatures. The Democratic wave continued into 2008, electing Barack Obama and increasing Democratic majorities at almost all these levels. Republican majorities returned to the House and Senate, in the gubernatorial offices, and in state legislatures after the 2010 election (see Table 1.1 in chapter 1) with an unremarkable off-year turnout (of 42 percent) that equaled the turnout that had swept the Democrats into power in 2006.

Democratic presidential victories that created the pro-Democratic turnout-vote slope bias in the 1990s served the same purpose in the 2002–2010 decade. Except that this relationship for the post-2000 era is driven by a single election: 2008. The average turnout–vote choice regression slope for the 2002–2010 period is 0.11. It is not a large coefficient, and there is significant variability among the districts, but the average is positive, as the bias thesis expects. When the 2008 election is removed, however, the regression slope for the turnout–vote choice link in congressional elections over this decade becomes slightly negative at −0.02; it is effectively flat because the 2008-induced distortion is absent.

Figure 5.9 illustrates the impact. The key feature of the two histograms is the roughly symmetrical distribution of the 339 slopes.[8] Considered together, the two distributions repeat those for the 1970s, 1980s, and 1990s, with the Republican vote boosted by turnout in some districts (all those on the left of the distribution), the Democrat vote helped by turnout in other districts (all those on the right side), and no effect in many districts (all those near zero). It is important to observe that this overall pattern masks substantial differences based on how one treats the 2008 data. When we include 2008 we produce a concentration of negative slopes (21 percent) or slopes near zero (23 percent), but we also see that over half of the districts have a positive slope, suggesting a slight link between higher turnout and the Democratic congressional vote share in the decade.

However, when 2008 is deleted from the calculation, the average of the slopes is effectively zero, though (numerically) slightly negative. Approximately 29 percent of the slopes are close to zero, 36 percent are

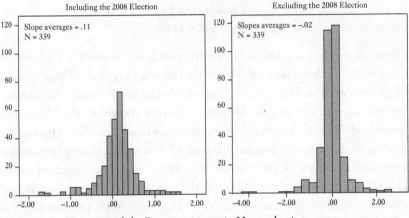

FIGURE 5.9 Turnout and the Democratic vote in House elections, 2002–2010.

negative, and only 34 percent are positive. Looked at with and without a control for the presidential surge in 2008, the congressional elections of the past decade repeat what we found in all the previous data: there is not a consistent positive relationship between turnout and the vote. Turnout sometimes helps the Democrats, sometimes the Republicans, but often helps neither—especially if the substantial variability around the slopes is considered.

The influence that matters is the tilt of the short-term influences that are shaping the political environment of the presidential election. When these influences benefit the Republicans the slopes are, on balance, negative; they are positive when Democrats are favored. In the aggregate, turnout barely moves congressional election results once the presidential disturbance is factored out.

Conclusion

This chapter examined whether the party vote consistently changed for either the Democrats or Republicans within states (for gubernatorial and presidential elections), Senate seats, and congressional districts over the past several decades. The design of the analysis matched exactly the way the bias proposition is most commonly formulated. Campaign planners and the commentariat invariably assert that most everything depends on turnout: if the Democrats get out their voters, they'll do well. We tested that by taking every congressional district, every Senate seat, every gubernatorial race, and every presidential election and compared whether, from one election to the next, the vote systematically changed with the turnout rate. We have found very little consistent with the bias hypothesis: the results are mostly null. The shape of the histograms and the variable correlation of turnout with the Democratic vote in the data makes a compelling case that turnout is not a reliable predictor of the vote for either party. For Senate and gubernatorial elections, the overall mean is slightly negative, but the sizable number of cases in which Democrats did better with increased turnout makes it wrong to suggest anything other than that the relationship between turnout and vote choice for both offices is unpredictable. This is even truer for House elections, in which the overall mean (while statistically insignificant) is also negative. The most promising data for those looking to establish that higher turnout helps the Democrats are found in presidential races, but even there support for the turnout bias thesis is weak.

The only sound, if unsatisfying, conclusion is that turnout does not consistently help either party. We hasten to add that we are not arguing that get-out-the-vote efforts in a particular race cannot help shape the outcome. Unbalanced turnout can decide an election. These effects, however, are unlikely to be a general feature of most national elections. Ascertaining why the turnout effect is small and variable compared to other influences is our next analytical task.

6

Congressional District Results

A FURTHER LOOK

FOR THE MOST part, the county-level data in chapter 4 establish no systematic association between turnout and the Democratic vote. The connection is weak and mixed. The U.S. House elections show comparable results in the analysis in chapter 5. As noted in the previous chapter, we can examine single, specific districts only over a decade because district lines change every ten years, after the Census and reapportionment and redistricting procedures are completed. However, there are vote influences, demographic and political, that matter for elections, and congressional districts are sufficiently small and homogeneous—certainly compared to the states—to permit an examination of turnout in the context of relevant political and demographic variables. That analysis is presented here.

For the two most recent decades, we built data sets that include relevant demographic and political variables for each of the congressional districts. We have collected information on the percentage of African Americans, Hispanics, and people under thirty years of age in each district. We have also gathered median household income to account for the effect of socioeconomic status on the Democratic vote share. This contextual information presses the analysis one level further. An estimation of the relationship between turnout and Democratic vote is strengthened when other factors that are known to influence support for the Democrats are considered and included in the models.

Consider U.S. House districts from 2002 through 2010, the first redistricting period of the new century and a time during which polarization seems to have been ascendant. Figure 6.1 shows how turnout correlates with Democratic vote share in House districts for each of the five elections across

The Turnout Myth. Daron R. Shaw and John R. Petrocik, Oxford University Press (2020). © Oxford University Press.
DOI: 10.1093/oso/9780190089450.001.0001

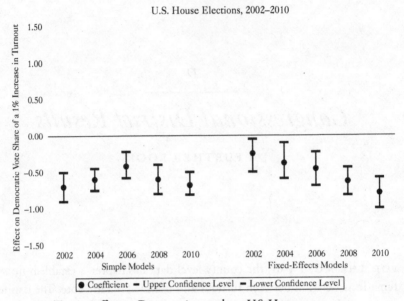

FIGURE 6.1 Turnout effect on Democratic vote share, U.S. House, 2002–2010.

the decade.[1] The question at hand is whether districts with higher turnout produce a higher Democratic vote share in an election. And the answer is no.

Turnout is negatively correlated with the Democratic vote in the simple bivariate models. The strongest negative association occurred in 2002 (with a regression coefficient of –0.72) and the weakest in 2006 (with a regression coefficient of –0.42). For the full models, which account for other correlates of partisan voting at the district level, the relationship remains slightly negative and gets progressively more so over the decade. The coefficients range from –0.28 in 2002 to –0.80 in 2010.

The regression coefficients derived from the full models, which include controls for individual states as well as district-by-district estimates of percentage black, percentage Hispanic, percentage under thirty-five years of age, and median income are intriguing but seem far from dispositive. From 2002 through 2006, the estimated negative turnout effects are substantively minimal. By 2008 and 2010, however, the negative association between turnout and Democratic vote share is notable. Even here, however, the demographic and political characteristics of the districts account for the lion's share of variation in the partisan vote: according to the models—between about one-quarter (2002, 2004, and 2006) and one-half (2010) of the total variance of the Democratic vote. Most notably, the African American percentage in a district is the powerful predictor of vote choice.

Still, the *negative* relationship between turnout and Democratic vote share does spike in the presidential election of 2008 and the midterm election of 2010. In the zero-order relationships and in the full models, districts with the highest turnout were voting against the Democratic candidate, *ceteris paribus*. It is therefore reasonable to speculate about a change in the association between turnout and vote choice in our most recent U.S. House elections.

Figure 6.2 displays the relationship between turnout and vote choice for the three congressional elections since the 2010 Census (2012, 2014, and 2016). We estimate six equations in total, two for each of the past three elections.[2] As with the 2002–2010 data, the simple bivariate regression models allow turnout in the district to predict the Democratic share of the two-party vote. The full model considers other factors (again, district-by-district estimates of percentage black, percentage Hispanic, percentage under thirty-five, and median income) that are likely to also influence Democratic vote share, thus offering a better estimate of the true impact of turnout on vote choice. The coefficients from the simple models indicate that higher turnout districts were casting fewer Democratic votes, although the relationship reaches conventional levels of statistical significance only in 2016. In the full models, the effect reverses: higher turnout is correlated with *higher* Democratic vote share.

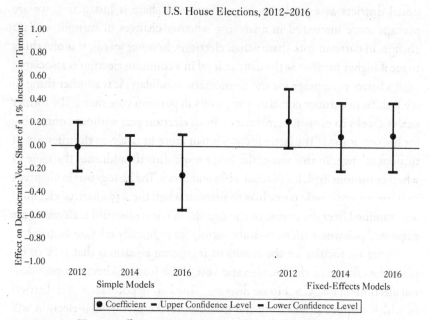

FIGURE 6.2 Turnout effect on Democratic vote share, U.S. House, 2012–2016.

The coefficients do not reach conventional levels of statistical significance, however. The reason for this is that there are many districts in which high turnout coincides with high Republican vote share—even controlling for factors such as race, ethnicity, and income—and the mixed nature of the relationship results in a regression coefficient with a substantial standard error.

Setting aside turnout, since 2012 we see that U.S. House elections are more powerfully predicted by simple demographic and political variables than they were during the previous decade. The adjusted R squared statistics indicate that between 58 and 68 percent of the variance in congressional election totals is explained by district-level race, ethnicity, age, income, and state dummy variables. This is almost twice again what we saw from 2002 through 2006. The vote share reflects the percentage of African Americans in the district and, in recent elections, the Hispanic and youth fraction (those under thirty-five) of the electorate; the latter two variables matter noticeably more than in previous elections. Put differently, since 2012 the existing congressional districts are party bastions in which the demographic traits of party loyalists shape the vote, with turnout having a trivial influence.

Election-to-Election Differences

Although examining the significance of turnout differences across congressional districts as a predictor of partisan vote share is instructive, we are perhaps more interested in analyzing whether changes in turnout explain changes in partisan vote share across elections. In other words, it is one thing to see if higher turnout at the district level in a common election is associated with a better percentage for the Democratic candidate; it is another thing to see if shifts in turnout correlate with shifts in partisan vote share. The former analysis seeks to explain performance in an election year without controlling for history or time. The latter focuses much more squarely on the question of turnout change. In this sense, the latter more directly addresses the issue of whether turnout explains partisan ebbs and flows. The histograms in chapter 5 indicate no systematic party bias to turnout when the 435 districts' elections are examined over the course of the decade. What is observed if elections are examined pairwise with statistical controls for politically relevant factors?

Figure 6.3 focuses on the results of regression equations that seek to explain the change in the Democratic vote share from midterm to presidential elections across U.S. House districts.[3] The bias hypothesis is that districts in which turnout surges from the midterm to the presidential election will also be the districts in which Democratic vote share rises. However, the data

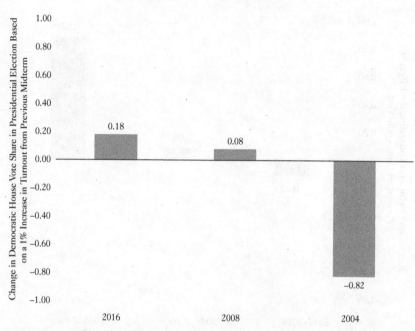

FIGURE 6.3 Effect of presidential turnout surge on the U.S. House vote, 2000 election cycles.

are not supportive. Positive numbers (regression coefficients) would indicate that the Democrats did better as turnout rose. But in 2004 increased turnout from the 2002 midterm elections was associated with a 0.82-point *decline* in Democratic vote share. In the 2008 and 2016 elections, increased turnout from the previous midterm election coincided with only modest spikes in Democratic candidate support (+0.08 and +0.18 points, respectively).

If surging turnout in presidential elections does not explain (relative) Democratic success at the House district level, perhaps declining turnout in midterm elections will explain (relative) Democratic failure. In Figure 6.4, we present the results of regression equations that explain the change in the Democratic vote share from presidential to midterm elections across U.S. House districts. Negative numbers would indicate that a decrease in turnout coincided with a decrease in support for Democratic House candidates. Our hypothesis here is that districts in which turnout declines from the presidential to the midterm election will also be the districts in which Democratic vote share decreases.

Once again, the data do not back the conventional wisdom. The midterm decline effects are positive for the Democrats in the 2006 and 2010 elections, indicating that decreased turnout coincided with a relative *increase* in

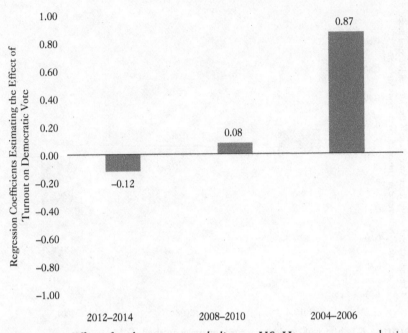
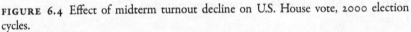

FIGURE 6.4 Effect of midterm turnout decline on U.S. House vote, 2000 election cycles.

Democratic vote share. In 2014 the relationship between decreased turnout and Democratic vote share is negative, but it is also marginal. All in all, the data provide little or no evidence that the fortunes of Democratic House candidates are driven by variation in district-level turnout from one election to the next, whether looked at from the off- to the on-year or from the presidential year to the off-year. More satisfying explanations of surge and decline require the introduction of contextual and political factors that are largely uncorrelated with turnout.

7

Why Is the Conventional Wisdom Wrong?

CHAPTERS 4 THROUGH 6, with different approaches, provide no support for the conventional wisdom that turnout oscillation has a consistent and predictable party bias. In fact the data show no party bias at all. Turnout increases have produced surges in the Republican vote in some elections and increases in the Democratic vote in others. That variability repeats itself across states for presidential, gubernatorial, and senatorial elections; it also characterizes congressional elections. Histograms of the distribution of the regression slopes estimating the dependence of the vote on turnout for these several types of elections in the states and congressional districts produce a pattern that is about as close to a persuasive refutation of the thesis as we observe for any political phenomenon. Equally significant, most of the regressions of turnout on the vote are small on both sides of zero and, even when larger, often fit the data so poorly that they are statistically insignificant. The only supportable conclusion is that election outcomes are not attributable to turnout. In some districts or states, an unusual surge or decline in turnout may play a role in shaping an outcome, especially when it is concentrated among politically distinctive groups (African Americans or religiously observant whites, for example), but there is no regular tendency for low turnout to help Republicans while high turnout aids Democrats. As a general proposition, turnout oscillation within the range that characterizes American presidential and midterm elections does not influence election results.[1]

The Turnout Myth. Daron R. Shaw and John R. Petrocik, Oxford University Press (2020). © Oxford University Press.
DOI: 10.1093/oso/9780190089450.001.0001

Why Do the Facts Not Fit the Myth?

As we noted earlier and will document in greater detail in this chapter, Republicans generally turn out at higher rates than Democrats due to predispositions that reflect socioeconomic and situational factors. That is, the kinds of people who tend to be Republican—whites, the middle class, the more upscale, religiously observant, married, and those with a longer residence in their community—are more likely to have the motivation and resources to vote in any given election. Thus, if people who are more likely to vote are also more likely to be Republican, a lower turnout election should tend to overrepresent them. When overall turnout increases, the less participatory are showing up and—by the logic underlying the bias thesis—bringing a more Democratic preference to the polling places than those who are voting when turnout is low. So, again, the question: If relatively more Democrats are showing up in high-turnout elections, and voters support the candidates of the party they prefer, why do the Democrats not do consistently and systematically better when turnout increases?

The answer has two parts. The first has to do with the magnitude of the turnout difference between Democrats and Republicans and how that affects the vote between or (for a few elections) among the candidates. As Table 7.1 documents, the difference in the turnout rate of Democrats and Republicans is not large.[2] Republicans have been about 6 percentage points more likely to vote by self-report; they were 7 points more likely to vote according to the validated vote measure that is available for some years. Furthermore, nothing has changed in recent years. Republican self-reported turnout averaged 79 percent in the presidential elections of 2000 through 2016; Democratic self-reported turnout averaged about 73 percent; it was 45 percent for independents.[3]

Table 7.1 Turnout Differences by Party Identification, in Percentages

	Self-Report	Validated Vote
Democrats	69	54
Independents	46	33
Republicans	75	61

Data are from ANES surveys, 1952–2012.

The 6- to 7-percentage-point difference between Democrats and Republicans is not trivial, but neither is it large when compared to other factors that need to be considered, particularly differential defection rates that reflect the short-term forces in the election. The more impressive turnout differences are between party identifiers and independents; the latter are 25 to 30 percentage points less likely to vote and—very important—the most responsive to the political currents of the election. This turnout similarity between the partisans will be expanded upon later.

The second part of the answer reflects the greater susceptibility of those not particularly motivated to vote (we call them "peripheral voters" hereafter) to respond strongly to short-term, election-specific influences.[4] Peripheral voters, unlike individuals who show up at the polls for most or all elections (we call them "core voters"), are easier to influence because they are less interested in government and politics, less partisan, and have fewer strong and established views with which to counter the issues and candidate advantages in the election. As a result, the content of the election environment is more influential for them. When turnout increases, therefore, elections become more susceptible to influence by a campaign or events because the ratio of peripheral to core voters changes in favor of the more easily influenced peripheral voters. We will demonstrate both features later. More immediately, however, we return to a topic discussed earlier in our study to more fruitfully explore what is wrong with the turnout bias argument: what correlates with voting and the turnout rate.

Who Votes? (Redux)

As demonstrated in chapter 3, those who are normatively disposed to vote or have a psychological investment in the outcome are the most consistent participators. As one might expect, the aggregate distribution of these pro-turnout attitudes varies depending upon the norm or notion that is invoked. For example, most Americans believe that it matters if you vote (nearly 90 percent) and that you should vote even if your candidate is unlikely to win (also 90 percent). In addition, they are inclined to agree that all elections are important; only about 15 percent believe that local elections are unimportant despite the typically low turnout for these contests. Americans are more divided, though, when it comes to a person's obligation to vote; about half think it is acceptable to skip an election if one does not care about the outcome, and exactly half think that Americans have a right *not* to vote.[5]

Table 7.2 Influences on Turnout, 2000–2016

Influences on Voter Turnout	Level of the Variable		
	Low	Moderate	High
Demographic Characteristics			
Religiosity	60	65	73
Education	53	68	82
Age	44	57	73
Marital status	56		70
Time lived in community	58		68
Attitudes and Beliefs			
Campaign interest	40	71	86
Strength of candidate preference	50	64	77
Strength of party preference	39	63	78
Care about election outcome	54		68
Perceived closeness of election	61		63

Data are from ANES surveys, 2000–2016. Entries are the percentages voting in the election who are characterized by the low, moderate, and high levels of the influences on turnout.

Perhaps even more relevant for the current discussion is that the impact on turnout of these normative commitments crosses party lines. There is little disagreement between Democrats and Republicans on the norms: Republicans are slightly more likely to believe in them and more likely to vote than similarly disposed Democrats—but the difference is only a few percentage points.[6]

Other characteristics and predispositions that encourage voting are also similarly distributed among Democrats and Republicans. Consider Table 7.2, which shows average turnout rates across the various levels of several demographic and attitudinal variables. As we see in the top half of the table, turnout varies by demography in part because the better educated, religiously observant, older, married, and longer-term residents of a community are likely to support the norms about voting mentioned earlier. The bottom half of the table shows how turnout varies with an individual's psychological investment in politics and governance. Those who vote are more interested in the campaigns, have strong feelings about the candidates and the parties, and care about the outcome of the election. The obvious consequence of interest and engagement: people with these attitudes are regular (core) voters.

Table 7.3 Turnout Predictors by Party Preference, 2000–2016

Traits and Orientations	Party Identification		
	Democrat	Independent	Republican
Demographic Characteristics			
Religiosity: Not observant	54	60	43
Religiosity: Observant	30	25	42
Education: High school or less	47	61	38
Education: College degree	25	14	32
Age: Under 25 years	14	17	9
Age: 40 and older	60	54	63
Married	57	58	73
Lived in community five years or more	68	64	68
Attitudes and Beliefs			
Campaign interest: Low	11	29	7
Campaign interest: High	25	11	27
Strength of party identification: Lean or weak	63		65
Strength of party identification: Strong	37		35
Strength of candidate preference: Weak	32	61	26
Strength of candidate preference: Strong	41	17	44
Care about election	80	86	79
Believe election is close	26	27	27

Data are from ANES surveys, 2000–2016. Entries are the percentage of the party category who have the trait or preference.

Again, as was the case for the general norms about voting, there are modest demographic differences between Democrats and Republicans (see Table 7.3). Religiously observant Republicans are as numerous as those who are unobservant; Democrats participate much less in religious services. The turnout-relevant sociodemographic distinctions continue: Republican identifiers are more likely to be college graduates, to be married, and to be older. Only residential stability does not differentiate Republicans from Democrats: identical fractions are long-term residents of their community (defined here as five or more years). Independents, by contrast, are characterized by all the traits associated with low turnout, and, correspondingly, they are the least likely to vote.

In contrast, the attitudes and orientations shown in the bottom half of the table, distinctions that are the proximate influence on voting participation, fail to differentiate the parties' supporters to any meaningful extent. Democrats and Republicans have approximately equal levels of interest in the campaign, are equally strong in their identification with their party, and equally likely to care about the election's result. Republicans display stronger feelings about their party's candidate (44 percent have a strong preference, while 26 percent have a weak preference) than Democrats (where the proportions are 41 and 32 percent). Overall, however, the parties' nominal supporters are not greatly different in attitudes that motivate turnout. Again, it is the independents who are marked by social traits and political dispositions that do not motivate people to vote.

There should be little surprise, therefore, that turnout differences have played such a small role in American elections (as documented in the previous chapters). Republicans are slightly more likely to vote, and they are slightly more likely to have the demographic characteristics and attitudinal predispositions that drive people to the polls. Those who are least likely to vote—and have the fewest traits and qualities that predispose people to vote—are independents. And when they do turn out, it is these independents who are the most likely to respond to short-term forces and who both shape and reinforce whatever shift or outcome is under way.

The Electorate at Different Turnout Levels

Almost all the data we have examined thus far have revealed minor and inconsistent correlations between turnout and partisan vote choice. One obvious analysis that we have not performed, however, is to estimate what the vote would look like across a comprehensive set of hypothetical turnout scenarios. In other words, given the differences in the preceding tables, what can be expected by way of a partisan division of the electorate at different turnout rates? More specifically, are the trivial differences in Tables 7.2 and 7.3 sufficient to produce electorates of significantly different party orientations when turnout is 50 percent rather than 60 percent, or 30 percent rather than 60 percent?

We answer that question by constructing a measure of the probability of voting using the demographic and attitudinal variables discussed in Tables 7.2 and 7.3. In addition to these, we include whether the respondent was contacted by anyone on behalf of a candidate. We add this last variable to capture any campaign effects that exist beyond the influences of the individual's

Table 7.4 Predicting Turnout in 2016

	Regression Coefficient	Standard Error	Wald Statistic	Statistical Significance	Odds Ratios: Exp(B)
Religious observance	.332	.061	29.66	.000	1.393
Education	.613	.075	67.142	.000	1.846
Age	.384	.088	19.087	.000	1.468
Married	.553	.118	22.142	.000	1.739
Time resident in community	.290	.124	5.483	.019	1.337
Campaign interest	.454	.104	19.053	.000	1.574
Strength of partisanship	.305	.096	10.111	.001	1.356
Strength of candidate preference	.252	.071	12.692	.000	1.286
Care about election outcome	.148	.061	5.801	.016	2.159
Contacted by campaign	.759	.130	34.125	.000	2.137
Constant	−6.872	.428	257.798	.000	0.001

Model Summary: -2 Log Likelihood 2030.8. Nagelkerke R Square = .31. Data are from the 2016 ANES survey. The dependent variable is an estimate of validated turnout (based on a model derived from 1988 data).

status and political motivations. The resultant equation, summarized in Table 7.4, estimates the probability that a person will be a voter. These results are also used to generate estimates of the likely electorate at different turnout levels (as is explained later).

Before turning to the data, a few facts about our validated turnout model are in order here. Most important, our turnout model was estimated using data—and, critically, the validated vote measure—from the 1988 ANES. Why do we rely on data from this distant election? One reason is practical: 1988 is the last year that ANES provided a reliable validated measure of turnout.[7] Another reason is theoretical: despite the recent tumult of American politics, the dynamics of turnout haven't changed very much. The factors that influence the decision to vote are basically the same today as they were in 1988. All of this is worth mentioning because we need a reliable validated vote estimation to generate an out-of-sample distribution of turnout likelihood for the most current (2016) election. In the event, as stated, the results based on our 1988 estimation of the validated vote are almost identical to those based on the self-reported vote from 2016 (see Appendix Table 7.1).

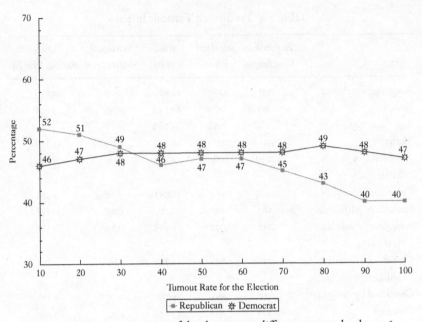

FIGURE 7.1 Partisan composition of the electorate at different turnout levels, 2016.

Turnout Levels and the Electorate's Partisanship

The problematic nature of the assumption that a drop-off in turnout corresponds with a drop-off in Democrats is documented with Figure 7.1, which reports the proportion of Democratic and Republican identifiers at various levels of turnout.[8] Contrary to the key assumption underlying the biased-turnout thesis, the balance of Democratic and Republican identifiers is almost identical at typical turnout levels. That is, the (negligible) net difference between Republican and Democratic voters when turnout is at presidential election levels (60 percent) is the same as when turnout is at midterm election levels (40 percent).[9]

Note that the turnout rate axis in the figure is a conversion of an estimate of the probability that an individual is likely to vote in an election.[10] The conversion inverts the probability and expresses it as a turnout level. In Figure 7.1, all individuals (respondents) with a calculated probability of voting that is 0.9 or greater are assumed to be voting when the turnout rate is 10 percent (the left most point in the figure). Any individual with a calculated probability of voting that is 0.8 or greater is represented at the second point on the graph, labeled as a 20 percent turnout rate. This logic carries across the graph; so, for example, the point that represents a 50 percent turnout rate includes all individuals whose calculated probability of voting is 0.5 or greater. The right-most point on the graph is all voters (respondents) and represents 100 percent turnout. It includes those who are calculated to have almost no likelihood of voting and those with the very highest probabilities.

The proportions on the left-most side of the figure show the expected higher turnout rate of Republicans. Although Democrats exceeded Republicans by 47 to 40 percent in the total 2016 electorate, Republicans exceed Democrats by about 6 percentage points when turnout is only about 10 percent.[11] They continue to outnumber Democrats (by 51 to 47 percent) when turnout is 20 percent (2 percent are independents). At 30 percent turnout, there is a partisan draw, with the proportion of Democrats at 48 percent compared to 49 percent who are Republican.[12] Democratic identifiers are also essentially tied with Republicans or may slightly exceed them in a 40 percent turnout election (a typical turnout rate in off-years), with a comparable balance of identifiers up through the 50 to 65 percent turnout level that is character- istic of presidential elections. Moreover the estimates of the balance of party identifiers at the various voting probabilities are approximately the same during the past forty years; 2016 is not an aberration.

In addition, the actual party distribution among self-reported voters typ- ically favored the Democrats by a wider margin than indicated in Figure 7.1. In a low-turnout presidential year—1988 or 1996, when turnout was slightly greater than 50 percent—Democrats were expected to enjoy a 2- or 3-percentage-point party-identification plurality among those whose proba- bility of voting was in the highest 50 percent. In the event, however, Democrats were about 50 percent of all voters in those two elections, while Republicans averaged 44 to 45 percent—a 5- to 6-percentage-point Democratic advantage. The observed advantage in identification among voters in the higher-turnout 2008 and 2012 elections was also slightly greater, at 7 or 8 percentage points. In 2016, when turnout was slightly lower than in 2008 but higher than in 2012, the observed Democratic identification among voters was 6 percentage points rather than the expected 3 or 4, but clearly the Democratic surplus of identifiers in 2016 did not yield a comparable vote advantage.

That said, the essential observation about Figure 7.1 is that the Democrats enjoyed a plurality of identifiers at all expected turnout levels except for the lowest. This was observed for all previous elections as well, going back to 1952. Within the band of likely turnout rates for U.S. elections, the balance of Democratic over Republican identification favored the Democrats in every election from 1952 through 2016, in presidential and off-years, regardless of the winner's party and irrespective of the vote margin. It is also worth noting that

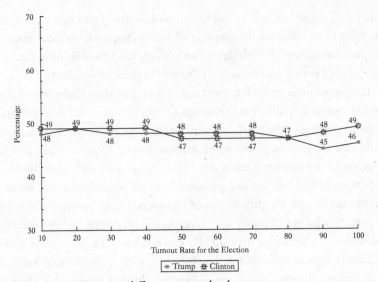

FIGURE 7.2 The 2016 vote at different turnout levels.

the expected turnout in the figure was corroborated by the partisanship among those who self-reported that they voted in the individual ANES surveys.

This way of portraying the electorate can also be used to estimate specific election results at different turnout levels. Figure 7.2, for example, uses self-reported vote choice and the same a priori turnout probabilities in Figure 7.1 to estimate the results of the 2016 presidential election at different turnout levels. From a low-turnout to a high-turnout scenario, the 2016 vote was virtually a dead heat. Hillary Clinton's margin in a 90- or 100-percent turnout election widened a bit. However, the dominant feature of the data is that Clinton's support hardly varied according to the electorate's size. The 2016 election was essentially a 2- to 3-percentage-point race throughout 2016, according to an average of the available polls, and it would have provided Clinton with a narrow national-vote win whether turnout was 33 percent or 75 percent. Put differently, Clinton would have had roughly the same edge on Trump had we seen turnout at 2004, 2008, or 2012 levels in the 2016 contest. Presidential preference in 2016 was uncorrelated with the likelihood of voting even though the Democrats enjoyed a larger share of the electorate (per Figure 7.1) as turnout increased.

The Unpredictable Peripheral Voter?

Clearly something besides a mechanical movement of voters into and out of the electorate is shaping the vote. That something is the short-term forces

(STFs) that help to define the issue contrasts and candidate appeals that give substance to an election and rationalize or motivate a voter's choice. The influence of STFs are not considered by the biased-turnout argument, which assumes, often explicitly, that peripheral voters will behave in the same way as otherwise similarly situated voters who are members of the core electorate (Bartels 2002; Citrin, Schickler, and Sides 2003). There is, however, no evidence to support this conjecture. On the contrary, the best evidence is that peripheral voters do not behave like core voters of a similar profile unless the STFs are pushing the political environment in the direction that corresponds to the political orientation of these core voters. STFs in an election will create a Democratic turnout bias if those forces are favorable to the Democratic candidate. If they favor the Republican candidate, the STFs will tip the peripheral electorate in a GOP direction because (again) the peripheral voters are particularly responsive to short-term directional forces. A citizen with a Republican profile—upscale, white, married, religiously observant—who is uninterested in government and politics and has few strong political viewpoints is less immunized against considerations that advantage the Democratic candidate. He or she is therefore much more likely to vote for that Democrat than a comparable person who votes regularly and pays at least the median amount of attention to public affairs.

This difference in susceptibility to STFs is the source of the greater elasticity of peripheral voters and why turnout can advantage Republicans as easily and as much in one election as it advantages Democrats in another. It also explains why midterm election results often differ so dramatically from their presidential predecessors (2004 to 2006, 2008 to 2010), why one presidential election can produce a solid GOP win only to be followed by a Democratic sweep (2004 to 2008), and why a big Democratic off-year sweep (2006) becomes a Republican wave in the next off-year (2010).

The short-term directional force has a couple of elements. One is the media and other social stimulation that increases interest in the election, a sense of its foremost importance, and, consequently, turnout rates. A second element is the issue debates of the elections and the relative appeal of the contesting candidates. This second element can be candidate-neutral, but usually it is not. The stimulation that promotes higher turnout typically includes a package of STFs than can greatly increase support for a party or candidate.[13] However, these directional forces are not uniformly influential. The responsiveness of voters to them varies as a function of the level of political interest and involvement of the individual. Highly partisan and politically interested individuals are less influenced by the STFs than their weakly partisan and politically disinterested neighbors (Campbell et al. 1960; Stokes 1966; Shanks and Miller 1996; Campbell 1997; Lewis-Beck et al. 2008).

These party- or candidate-favoring STFs also influence turnout. Many voters show up at the polls because of their inherent sense of citizen duty (which is often linked to their partisanship), but most of these core voters (who probably represent about 40 percent of the eligible electorate) can be expected to show up at the polls regardless of the excitement or putative significance of the election. Short-term forces, on the other hand, mobilize the participation of those with a weak sense of citizen duty, less interest in public affairs, and little emotional commitment to any political party—the principal driving force in U.S. elections. When these peripheral voters show up on Election Day, they disproportionately contribute to the swing between a less and a more stimulating election. The effect can occur across the electorate and subgroups.

Figure 7.3 illustrates this effect by plotting (1) turnout and (2) vote change from one party to the other as a function of a summary measure of the

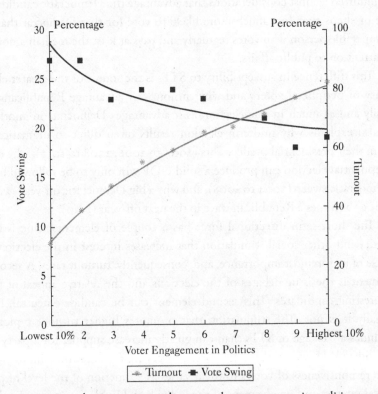

FIGURE 7.3 Interelection swing and turnout by engagement in politics, average relationship.

individual's level of engagement in politics and public affairs.[14] The turnout line (plotted through the asterisks) presents the mean turnout rate across ten elections; the vote swing line (plotted through the squares) indicates the percentage of respondents who reported changing their vote from one party to the other for each of the engagement deciles. The effect of engagement, and of being a core rather than a peripheral voter, on turnout and voting for the same party is apparent. The rate of increase in turnout is greatest for those at the lowest levels of engagement, where the peripheral voters are located. If one can imagine (for illustrative purposes) that the stimulation associated with an election equals a difference of 1 unit across the engagement deciles, a high-stimulation election boosts the engagement—and therefore the turnout—of voters on the low end (left) of the measure more than it increases turnout for voters on the higher (right) end. Correspondingly, core voters on the high end of the engagement index are less susceptible to the directional content of the STFs. Their vote did not change as much as the vote of less involved voters on the left side of the graph who experience a similar jump in their interest. Some fraction changes their vote compared to the previous election, but significantly fewer switch compared to the less engaged peripheral voters on the left of the measure.

Figure 7.4 reports the vote swing line in Figure 7.3 for several elections, focusing on the interelection swing for elections in which the incumbent party was defeated. A nontrivial portion of high-engagement core voters switched their votes. The several landslide elections of the past fifty years were notable for the defection rates of even the strongly identified partisans of the party that was swept away—1964 and 1972 come to mind. However, the less engaged peripheral voters were more influenced by the STFs at play, and they contribute significantly more to the swing in the fortunes of the parties, as Figure 7.4 shows.

Vote Switching and Turnout Oscillation between Elections

Our claim that STFs and the distinction between core and peripheral voters is key to understanding shifts in voting and turnout across elections merits both theoretical and empirical elaboration. The following two tables use three ANES survey panels to analyze individual-level data on vote switching and turnout changes. The first table permits comparisons between adjacent presidential elections: 1956–1960, 1972–1976, and 1992–1996. The second table examines changes in the vote and turnout for three pairs of House elections: the House vote and turnout between the adjacent presidential

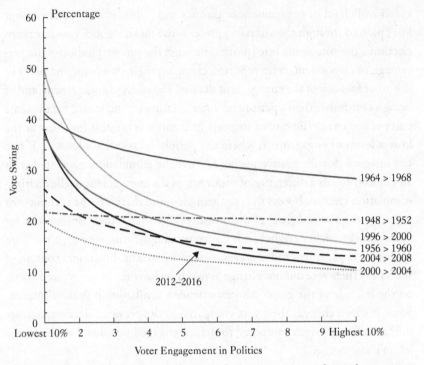

FIGURE 7.4 Interelection swing and turnout by engagement in politics, elections won by the challenger.

elections (e.g., 1992–1996), the pattern from the presidential year to the following off-year (e.g., 1992–1994), and from the off-year to the following presidential election (e.g., 1994–1996).

The election pairs provide some variance in election environments and offer an opportunity to examine whether longer term secular changes in the American political system might influence vote switching and turnout. For example, the 1956–1960 and 1972–1976 panels are similar in contrasting a big GOP presidential win with a narrow Democratic win in the subsequent election. They also share an intervening off-year election that produced a large defeat for the Republicans in both the House and the Senate elections. Those similarities tie together election sequences that are otherwise distinguished by a twenty-year gap of significant changes in the party coalitions, as well as in broader contours of American politics (which was marked by the civil rights revolution, a divisive foreign war, and significant cultural shifts that roiled the country). The 1992–1996 elections are distinct from the earlier panels by being more recent and by featuring unique partisan results. The

Democrat (Bill Clinton) won both times, although with only a plurality of support. Turnout surged in 1992 but dropped off significantly in 1996, while the Democrats lost control of Congress in the off-year—for the first time in forty years. And again, the twenty-year gap between the 1972–1976 and 1992–1996 panels allows political variance that would be expected to make consistent findings less likely.

Also, the panel design of the surveys is important since recall errors and bandwagon effects are minimized. That is, respondents tend to overreport, sometimes by a wide margin, their support for the winning candidate; 2012 is a prominent recent example. Panel attrition might have a bias, but it is hard a priori to argue that it would intrude on the question examined here. In brief, while these elections will never be a natural experiment that controlled for all the rival alternative hypotheses about vote switching and turnout, the mix of influences is large enough to believe that they do not share a consistent bias that could explain whatever similarities we observe.

Switching between Presidential Elections

Consistency in the vote was the central feature of all three cycles. However, changes in the election outcomes were shaped by changes in individual votes. Switching dominated both mobilization and demobilization among the three panels over the forty-year period displayed in Table 7.5. Kennedy's win in 1960 and Carter's in 1976 were brought about by a lopsided switch from a GOP vote in the preceding presidential election to support for the Democrat in 1960 and 1976. Voters who switched their ballots from 1956 to 1960 or from 1972 to 1976 moved to the Democrats by a 3:1 margin or better. Some mobilization occurred, but it was balanced; the Democrat and Republican in both years drew almost equal support from new voters.[15] Voters who dropped out in 1960 and 1976 took votes equally out of the candidates on both sides.

The 1992–1996 elections essentially repeat the pattern. Clinton's margin increased in 1996, with most of the change coming from Bush voters in 1992 who preferred Clinton to Dole in the succeeding election. Turnout declined in 1996—not the case in 1960 or 1976—but it took votes from both party's candidates equally, while those who voted in 1996 but not in 1992 supported Dole and Clinton equally. Put succinctly, vote switching and not mobilization of new voters or a demobilization of voters from the preceding election is the central feature of the story in both years.

Table 7.5 Switching and Mobilization between Presidential Elections
The ANES Panels

	The Panels		
	1956–1960	1972–1976	1992–1996
Consistent party vote	52%	50%	56%
Switch	16	19	17
Democrat to Republican	4	4	2
Republican to Democrat	11	14	5
Other to Democrat			4
Other to Republican			5
Mobilized for second election	11	9	6
Nonvoter to Democrat	5	5	3
Nonvoter to Republican	6	4	3
Demobilized	7	7	9
Democrat to nonvoter	3	3	4
Republican to nonvoter	3	4	3
Nonvoter	16	14	12

Note: Cells may not total to 100% because of votes for candidates who are neither Democrat nor Republican. The 1992 election provides additional detail because of Ross Perot's large vote share. Other candidates' proportions in other years are too small to yield meaningful percentages.

Switching and Mobilization in House Elections

In Table 7.6 the three House elections in each of the three panel studies follow the same dynamic that characterized the presidential elections, with the added proviso that the House elections display the surge and decline that join the outcomes down-ballot to the level of support for the presidential candidates.

Consider the 1956–1960 panel. Turnout increased between the two elections, but vote switching (at 12 percent) mattered as much if not more than mobilization (at 11 percent) to the outcome. Democrats gained a small advantage from switching (7 percent over 5 percent), but the increased support from those who sat out the 1956 election was lost among those who voted in 1956 but then abstained in 1960 (again, 7 percent compared to 5 percent). Without spinning a completely hypothetical and conjectural tale, it seems likely that Kennedy's relatively greater attractiveness over Nixon compared

Table 7.6 Switching and Mobilization between House Elections
The ANES Panels

	1956–1960			1972–1976			1992–1996		
	1956–1960	1956–1958	1958–1960	1972–1976	1972–1974	1974–1976	1992–1996	1992–1994	1994–1996
Consistent party vote	46%	41%	37%	49%	43%	40%	51%	48%	50%
Switchers	12	9	8	16	11	14	18	10	10
Democrat to Republican	5	3	5	8	5	7	11	7	5
Republican to Democrat	7	6	2	8	6	5	6	3	5
Mobilized	11	6	21	8	4	19	6	3	15
Nonvoter to Democrat	7	4	12	5	3	12	3	1	7
Nonvoter to Republican	4	2	9	3	1	6	3	2	8
Demobilized	11	19	8	7	16	4	9	17	4
Democrat to nonvoter	7	10	5	4	9	3	6	10	2
Republican to nonvoter	5	9	2	3	7	1	3	7	2
Nonvoter	21	26	27	18	29	24	15	24	20

Note: Cells may not total to 100% because of votes for candidates who are neither Democrat nor Republican.

to Stevenson's deficit relative to Eisenhower proved an asset for Democratic congressional candidates in 1960.

The off-year pairs also demonstrate the power of STFs that supported Democratic voting, without any mobilization or demobilization effect. Those who joined the electorate in 1958 after sitting out the 1956 election (some because they became age-eligible to vote) gave Democrats a slight boost (see the 4 percent versus the 2 percent in the mobilized cells). Those who voted in 1956 but were not stimulated to vote by the 1958 campaign were as likely to be Republican as Democrat (Democrats lost 10 percentage points compared to the Republicans' 9-point loss). If one felt confident in doing precise calculations from survey data—and we do not—the patterns of gains and losses tilts slightly toward the Democrats because of the shift from a GOP vote in 1956 to a Democratic vote in 1958.

The 1958 breakdown shows surge effects that were in equal parts voter mobilization and voter persuasion—a surge among the switchers. Democrats netted a 3-point gain from switchers and another 3 points from the surge in mobilization created by the relative excitement of presidential elections. However, they also lost a net of 3 points because people shifted from voters in 1958 to nonvoters in 1960.

The 1972–1974–1976 and 1992–1994–1996 panels show the same pattern as the 1956–1958–1960 panel, with the added wrinkle of some short-term issue tides. In the 1972–1974–1976 panel, the anti-Republican environment driven by Watergate magnified GOP losses in the low-turnout off-year election in 1974. In the 1992–1994–1996 panel, the anti-Democratic environment driven by the failure of Clinton's health care reform initiatives (among other things) magnified Democratic losses in the equally low turnout off-year election in 1994.

Caveats and Further Discussion

There are, of course, limits to the accuracy of the preceding decomposition of changes with survey data. We are particularly attentive to the fact that the sampling and measurement errors of surveys limit their utility for decomposing small, individual-level shifts in voter behavior, and that these shifts are our focus. However, there are several reasons we remain confident in our analyses. First, these survey data come from panels, which control for misremembered and misreported past behavior. Moreover the patterns in the preceding tables are consistent with the aggregate tides presented earlier in this chapter. On balance, therefore, the survey data constitute evidence that is weighty because of its consistency with other patterns.

The takeaway point seems unassailable. The short-term forces shape the vote that defines the substantive meaning of an election change. They produce shifts in the decisions of participants who consistently show up for elections. They have an even larger effect on those who are not consistent participants. In each case, the mobilized and demobilized move toward the same party or candidate as the switchers, sometimes more so.

This points out an important and flawed assumption supporting the conventional wisdom of a turnout bias: that a nonvoting partisan is approximately as likely to support his or her party's candidate as are the partisans who actually turn out to vote. This assumption undergirds several prominent studies of the effects of turnout on partisan vote choice and (erroneously, in our view) marginalizes the importance of context and campaigns for political outcomes. The data at hand suggest that politics matters, and that it matters most for those who are only occasional participants in the electoral process. This is a theme central to our understanding of U.S. elections, and one we return to later in this study.

8

If Turnout Isn't Driving Election Swings, What Is?

ALMOST NO EVIDENCE supports the turnout bias assumption that grips practitioners, pundits, and many academics. There are elections (probably every observer can name one) in which differential turnout swung the result, but such cases are not a common feature of American elections. In documenting this fact, we have spent a considerable amount of time and energy on something that *doesn't* affect vote choice. While we think this a worthwhile endeavor—particularly given the narrative offered to explain elections such as 2010 and 2014—it is reasonable to expect this analysis to provide a theoretically satisfying empirical explanation for what *does* account for the oscillations in partisan fortunes between elections.

In this chapter we do our best to delineate just such an explanation. We do not include a detailed discussion of the determinants of vote choice; we assume the reader is familiar with it. The reassessment of *The American Voter* (Campbell et al. 1960) by Lewis-Beck et al. in 2008 (*The American Voter Revisited*) summarizes most of the themes and findings of the literature on what influences an individuals' vote. The concern here is the contribution of turnout oscillation to the result. Specifically, we focus on the concept of surge and decline, an idea formulated decades ago by Angus Campbell (1960), elaborated upon by many since (most notably, Kernell 1977; Campbell 1991), but mostly lost due to the recent obsession with turnout differences between the parties. In so doing, we expand on our core assumptions—articulated in chapter 3 and again in chapter 7—about the greater susceptibility of peripheral voters to information about extant circumstances and to institutional arrangements, which can affect the marginal costs of voting.

The Turnout Myth. Daron R. Shaw and John R. Petrocik, Oxford University Press (2020). © Oxford University Press.
DOI: 10.1093/oso/9780190089450.001.0001

Economic Conditions and Incumbent Performance

As discussed in chapter 3, most theories of vote choice treat turnout as an afterthought. Indeed there is no shortage of proposed alternatives to turnout as a predictor of election outcomes. Perhaps the most familiar to academics, commentators, and the average citizen is the condition of the economy. It is often doubted whether incumbents—mayors, governors, members of Congress, or presidents—can materially affect the state of the economy, but incumbents have never shied from claiming credit for good times, while challenging opponents have enthusiastically attributed responsibility to them for economic decline or turmoil. Of course the causation may run the other way; in some primordial political order, challengers may have used economic hard times as a reason to replace the incumbent with themselves, so incumbents learned to take credit for good times. Whatever began the cycle of blame and credit taking, though, there is a long record of hard times defeating elected officials while good times frequently help the incumbent hold on to his or her job.[1]

Academics have used this association as the basis for extensive and intensive election analysis. At the conceptual level, it gave rise to the idea of retrospective voting, which, reduced to its essentials, assumes that (1) officeholders take credit for good times, (2) challengers blame incumbents for hard times, and (3) voters make defensible choices by reelecting incumbents who preside over good times and replacing them otherwise. On the empirical front, it spawned a cottage industry of statistical modeling that permitted predictions about how the incumbent and his or her party would be aided or handicapped by economic circumstances at the time of the election.[2] Those involved in this effort have proffered a variety of predictive formulations using different measures of the condition of the economy, at different months removed from the voting (see, e.g., Fair 1978; Tufte 1978; Lewis-Beck and Tien 2016; Campbell 2016; Abramowitz 2016). Conceptual considerations make some of these algorithms more attractive to various analysts, but the minor differences yield equally minor differences in the accuracy of the resulting predictions. The varying estimations usually correctly identify the winner and often get very close to the vote margin (for an overview, see Campbell 2016).

Figure 8.1 illustrates the strength of the approach. Most outcomes are well predicted, with the most obvious outliers (1956, 1964, and 1972) easily explained by voter assessments of foreign policy and adverse personal judgments about the challengers. Noneconomic factors matter. Personal scandals, corruption, malfeasance, and poor administrative performance

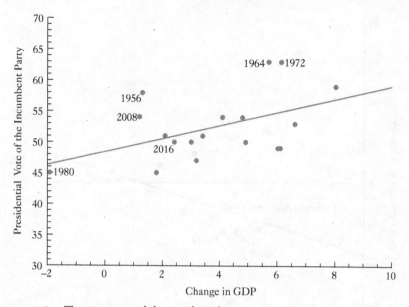

FIGURE 8.1 The economy and the presidential vote, 1948–2016.

give voters reasons to "throw the bum out," while a reputation for providing effective government explains why citizens reelect the incumbent. These noneconomic measures of governmental performance have been less prominent in our statistical models simply because we lack easily accessed measures of them. However, they are always discussed during election campaigns. Incumbents widely and loudly tout their achievements on these matters, while challengers emphasize shortcomings and failures as they insist that they will do better.

Even though we often lack satisfying measures for many of these noneconomic influences, we capture satisfaction with the incumbent's performance by asking whether the respondent approves of how the the incumbent is performing his or her job, overall and by specific area. These approval questions leave many opportunities to disagree about the source of the approval or disapproval, even when we ask specific questions about how well the incumbent is handling foreign affairs, the economy, education, and so forth. Still, the approval questions give us a measure for assessing how the vote is shaped by incumbent performance compared to other factors (including turnout). The relationship between job approval and how well the incumbent (or the incumbent's party) fares in a subsequent election is quite strong. An illustration appears in Figure 8.2, which documents the well-known fact that

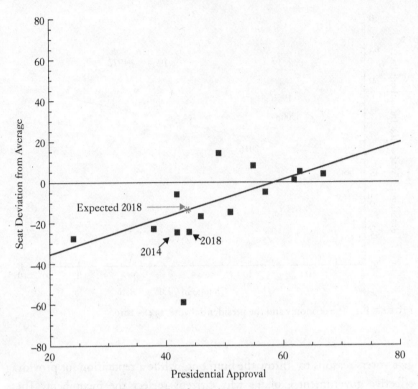

FIGURE 8.2 Incumbent's approval and party's House seat wins.

support for the president's congressional candidates in the off-year election varies with the incumbent's approval level.

This is a particularly relevant relationship given the conventional wisdom that turnout declines (particularly from the presidential election to the subsequent midterm election) explain losses by the president's party, especially when that president is a Democrat. The close fit of the slope to the scatter in Figure 8.2 makes it obvious that judgments about the president's job performance matter consistently. This comparison between the correlation of the vote with turnout and approval and its related factors is a point we will return to throughout this chapter.

Institutional Influences

The political and governing dynamics that shape election swings are not the only factors that trump turnout oscillation. Institutional influences—such as the type of ballot form (office block vs. party block), whether the ballot makes straight-ticket voting an option, and how many and which offices are scheduled for election simultaneously—also have a significant effect.

According to familiar lore, throughout U.S. history party leaders have promoted laws that created ballot forms and election cycles that advantaged themselves. Reformers often objected that these ballot variations exploited and confused voters. Perhaps they did, but the effectiveness of these ballot differences depended on the appeal of candidates at the top of the ballot: the candidates for mayor, governor, and, especially, president. Promoting popular top-of-the-ticket candidates produced dividends down the ballot as voters responded positively to lower-office candidates who touted the top candidate. More important, perhaps, was the susceptibility of marginally interested voters to their enthusiasm for the top candidate. Feelings about FDR and a ringing chant of "I Like Ike" could produce a straight Democratic or Republican vote that was mechanically facilitated by a party column ballot that may have even provided an option to vote for the complete party ticket with a single selection.

An illustration of how ballot forms are consequential occurred in the 1986 Illinois gubernatorial election in which all indicators pointed to a GOP sweep, except that this possibility was compromised by a vigorous effort by the Democrats to promote a straight-ticket vote. The campaign theme that year was "Punch 10," where "10" was the ballot key that produced a straight Democratic vote. It was especially effective in Chicago, which produced an unusual (even for Chicago) Democratic plurality that almost defeated the Republican incumbent seeking reelection.

The decline of party column ballots and straight-ticket options has limited ballot-form effects. Outcomes are further separated by the practice of holding elections for statewide offices in midterm or even odd years, when presidential candidates, the top-of-the-ticket candidates with the most influence, are not on the ballot. In fact most states hold elections for statewide offices in the off-years, while a few (Louisiana, New Jersey, and Virginia) hold them in odd-numbered years, when no elections for national government offices are held and voter attention is typically very low.

The influence of ballot form did not end with the elimination of party column ballots and straight-ticket voting options, though, because the motivation to vote for a "ticket" was always centered on the candidate at the top of the ballot. In other words, the ballots facilitated voting choices that were motivated by the candidates (Campbell et al. 1960). A lack of understanding about this dynamic has led to the conventional wisdom that straight-ticket (also known as "top-of-the-ticket") voting collapsed throughout the second half of the previous century. It has become less common, but it has not disappeared. Indeed it continues to influence election outcomes and remains a strong influence on the swings from on-year to off-year elections.

Coattail Voting

Implicit in the previous section is the notion that vote choices in down-ballot contests are influenced by preferences for candidates running for the most salient office. This is "coattail" voting, formally understood as the extent to which a popular candidate at the top of the ticket (usually the presidential candidate but sometimes a U.S. Senate or gubernatorial candidate) will lead voters to support candidates of that party for lower offices.

We offer three different but related pieces of data on the phenomenon to measure its prominence in contemporary elections. First, Table 8.1 examines the House vote by the presidential vote while controlling for party preference. Second, Table 8.2 examines the House vote by party preference and the party of the incumbent. Third, Table 8.3 examines how much the House vote follows the presidential vote after controlling for both party preference and incumbency. That is, we test for the effect of top-of-the-ticket coattails in congressional elections, controlling for the two influences that are strong proximate influences on the voter's assessment of candidates, especially legislative candidates: party preference and the evaluations linked to a familiar incumbent. The number of cases is very large, reflecting a data set of all the ANES surveys from presidential years. To eliminate any sample-size effect, all surveys are weighted to have a common number of respondents (N = 3,000).

One of the first things observed from the examination of coattails is that the appeal of the presidential candidate deflects the congressional vote from party identification in the same way and to an almost identical degree as

Table 8.1 Effects of the Presidential Vote in House Elections

	Party Identification		
Presidential vote	Democrat	Independent	Republican
Democrat	89	73	55
Republican	58	38	15
Total	83	51	20

Note: Cell entries are the percentage voting for the Democrat for the House.

Table 8.2 Effects of Incumbency and Partisanship in House Elections

House seat	Party Identification		
	Democrat	Independent	Republican
Democrat	94	76	44
Open Seat	81	46	17
Republican	58	21	5
Total	83	51	20

Note: Cell entries are the percentage voting for the Democrat for the House.

Table 8.3 Coattail Effects in the Face of Incumbency and Partisanship in House Elections

Party Identification	Democrat		Independent		Republican	
Presidential vote	Democrat	Republican	Democrat	Republican	Democrat	Republican
House seat						
Democrat	97	75	91	65	78	37
Open Seat	88	52	65	39	54	13
Republican	67	26	35	39	17	3

Note: Cell entries are the percentage voting for the Democrat for the House.

incumbency.[3] For example, in Table 8.1, the House vote swung 31 percentage points in response to the presidential vote, controlling for the voter's party identification. Eighty-nine percent of these Democrats who voted for the Democratic candidate for president also voted Democratic in the House, while only 58 percent voted Democratic for the House race when they cast their vote for the Republican presidential candidate. Republican partisans were similarly affected: their vote for the GOP House candidate declined 40 percentage points when they voted for the Democratic candidate for president. Clearly the coattail effect is substantial even though it receives less attention now than in the past, when ballot forms encouraged top-of-the-ticket effects and coattail voting was a prominent factor in candidate selection.

Although the ability of candidates, especially legislative candidates, to personalize their vote limits the influence of the top of the ticket on down-ballot offices today, the top candidate's influence is substantial. This insulating incumbency effect is easily observed in Table 8.2. Democratic identifiers have been 36 percentage points less likely to vote for the Democratic House candidate when a Republican holds the seat (94 percent vs. 58 percent). Republicans have responded similarly to incumbency: only 5 percent of Republican identifiers voted for the Democrat for Congress when a Republican was their sitting representative, whereas 39 percent defected when the Democrat held the seat.

Table 8.3 brings these influences—partisanship, coattails, and incumbency—together. It contrasts those who voted for the Democratic as opposed to the Republican presidential candidate, controlling for partisanship and the incumbency advantage. The effect of the presidential vote is large and cuts across both competing influences. Consider the first two columns. The voters in both columns are Democratic identifiers; most voted for the Democrat for the House and for president.

However, when they voted for the Republican presidential candidate, their support for the Democratic House candidate declined significantly, whether their representative was a Democrat or a Republican or the seat was open. Among these Democratic identifiers, support for the Democratic congressional candidate declined over 22 percentage points when the seat was held by a Democrat (97 percent vs. 75 percent), 36 points when it was an open seat (88 percent vs. 52 percent), and over 40 points when the Republican held the seat (67 percent vs. 26 percent).

The voting choices of the Republican identifiers—the last two columns of the table—are a mirror image of those observed for Democrats. Independents—the two columns in the center of the table—behaved like the partisans. A vote for the GOP presidential candidate by independents produced more support for the GOP congressional candidate regardless of the incumbency of the district; support for the Democratic presidential candidate helped the Democratic House candidate.

To summarize: The effects of incumbency are strong. Republicans voting for the Republican presidential candidate were much more likely to defect in the House race if the incumbent was a Democrat. Democrats behave similarly. Incumbency and partisanship work to dampen electoral waves. But, as the columns for the presidential vote document, presidential preferences can produce waves depending upon the short-term force of issues and personalities captured by the presidential candidates. Importantly, the effect of the presidential vote on the House vote—net of partisanship and incumbency—is large. Presidential candidates provided coattails to their down-ballot House candidates, irrespective of incumbency and voter party preference. We suspect this is also true for their copartisans all the way down the ballot. The net effect certainly depends on how well the presidential candidate fares. A close presidential race in which defection is minimal will not produce enough of a wave among partisans or independents. On the other hand, an electoral tidal wave (1964, 1972, 1980, and 2008 are possible examples) will work against House candidates of the losing presidential party by defeating more of them than the district's partisanship or incumbent's status would predict.

Surge and Decline

Coattail voting is the proximate cause of the partisan surge in down-ballot races. Moreover, because the surge is a short-term force that is almost always gone by the subsequent election, it presages a decline in that election unless the surge has been part of a reset of the party balance, something that occurs rarely. The surge and decline cycle in the on-year presidential election and the succeeding off-year congressional election was noticed decades ago and has been examined carefully by several scholars (see, e.g., A. Campbell, 1960, 1966: J. Campbell, 1987, 1991: Kernell 1977).[4] Coattails ensure that the following congressional election is held in the shadow of the presidential election that preceded it. The shadow has a direct influence on the outcome of the congressional election contests during the presidential election year; it has a second-order effect in the succeeding midterm. Presidential elections influence congressional elections because presidents have coattail effects on congressional candidates and virtually all down-ballot races. Congressional candidates of the winning presidential party do better in rough proportion to the success of the presidential candidate. The coattail effect seems to be weaker and less consistent than it was a half-century or more ago, but it is still felt by congressional candidates.

The linkage of congressional and presidential elections is not confined to the on-year contest. The shadow of the presidential election also covers the succeeding congressional election. Specifically, the midterm congressional results are dependent on how many seats were won by the party that won the presidency (and we know that the bigger the presidential win, the bigger the accompanying congressional majority). This cycle coincides with the rise and decline of turnout in presidential and congressional elections and explains why turnout has so often (incorrectly) been identified as causing changes that occur in off-year elections compared to the outcomes in the preceding presidential election.[5] The following data and analyses illustrate and consider the pattern, beginning with the presidential election.

Presidential Surges

Figure 8.3 plots the relationship between the vote share won by the winning presidential candidate and the vote share won by House candidates from his party between 1952 and 2016. The close relationship is obvious, although only after removing four outliers. Three of the four outliers—1960, 1976, and 2008—are presidential elections that produced substantial Democratic congressional majorities despite presidential wins that were not noticeably large; that is, the presidential surge did not seem large enough to justify the Democratic congressional surges in these years.

The anomalous results disappear when the preceding off-year contests in 1958, 1974, and 2006 are considered. The 1958 off-year election was a Democratic sweep in response to a significant economic recession. The stagnant economy carried Democrats into office throughout the country in that year, and probably burdened Nixon's campaign in 1960. The Democrats held on to most of those seats in 1960 but did not gain significantly more than they held going into the election.[6] The departure of the 1976 election from expectations has a similar etymology, although it was not a faulty economy but the

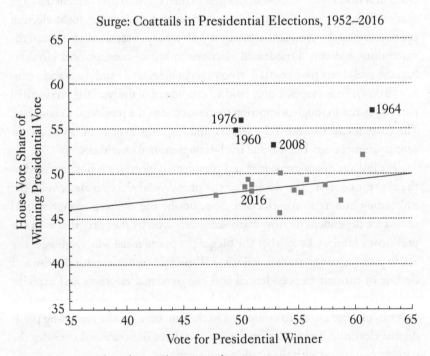

FIGURE 8.3 Presidential coattails: surge in the vote, 1952–2016.

Watergate scandal that produced (1) the near-impeachment of Nixon in the first half of 1974, (2) his resignation in mid-1974, (3) a pardon by President Gerald Ford in September 1974, and finally (4) a major rejection of the GOP throughout the country in November 1974.[7] The Democrats gained 49 House seats in 1974 (ending with 291), totaling well over the 242 they won in 1972, but then only one additional seat in 1976.

The 2008 election was a bit different. The Democrats gained 31 seats in the 2006 off-year election as Americans soured on the Republicans because of the Iraq conflict and the mishandling of the Hurricane Katrina–induced New Orleans flood, and then another 21 seats in 2008 as the recession of 2007–2008 became ever more severe. In short, there was a strong pro-Democratic environment in 2008 as well as 2006. In contrast, the 1960 and 1976 elections were won by the Democrats but were closely fought; Kennedy and Carter were only marginally more popular than Nixon and Ford, respectively, and no issues generated surges in either year.

The three elections fit our expectations about retrospective election dynamics. What appears to be ill-fitting results are not a challenge to the notion that presidential success generates congressional surges and declines in a predictable manner. The 1964 result, on the other hand, stands apart. However, this is only because Lyndon Johnson's landslide paid greater than normal political dividends down ballot. Furthermore, that feature does not invalidate the overall surge and decline pattern; it only constitutes an example of a top-of-the-ticket victory producing an unusually large down-ballot surge. Figure 8.4 summarizes the history of surges for these elections, highlighting the number of seats won relative to the party's average, allowing us to highlight elections in which the number of seats won was above (or below) the norm for the period.[8]

Off-Year Declines

The surge, whether measured by a vote percentage (Figure 8.3) or by seats won (Figure 8.4, and probably a more meaningful number politically), produces a high tide for the winning party in proportion to the magnitude of the margin for the winning presidential candidate. The increase in seats is, *ceteris paribus,* destined to return to an equilibrium, that is, the vote share the party typically receives and the seats that it usually wins. When the tide of the presidential surge recedes, support for many (and perhaps almost all) of the candidates who won on the coattails of the presidential wave declines and they lose their reelection bid. There is a political hydraulic process at work, which

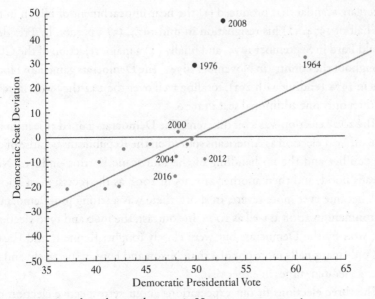

FIGURE 8.4 Presidential coattails: surge in House seats, 1952–2016.

dictates that the more a party wins by virtue of a presidential wave, the more it is destined to lose in the following election. This process occurs irrespective of turnout (again, *ceteris paribus*). It is always possible that an electoral triumph—like Roosevelt's win in 1932—reflects a shift that resets the party balance. Absent that, however, a top-of-the-ticket blowout that yields an unusually substantial number of down-ballot victories will be undone down ballot in the succeeding off-year contests.

Figure 8.5 illustrates the off-year declines for the elections in Figure 8.4. It plots the relationship between the numbers of congressional seats lost by the president's party in the midterm election against the numbers of seats won in the preceding presidential election. Since it is necessary to account for the post-1994 decline in Democratic congressional strength, the variable on the horizontal axis is the number of seats won in the presidential year *minus* the number of seats the party normally won during the period. The Democrats averaged 263 seats in the House from 1960 through the 1992 election. From 1994 through 2016, they averaged 210 seats. These averages thus adjust the "seats won" count for the presidential year. The resulting pattern is easier to discern in graphical form but, more important, it measures the underlying phenomenon directly: how many seats above the norm— the equilibrium value—were won in the presidential election? The figure uses the Democratic count, but in a two-party system that is immaterial.

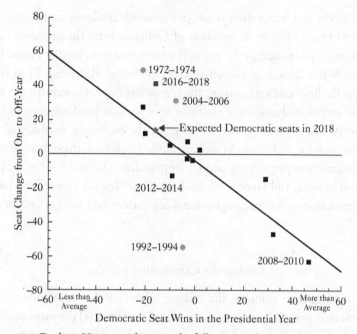

FIGURE 8.5 Decline: House seat losses in the following midterm, 1962–2018.

Either party's number tells the same story, with no misrepresentation of the relationship.

Figure 8.5 provides a graphic illustration of the basic proposition that the magnitude of the midterm loss is proportional to the "excess" congressional victories of the preceding presidential election. Moreover, from the data we clearly see the dependence of the midterm result on the party's congressional fortunes in the presidential election. Many factors are at work, but the regression slope in Figure 8.5 displays the link between each presidential-congressional election pair. Its negative value documents that seat losses in the subsequent midterm tend to be greatest when the seat gains in the presidential election were greatest. When the presidential election did not yield a surplus of congressional wins, the succeeding midterm did not produce a big loss for the president's party. Furthermore, there are relatively few on-/off-year pairs where the observed outcome in the succeeding off-year was substantially different from expected given the general pattern.

Surge and decline dynamics would lead a disinterested person to propose an outcome for the following off-year election as soon as the final total of House seats by the newly elected president's party is provided. All other things being equal, losses will be proportional to the gains in the presidential year. The key fact is that there is not an inexorable tendency for the electorate to defeat twenty-five or so members of Congress from the president's party (the number often used by the political commentariat to predict House losses for the White House in the off-year congressional elections). Most of the off-year declines run very close to the regression slope. Unsurprisingly, based on our earlier analyses, three elections stand out as producing much larger than expected declines, given the surge of the preceding presidential election: 1974, 1994, and 2006. As we have already observed, these three elections have in common particularly unpopular presidents: Gerald Ford in 1974, Bill Clinton in 1994, and George W. Bush in 2006.[9] The off-year referendum on the president struck their congressional delegations very hard in each of these years.[10]

Testing the Competing Effects

It is important to compare the relative effects of the three influences on off-year changes in House seats that we have set forth: (1) the turnout decline from the presidential year, (2) the job approval of the incumbent president, and (3) the magnitude of the surge in the preceding presidential election. In doing this, we expect to observe three results:

1. The magnitude of the surge in House seats by the party of the winning presidential candidate sets the stage for the decline in the succeeding off-year election. Presidential coattails resulted in more House victories than the presidential winner's party should normally expect, leading to losses in the off-year election. Briefly, the bigger the on-year win, the greater the off-year loss.

2. Current conditions intervene to moderate the decline in the aftermath of the surge. An exceptionally unpopular president produces losses directly and indirectly. Directly, voters express their disapproval by supporting the out-party candidate who represents it. Indirectly, presidents with low job approval encourage strong candidates from the out-party to run, and they encourage greater contributions to these out-party candidates because contributions flow toward likely winners. On the other side of the ledger, they discourage strong candidates of the in-party from running, and (if they do run) they discourage contributors from backing these candidates. Conversely, a popular incumbent will moderate House losses by reversing the processes just described, with the result that the loss of seats may be negligible. Indeed it is possible that an off-year election can produce

additional seats if the president is unusually well-regarded. The 1934 election is perhaps the first and most prominent historical example, and of course 2002 is a significant recent one.

3. Turnout declines from the on-year to the off-year congressional elections have averaged 15 percentage points and been as small as 8 points (in 1974). However, as has been repeatedly demonstrated, the turnout change will be an insignificant influence on the outcome.

Table 8.4 presents our estimates of the effects of these variables on midterm seat losses from 1962 through 2014. Turnout is insignificant, with only about a 27 percent chance that there is any relationship between it and the number of seats lost in the off-year election. By contrast, the incumbent president's approval rating (our proxy for the existing political environment) and the on-year surge are both strong predictors of the off-year loss of seats by the president's party.[11] Since 1960, the average on-year election has added seven seats to the winning presidential candidate's caucus in the House, which leads to an expected loss of eight seats in the succeeding off-year election. Incumbent approval has averaged about 49 percent, which leads to an expected loss of twelve seats in the off-year. Together the on-year surge and typical president's approval level lead us to expect about a twenty-seat loss in the House for the incumbent president's party. Turnout adds nothing to that oscillation. However, low approval levels just before the off-year election, regardless of the magnitude of the on-year surge, can yield big off-year

Table 8.4 Modeling Off-Year Losses in the House, 1954–2014

	Unstandardized Coefficients		Standardized Coefficients	t-statistic	Statistical Significance
	B	Standard error	Beta		
(Constant)	−66.62	29.94		−2.23	.05
President's job approval in early October of off-year	1.31	.44	.59	3.59	.01
Presidential party's seat surge in on-year	−1.18	.33	−.59	−3.59	.01
Change in turnout from the on-year	1.43	1.56	.15	.91	.38

drops. Perhaps the most obvious recent example is 2006, when low approval cost George W. Bush and the Republicans twenty-nine seats. Conversely, a big on-year surge can produce a substantial midterm decline irrespective of the president's approval level. For example, the Obama-led surge of 2008 produced a sixty-three-seat loss in 2010 even though Obama's job approval on the eve of the November balloting was 45 percent—only slightly below the average presidential approval-level since 1962.[12]

Other Effects

The issue environment shaped by the campaigns adds to the structural decline directly, as it did in 2006, for example. Some of the effect is direct (voters supported Democrats who criticized Bush and the Republicans for Iraq and the ineffective efforts by the federal government to help New Orleans after the hurricane), and some of it is indirect, reflecting and magnifying the issue influence on the vote.

One indirect effect that is especially consequential is who decides to run in these election environments. Ambitious politicians, always mindful of their next promotion, must calculate how long to stay in their current office (where factors associated with their incumbent status virtually assure continued reelection) and when to run for the next office up the hierarchy (something that is usually riskier than staying put). One rule they use to decide is how good they *expect* the political environment to be for their candidacy. The party that seems disadvantaged by short-term forces typically produces a surplus of retirements, as the GOP experiences in the run-up to the 2018 congressional elections and seems to be experiencing as the 2020 election approaches. Simultaneously the favored party often produces a crop of strong candidates because they see such years as an opportunity to move up from local and state offices they currently occupy.

The data that political scientists have collected on this recruitment differential are consistent and unequivocal (see, e.g., Jacobson 1978; Jacobson and Kernell 1982). When the political environment favors the Republicans, the GOP tends to have the better crop of candidates, and these candidates seem to be well-financed. Conversely, the Democrats have the better candidates (also better financed) when the political environment favors the Democrats. Of course, better candidates who are better funded typically have more success. This dynamic has been evident in recent landslide elections. For example, charges of Republican failure during the months leading up to the November

2006 election were aided by candidate selection and campaign processes that preceded the vote by many months.

The underlying propositions in this "strategic politician" model are straightforward. Many to most politicians in contemporary America are professional, lifelong office seekers. The example of Cincinnatus—four or so years of public service and back to the farm, law office, or insurance business—is uncommon except for the lowest-level offices. Consequently most political careers are planned movements up the hierarchy of offices (city council or prosecutor, to state legislature, to the House, to governor, to the Senate, topping out at the presidency). Not every politician follows the same route and not all continue to climb, but there is a clear path on which pols-in-training learn their craft. Every now and again, a Donald Trump moves laterally to high office—but only rarely. Finally, losing does little or nothing to promote a successful political career. A core rule requires the career politician to always win reelection and to *carefully calculate when to seek that next office up the ladder*.

The key to understanding the better than expected gains for the out-party in 1974, 1994, and 2006 is the strategic politician's calculation of *when to seek that next office up the ladder*. The expected political environment is calculated a year or more before the election. Final decisions to begin planning a campaign, identifying key staff and consultants, touching base with key supporters, laying the foundation for raising the necessary money, and so forth typically are made twelve to eighteen months before the election.

In November and December 2005, when strategic politicians who contemplated moving up to the House had to decide whether to do so, the accusations of failure directed at Bush persuaded ambitious Democrats to start a campaign. On the other side of the aisle, these accusations prompted ambitious Republicans to await a better year, where "better" is a summary assessment of the election environment.

The environment influenced activists, consultants, and campaign contributors. Contributors, unless they are ideologically committed, are unlikely to donate large sums to candidates who are not expected to win. Similarly, on the other side, pragmatic campaign contributors are inclined to support prospective winners with large donations since the companies and unions that have business before Congress want to be able to remind their representatives that they were supportive. Senate seats, governorships, and other offices are affected by the same influences and in the same fashion, often to as large a degree.

At this point, one might reasonably ask how much shifts in candidate spending—perhaps the most effective indicator of campaigning—contribute to election surges and declines. Table 8.5 allows at least a partial assessment of how a variety of factors (including turnout and candidate spending) affect electoral change in our most recent elections. More precisely, the results are based on regression equations that allow turnout, along with contextual and political variables—such as presidential approval, unemployment rates, and campaign spending— to predict the shifts in Democratic vote choice for two U.S. Senate election cycles. We wish to explore the surge from 2010 to 2016, as well as the decline from 2008 to 2014.[13]

The first data column offers the surge equation for the thirty-one U.S. Senate seats up in both 2010 and 2016; given the data presented throughout

Table 8.5 Turnout and Election Environments

Change in	2010–2016 Surge		2008–2014 Decline	
	Unstandardized regression coefficient	Standard error	Unstandardized regression coefficient	Standard error
Turnout	−0.394	0.375	−0.159	0.098
Unemployment rate	−0.013	0.010	−0.022	0.026
Presidential approval	0.002	0.008	0.002	0.002
Candidate campaign spending	0.007**	0.003	0.008**	0.003
Democratic incumbent	−0.030	0.062	−0.035	0.069
Republican incumbent	0.050	0.057	0.066	0.060
Intercept	0.024	0.109	−0.159	0.098
N	31		32	
Standard error	0.091		0.116	
Adjusted R-square	0.252		0.263	

Notes: The dependent variable is the change in the Democratic share of the two-party vote for U.S. Senate. Unemployment data come from the Bureau of Labor Statistics, 2010–2016. Presidential approval ratings consist of the percentage saying they approve of the president's job handling; these data come from Gallup, 2010–2016. Campaign spending differentials consist of Democratic expenditures minus Republican expenditures; these data come from the Federal Election Commission, 2010–2016.

***$p < 0.01$, one-tailed; **$p < 0.01$, one-tailed; *$p < 0.05$, one-tailed.*

this book, it is unsurprising that turnout has no significant effect on shifts in the Democratic share of the two-party vote for U.S. Senate. The regression coefficient is negatively signed (though the correlation is statistically insignificant). Interestingly, the surge in the Democratic Senate vote from 2010 to 2016 appears to have been immune to economic and presidential approval shifts as well. While contrary to a priori expectations, these findings fit with what we observed in 2016; that is, improved unemployment numbers and solid (if not spectacular) job approval ratings for President Obama did not help the Democrats much. The headwinds faced by all incumbents in 2016 are evident in the fact that the increase in the Democratic vote share from 2010 to 2016 diminishes where there are Democratic incumbents; similarly, the Democratic surge is greater where GOP incumbents hold the seat.

On the other hand, candidates did much better when they were able to improve the campaign spending differential. This effect is both statistically and substantively significant. A Democrat who was able to turn a $1 million spending deficit in 2010 into a $1 million advantage in 2016 could expect, on average, an improvement of 1.4 points in the Democratic vote share.

The third data column of Table 8.5 displays the results of a parallel equation for the decline in Democratic vote share across the thirty-two Senate seats that were up in both 2008 and 2014. Once again turnout does not explain vote share: the data indicate that decreased turnout is insignificantly correlated with a decline in the Democratic Senate vote. In fact, the regression coefficient is (again) negative. As we saw with the surge equation, the decline model suggests that unemployment and presidential job approval numbers do not explain much of the shift in the Democratic vote—at least, not across these particular contests.[14] As before, we are inclined to think that this is largely a function of the peculiar economic circumstances of this era (when a sluggish recovery is viewed as poor economic performance) rather than an indictment of the power of conditional factors. There is also a repeat of the finding that incumbency was less of a conduit and more of an impediment to vote share, though the relationship was insignificant in statistical terms.

What does matter for the decline—as it did for the surge—is the campaign spending differential between candidates. Democrats who saw their spending differentials decrease tended to have a more substantial vote share decline. More specifically, a Democratic candidate who had a $1 million spending advantage in 2008 and a $1 million spending deficit in 2014 was likely to experience a vote share decrease of 1.6 percentage points. The larger point for our story is that campaign spending often tracks with how the candidates and parties assess conditions and their prospects for victory. The significance of the spending differentials therefore suggests that both money and the strategic assessments of opportunity that influence contributions are important explanations for variance in electoral performance. Turnout, on the other hand, has neither a consistent nor an especially powerful affect.

Conclusion

Much of this study has focused on the weak and inconsistent relationship between turnout and partisan vote share. In this chapter, we shifted our sights from what *does not* influence election swings to what *does*. In so doing, we expand on the theoretical perspective offered in chapter 3. Most notably, we assume that the short-term forces that exercise disproportionate sway on peripheral voters also shape the broader contours of election outcomes. Furthermore, the coattails that result from the surge not only affect the presidential election but also establish the baseline against which the subsequent decline occurs. In sum, a substantial presidential election surge creates the opportunity, conditioned by extant conditions and circumstances, for a massive off-year decline. Of course the surge and decline argument is not new. And even though we think it is interesting to test some of its assumptions with new data, the central finding again is that turnout plays almost no role with respect to the shifts in vote choice that animate the surge and decline story.

At this point, the data—both the survey and aggregate-level data—largely speak against a turnout bias. Assuming one is convinced that the conventional wisdom about higher turnout leading to greater Democratic vote share is wrong, several questions remain: Why is the conventional wisdom's hold on academics and practitioners so persistent? Does it matter if the conventional wisdom is wrong? We turn to these and other, more expansive and more normative notions in the concluding chapter.

9

Some Final Data and Thoughts on the Link between Turnout and Vote Choice

IT IS SOBERING to find so little empirical support for a perspective that seems so plausible and is compelling to so many knowledgeable people. On the one hand, we are disciples of the "Trust the data" school of social science. And we are particularly impressed by the consistency of the null finding here—over time with electoral units, across election types, and across levels. There is a time-honored saying among social scientists: "If you torture the data enough, they'll confess to anything." Yet despite our insistence on poking and prodding and on viewing things from every conceivable angle, the data refuse to report that turnout influences partisan vote choice in American elections. On the other hand, null findings for such a popular convention deserve intense scrutiny. Perhaps a key variable has been mismeasured; perhaps a key relationship is obscured by some effect hiding in plain sight. As we conclude our study, we return to the possibility that a single factor might be exerting an unseen effect on the relationship between turnout and partisan vote choice. More precisely, as suggested by Michels (1962) and DeNardo (1980), we return to the concept of partisanship and the idea that turnout affects vote choice, but only if one takes account of the majority party and the competitive balance in the state or district.

The Curious Case of Partisanship

Though mindful of the potential for conditioning or mediating effects, we have been unable to identify a variable that strongly influences the relationship between turnout and vote choice. One variable that seemed likely to play some role is the partisanship of the statewide electorates and how it changed.

The Turnout Myth. Daron R. Shaw and John R. Petrocik, Oxford University Press (2020). © Oxford University Press.
DOI: 10.1093/oso/9780190089450.001.0001

However, whether the electorate was Democratic or Republican, whether the competitive margin was narrow or wide, and whether this balance was changing or static, the fundamental lack of a relationship between turnout and partisan vote choice remained consistent. Still, tracking party identification over time within the different states allowed us to observe some interesting patterns.

Table 9.1 profiles the partisanship of the states along two dimensions. The first is the relative proportions of Democrats and Republicans; we label this the competitiveness of the electorates (the rows of the table). The second dimension is how those proportions have changed over the past three decades; we label this the direction of partisan change (the columns). Gallup's yearly estimates of partisanship in the states from 1990–2016 provide the raw data (Shaw et. al. 2019). For those years and states for which Gallup does not provide the necessary data, we rely on an equation derived from statewide exit polling data (again, see Shaw et. al. 2019). The table identifies the states by these characteristics, while the cells of the table also report a value labeled "PDI" (percentage difference index), which is the arithmetical difference between the proportion of Democratic and Republican identifiers from our estimate. Negative numbers indicate that the Democratic percentage is larger (by the PDI value), and positive values indicate that Republicans are more numerous.

This juxtaposition of partisan balance and competitiveness offers a possible insight into the weak and erratic effect of turnout on vote choice. States with electorates tilted toward the Democratic Party tend to be more lopsided in their party identification than states that tilt toward the GOP. More important, the partisan balance among states that have been stable and tilted toward the Democrats or moved toward the Democrats tend to be so heavily Democratic in party identification that elections are unlikely to be competitive given the dominant influence of party identification on candidate choice. Nine of the states whose electorate adopted a significantly more Republican identification during the past three decades (the upper left-most cell in the table) are evenly balanced between Democratic and Republican identifiers. The seven states below them (headed by Alabama) have a party identification balance that is approximately 12 percentage points more Republican than Democratic. The six states (in the second column of the table) whose party preference has been stable are less competitive overall, with Nebraska, Utah, and Wyoming being GOP bastions where Republican identifiers outnumber Democratic partisans by more than 24 percentage points. Collectively, however, twelve of the twenty-two most Republican states are not so Republican

Table 9.1 Assessing Partisan Identification and Election Competitiveness Over Time

	Direction of Party Identification Change					
	Moved to Republicans	Stable Republican	Balanced	Stable Democratic	Moved to Democrats	TOTAL
Party ID balance is competitive	Arkansas Kentucky Louisiana Mississippi Missouri Oklahoma Tennessee Texas West Virginia	Arizona Indiana Kansas	Colorado Florida Georgia Iowa Maine Nevada North Hampshire North Carolina Ohio Virginia Wisconsin	Michigan Minnesota Oregon Pennsylvania		
	PDI = 0	PDI = 6	PDI = −2	PDI = −7		
N	9	3	11	4	0	27
Party ID balance is not competitive	Alabama Alaska Idaho Montana North Dakota South Carolina South Dakota	Nebraska Utah Wyoming		Hawaii Maryland Massachusetts New Mexico Rhode Island Washington	California Connecticut Delaware Illinois New Jersey New York Vermont	
	PDI = 12	PDI = 25		PDI = 25	PDI = −15	
N	7	3	0	6	7	23
TOTAL	16	6	11	10	7	50

in their partisanship that Democrats face lopsided odds. On the right side of the table, by contrast, where seventeen states tilt toward the Democrats, only four—Michigan, Minnesota, Oregon, and Pennsylvania—have electorates that are not heavily tipped toward the Democratic Party.[1] Three-quarters of these states—thirteen of the seventeen—have lopsided Democratic electorates, as the PDI values indicate.[2]

If turnout were to have an influence on the vote, one would expect states that are the most balanced in their partisanship to exhibit the effect. States that are the least competitive—California and Connecticut, for example—would be the least influenced by the kind of turnout oscillation that is normally observed. By contrast, states in the same category as Arkansas, whose voters have adopted a more Republican partisanship, or Arizona, where partisanship has been stable but tilted Republican, might be influenced by turnout changes if there was any bias in turnout.

In fact there is such a relationship, but not in the direction expected. The effect of the PDI on the turnout–vote choice linkage is strongest for gubernatorial elections and weakest for presidential elections, while contests for Senate seats fall between them. The following figures plots the relationship.

Figure 9.1A focuses on presidential elections, where the correlation between the turnout bias slope and partisanship is −.02. Figure 9.1B is for gubernatorial elections, where the correlation is .39. Figure 9.1C is for Senate seats, where the correlation is .19. By conventional standards the gubernatorial and Senate results are statistically significant, while the presidential data are effectively random.[3] That is, the balance of Democrats and Republicans in the states is correlated with a turnout bias for gubernatorial and Senate elections, but not for presidential contests.

However, the substantive pattern demonstrated by the data is more noteworthy by far: *turnout helps the minority party*. As Michels (1962) asserted decades ago, and DeNardo (1980) confirmed when he concluded that "the joke is on the Democrats," the peripheral electorate is more likely to support the minority party when turnout increases. For gubernatorial, Senate, and presidential elections a positive-slope relationship between turnout and the party vote—which indicates that higher turnout is increasing Democratic support—*occurs in states where Democrats are in a minority*, or at least not dominant. More specifically, the posited pro-Democratic effect of turnout appears to hold among the Republican-leaning states (the right side of Figures 9.1A to 9.1C). By contrast, turnout increases tend to boost the Republican vote in states where Democrats are dominant (the left side of each figure). Moreover these effects are strongest for gubernatorial and Senate elections but mostly absent for presidential races.

But is this right? Recall Michels's (1962) suggestion (which others have embraced to various degrees) that anyone not regularly supporting the majority party is alienated from it to some degree but available to support the minority when they are politically activated. This seems quite plausible. Indeed this phenomenon is observed in many places in the United States where one

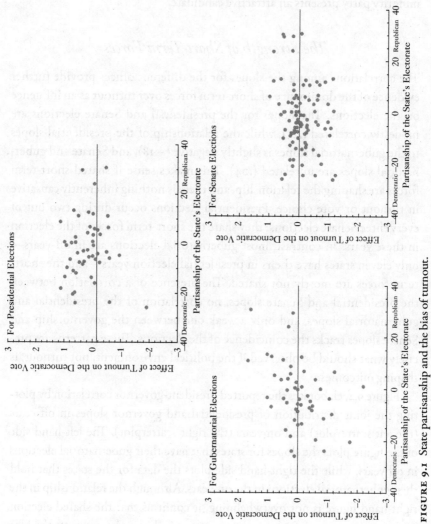

FIGURE 9.1 State partisanship and the bias of turnout.

party is dominant. In these places—examples include California, where the minority Republicans are less numerous than self-described independents or those who refuse to register with a party preference—such voters typically cannot bring themselves to support the minority party, but their unwillingness to commit to the majority makes them relatively more available when the minority party presents an attractive candidate.

The Strength of Short-Term Forces

The correlations among the slopes for the different offices provide further evidence of the dominance of short-term forces over turnout as an influence on the elections. The slopes for the presidential and Senate elections are modestly correlated (.23), while the relationship of the presidential slopes to the gubernatorial slopes is slightly negative (−.18), and Senate and gubernatorial slopes are unrelated (.04). This makes sense if shared short-term forces are shaping the relationship, and there is nothing inherently causative in turnout or vote choice. Presidential elections occur during two out of every three Senate elections; they share the short-term forces of the election in these years. In contrast, most gubernatorial elections are in off-years—only eleven states have theirs in presidential election years—and the short-term forces are mostly not shared. The presence of a correlation between the presidential and Senate slopes, no correlation of the presidential and gubernatorial slopes, and only a weak one between the governorship and Senate slopes tracks the coincidence of the elections. These patterns are precisely what should be observed if the political environment, not turnout, is shaping outcomes.

Figure 9.2, elaborates the reported president-governor correlation by plotting the joint distribution of presidential and governor slopes in off-years (the left scatterplot) and on-years (the right scatterplot). The left-hand side of the figure plots the slopes for states that have their gubernatorial elections in off years, while the right-hand side plots the data for the states that hold their gubernatorial elections in the on-years. Although the relationship in the right-hand figure is not overwhelming, it confirms that the shared election environment matters. Perhaps more germane is that it also supports the idea that the election environment, and not turnout, shapes election outcomes. Put differently, short-term issues and candidate forces connect the outcomes of the elections, not turnout rates.

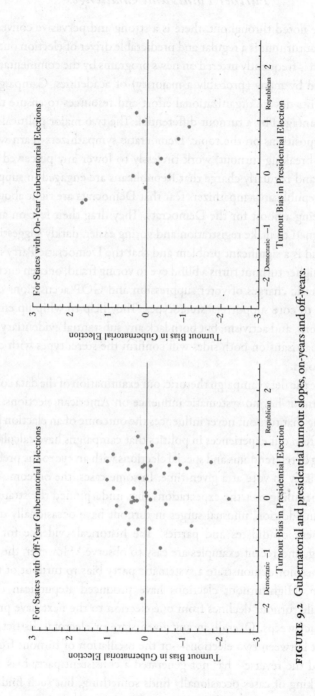

FIGURE 9.2 Gubernatorial and presidential turnout slopes, on-years and off-years.

Further Points and Challenges

As we have noted throughout, there is a strong and pervasive conventional wisdom that turnout is a regular and predictable driver of election outcomes. This notion is frequently uttered on news programs by the commentariat and is embraced by many (probably a majority) of academics. Campaigns and party activists devote organizational effort and resources to ensure they are not disadvantaged by a turnout differential. The two major political parties have clear positions on the topic. Democratic sympathizers yearn wistfully for record-breaking turnout, work tirelessly to lower any perceived barrier to voting, and regularly charge that Republicans are engaged in suppressing turnout. Republican sympathizers fear that Democrats are right about more turnout being a boost for the Democrats. They drag their feet on any proposal designed to make registration and voting easier, darkly suggesting that voting fraud is a significant problem and that the Democratic Party's enthusiasm for higher turnout turns a blind eye to voting fraud, or even encourages it. Democratic charges of voter suppression and GOP accusations of voter fraud play to core supporters' stereotypes. They help to whip up emotions, contributions, and activism, but both lack any substantial evidentiary base—although partisans on both sides will confirm the stereotypes with compelling anecdotes.

Despite the fiery campaign rhetoric, our examination of the data convinces us that turnout has no systematic influence on American elections. We are not arguing that turnout never influences the outcome of an election because we know from our experiences in politics that campaigns have calculated the scheduling of referendums and special elections with an eye to the preferences of voters likely to vote at a given time. In some cases, the outcome of such careful scheduling met the expectations that underpinned the strategic calculation. In addition, unusual surges in turnout have occasionally upended establishment candidates and parties. The historical evidence for that is compelling, and recent examples are easy to observe.[4] However, the general pattern does not demonstrate a systematic party bias to turnout or turnout fluctuation. High-turnout elections have produced Republican electoral waves, while turnout declines from one election to the next have produced Democratic sweeps. Overall, in any given state or electoral district a surge in turnout between two elections—or the oscillation of turnout from high to low and the reverse—has not generated a consistent party bias. Careful cherry-picking of cases occasionally finds something, but such findings are little more than a confirmatory analysis effort that ignores the general effect.

We have methodically considered the validity of the conventional wisdom that shifts in turnout are correlated with changes in partisan vote choice. What we repeatedly find is that partisan vote choice is weakly and inconsistently related to the vote share. Short-term forces that alter the vote choices of the less partisan drive turnout and the direction of the vote are the key exogenous influence on elections. Turnout and vote choice are consequences, and neither is a cause of the other. Our conclusion is that Democrats who yearn wistfully for record-breaking turnout and work tirelessly to lower the barriers to voting in the United States are engaged in a morally laudable democratic endeavor, while Republicans who are spooked by every uptick in turnout and scheme to enact and enforce anti–voter fraud laws are only creating an image problem for themselves.

Unfortunately, many are loath to accept that politics—in the form of short-term forces—can cast an adverse judgment on their candidate or party in a given election, and therefore look to blame some mechanical and inexorable Newtonian-esque law. This is part of the appeal of the conventional wisdom regarding turnout and vote choice. We therefore expect our evidence and argument to be met with resistance. However, we do not expect to be presented with persuasive contradicting findings since our data, by virtue of their face validity and straightforward quality, are hard to refute. Nevertheless we can anticipate objections that should be addressed. Thus, in this valedictory chapter, we explore these considerations and then extend our own line of thinking (hopefully) to say something about the future of electoral politics in the U.S.

Are There Endogeneity Concerns to Address?

Is it possible that the vote and turnout are linked, not with turnout as the cause but as a product of candidate preference? Perhaps more to the point, would our findings look different if vote choice affected turnout? We do not think so. Endogeneity arguments typically seem plausible and are certainly popular in political science because there is considerable simultaneity among the things we study. Many of the phenomena political science examines occur at the same time, allowing us to establish correlations but not causation because we cannot determine time order, even when we can decide mutability. Ergo the specter of endogeneity is summoned.

Given this general concern, what is plausible in this specific case? In the American voluntary voting system, the more likely sequencing in the turnout–vote choice decision is that the voter makes a judgment about candidates (schematized by Downs's model) and decides to vote for that candidate if (and when) the judgment generates a sufficiently lopsided preference.[5] At the individual level, this formulation makes candidate preference the motivator to vote. Aggregated across the electorate it is therefore possible to assert that candidate preference determines turnout levels. Although much voting is habitual behavior and not everyone with a candidate preference turns out, Downs's formula provides a way to understand voting that is too rich to ignore, and our conceptualization of the voting decision assumes that candidate preferences motivate people to vote (see chapter 3).

However, as we suggested earlier, there is nothing in this formulation that suggests (let alone mandates) a consistent turnout bias in which high turnout always advantages the Democrats. At the individual level, the strong candidate preference that motivated a decision to vote (à la Downs) could easily advantage the Republican candidate—as can be observed in the open-ended like/dislike questions from the American National Election Surveys. The most fundamental problem for endogeneity critiques is the failure to recognize the simple fact that the bivariate correlations between turnout and the vote are (a) trivial and (b) often the reverse of what is expected by the conventional notion that turnout has a Democratic bias. Whether one sets up assessments that view turnout as an influence on the vote or the vote choice as an influence on turnout, the record produces an unrelated joint distribution of turnout and vote choice across elections overall, over time within congressional districts, by Senate seats, and for gubernatorial and presidential elections for the same state. Put differently, the zero-order relationship between turnout and vote choice, regardless of which is deemed causal, is most often numerically equal to zero, with the measured slope coefficients yielding near-normal distributions around zero.

Further, we think that understanding the place of turnout in any story of election oscillations does not require sometimes impenetrable statistical massaging. There are relevant variables whose time order can be established. There are also groups of relevant variables that can be distinguished by their mutability. There is a time order that must occur for a variable to be a cause. That is, the cause must precede what is presumed to be the effect. And while we may be correct (per Downs) in believing that a candidate preference is generally a necessary precondition to a decision to vote, that connection does not support any speculation about a partisan bias in turnout because, as we have documented, there is no correlation between turnout rates among and between elections and the outcome of the elections. Minor differences in turnout between Democrats and Republicans are consistently swamped by much larger interelection variance in defection rates and the choices of independents.

Confounding Considerations

Recent research (Stolwijk, Schuck, and de Vreese 2016; Dahlgaard et al. 2017) seems to be reconsidering the importance of bandwagons, sometimes referred to as electoral waves. However, bandwagons do not, either conceptually or empirically, have a necessary relationship to turnout. They are about swings and, often, a tendency for down-ballot candidates to prosper because of the popularity of top-of-the-ticket candidates (see, e.g., Table 8.3). But bandwagons do not have an inherent party bias. Bandwagon elections have benefited both parties; defection has helped the Democrats (1964 and 2008) and the Republicans (1972 and 1984). Furthermore, electoral waves sometimes generate substantial coattails (2008) and sometimes none (2012). The same sort of variance occurs with respect to bandwagons and turnout. Sometimes a party's loyalists respond with an unusual turnout bump, as African American voters did for Barack Obama and the Democrats in 2008 and, especially, 2012; sometimes the expected loser faces apathy and diminished turnout among his or her nominal loyalists (Republicans in 2012). But we have also had blowout elections with unexceptional turnout rates (1964). A substantial margin between the major party candidates at the top of the ticket does not necessarily reflect or affect turnout.

Once again the result in every election is shaped by the short-term influences—the political environment, if you will—of that election. V. O. Key stated it well almost fifty years ago: "Voters are not fools" (1966, 7). Most may not have preferences on complex policy questions, but they appreciate whether the economy is producing employment and good wages, whether the nation is secure against potential enemies abroad, if a military or foreign policy has succeeded or gone awry, and whether the incumbents are in court or jail for malfeasance. The electorate's collective judgment about egregious failure or conspicuous success determines candidate preference, enthusiasm, and the outcome of elections. Modeling turnout as a function of candidate preference attributes causation, candidate preference, to what is an intervening variable. The central exogenous influence is the political, social, and economic environment that shapes candidate assessments and preference. That political environment within which an election is occurring—what we have usually referenced as the short-term forces (STFs)—is the relevant exogeneous influence on individual voters and, in the aggregate, the electorate. Understanding and predicting the impact of these STFs does not require every voter to re-spond identically. The most highly partisan are capable of perceiving successful stewardship by their party's candidates no matter what an unprejudiced view might conclude. However, electoral tides are determined by the assessments of voters who respond to the political environment, as Key formulated; the benefiting candidate is the expression of the exogenous variables.

Polarization

Over fifty years ago Seymour Martin Lipset and Stein Rokkan (1967) considered party systems in terms of their polarization and rigidity. They contrasted party systems in which the parties functioned as "agents of con-flict or instruments of integration." The American parties, despite occa-sional turns toward representation and conflict, have generally functioned as instruments of integration. The two major parties each cobbled together diverse constituencies that were sufficiently divided on enough of the issues of the day so that the central cleavages between the parties were effectively moderated by the heterogeneous views of both party's elites, activists, and voters. Since the mid-1980s, however, the parties' constituencies have tended toward greater homogeneity, like Lipset and Rokkan's "parties of conflict." Does the relevant electoral environment substantively change as fewer partisans view the world independent of the defining conflicts of their party? Will persuasive effects be minimal? Will rigid partisanship reduce elections to events in which the previous outcome is simply confirmed, because no one will view anything differently? Recall that Lipset and Rokkan's "frozen cleavages" yielded election outcomes that usually repeated the results of the preceding one. Our emphasis has been on short-term forces that generate changes and tides, but what if reality is increasingly conditional upon the par-tisan lens through which someone views things? Partisan and ideological in-formation, transmitted and amplified by partisan news sources, could create information environments in which partisans have many, perhaps mostly par-tisan facts, leading to sectarian worldviews in which prior viewpoints allow citizens to have their own facts, and perhaps not the facts known by their political opposition.

A popular aphorism insists that we should "never say never," but the country is far from that level of polarization. Divisions were sharp and antagonisms across party lines were substantial by 2006, but a backlash against the Republican administration's unpopular policy in the Middle East and its poor response to the suffering in New Orleans after Hurricane Katrina swept out the GOP's congressional majority. The banking and economic collapse of 2007–2008 and Obama's ability to project a possible recovery amplified the electorate's assessment of 2006 and produced more Republican congressional losses and John McCain's defeat in 2008. Less partisan voters still matter, and they have proven particularly important as conduits of short-term forces even in these polarized times.

But what about the broader trend toward unyielding partisan conflict and the politics of the 2010s? Have the parties moved even further into the realm of conflict and away from integration? Has a search for "responsible parties" (see the famed APSA Report, 1950) taken us too far and created parties of warring coalitions? We can see the trace evidence for this in many recent developments: the geographic polarization of the 2016 election; the lopsided margins within the states in 2016; a very popular movement to resist what was seen as a democratically illegitimate Trump win; contentious postelection demonstrations; and the personal harassment of some administration figures by Trump opponents. On the other hand, several heretofore strongly Democratic states (Michigan, Pennsylvania, and Wisconsin) voted for Trump in 2016, and other typically Democratic states (Minnesota) supported Hillary Clinton by much less than they went for other recent Democratic presidential candidates. Almost coincidentally, special elections held in the heretofore reliable Republican bastions of Georgia and Alabama produced Democratic victories. Overall we think the arguments for transformational change should not be based on events of a brief period. The most vocal activists invariably attract attention and the current crop of anti-Trump activists is vociferous. We do not see much evidence that the remainder of the electorate is so engaged or shares their hardened views. The unyielding proportion may have grown, and some issues with significant symbolic content that is hard to compromise have emerged (particularly around immigration). Even so, voters still seem to fit Key's summary with their inclination to tilt toward candidates who are reasonable stewards of the domestic economy, foreign relations, and government performance.

The 2018 Midterm Election

It is the rare obligation of a few professions—meteorology, economics, and political science come to mind—to not simply explain the present but to use this expertise to predict the future. And the success of those predictions is taken as some indication of the prognosticator's underlying competence. The truth is that we shouldn't engage in these exercises. We do not know 5 percent of what we need to know to forecast successfully political outcomes. We don't know which candidates are boning up on the issues and working on their communication skills, and which are ignoring their constituents and getting kickbacks on government contracts. Still, we can't resist. Furthermore, we do have information on a sufficient number of crucial factors to offer a few broad statements about what the future holds.

What did we expect for the 2018 midterm elections? For starters, we return to the regression slopes estimating the effects of turnout as well as short-term forces on election outcomes. The slopes in Table 8.4 indicate that turnout was unlikely to have been a consequential factor across the electorate, although the chatter from the commentariat and sundry mavens suggested otherwise. Instead the outcome in 2018 was most likely shaped by two factors: (1) the minimal down-ballot surge produced by 2016's presidential candidates and (2) attitudes toward Trump, commonly measured by his job approval.

There was not a down-ballot surge for the Republicans in 2016. In fact Clinton's win in the popular vote produced an *increase* in Democratic House seats in 2016. This should have limited Republican losses in 2018. An analogue would be 2002; the Republicans did not gain seats in the House or Senate despite Bush's Electoral College victory in 2000 and thus experienced no appreciable decline in the subsequent midterm election. But the 2002 analogy goes only so far, as Bush had extraordinarily strong approval ratings in the aftermath of the 9/11 attacks. The Gallup Organization had Bush at 63 percent approval just before the 2002 election. Trump's approval rating, according to Gallup, was 43 percent in the run-up to November 2018.

Besides Trump's middling approval ratings, a variety of challenges to state district plans probably helped the Democrats in 2018 (especially in Pennsylvania). Trump's effect on GOP losses probably equally the effect of Obama's similarly low approval level in 2010. Despite the surge in turnout in 2018 there is no reason to think that it explains what amounted to GOP seat losses that were only slightly greater than Trump's relatively low approval numbers would have predicted.

A Final Word

We think it is important to end by noting that turnout matters. The turnout rate is an indication of the health of a country's body politic. Since the time of Tocqueville, foreigners have commented appreciatively on the level of political engagement of Americans. And turnout is the ultimate expression of the connection between a people and its governing institutions. It is something the country has rightly taken pride in over time. We also reject the notion that lower turnout and participation rates evince a satisfaction on the part of the people with their government.

But while we think that turnout is important, we do not think it has been a major factor for which side wins elections. The fact that so many seem to point reflexively to turnout when assessing the cause of their joy or sadness seems, based on the data, fundamentally misguided. Instead we see this analysis as an affirmation of the centrality of issues, candidate qualities, and campaigns for understanding outcomes, even as they work in conjunction with broader forces and institutions.

Appendices

Appendices

Appendix 4.1 Predicting the Democratic Vote Share, All U.S. Counties

	Model 1: Simple Bivariate, 1948–2004	Model 2: With Controls, 1948–2004	Model 3: With Controls, 2000–2004
Constant	0.520*** (.003)	0.508*** (.007)	0.539*** (.019)
Turnout	−0.156*** (.005)	−0.065*** (.006)	−0.283*** (.021)
Southern	—	−0.144*** (.007)	−0.110*** (.018)
Rural	—	0.006*** (.001)	−0.016*** (.004)
% Black	—	0.260*** (.006)	0.420*** (.014)
% Foreign Born	—	0.214*** (.033)	0.717*** (.102)
Competitive	—	0.011*** (.002)	—
Statewide dummy variables	—	Yes	Yes
Election dummy variables	—	Yes	Yes
N	47,138	47,138	3,147
SE	0.142	0.118	0.083
Adjusted R-square	0.025	0.338	0.520

Notes: These estimates are unstandardized regression coefficients and include all cases (counties). In models 2 and 3, we include cross-sectional dummy variables for the states (Oregon is the baseline) and time-series variables for the election years (2004 is the baseline). In these models we also estimate the effects of six-month change in unemployment, September unemployment, two-quarter lag in local consumer price index, and the local crime rate. None were statistically significant. Standard errors are in parentheses.

***p significant at 0.001, **0.01, *0.05.

Appendix 4.2 Predicting the Democratic Vote Share, Rural and Urban Counties

	Rural Counties, 1948–2004	Urban Counties, 1948–2004
Constant	0.529***	0.483***
	(.008)	(.035)
Turnout	−0.034***	0.066
	(.007)	(.043)
Southern	−0.129***	—
	(.008)	—
% Black	0.207***	0.285***
	(.007)	(.058)
% Foreign Born	−0.585***	−0.062
	(.068)	(.270)
Statewide dummy variables	Yes	Yes
Election dummy variables	Yes	Yes
N	31,077	528
SE	0.120	0.075
Adjusted R-square	0.353	0.543

Notes: These unstandardized regression coefficient estimates include all cases (counties). Standard errors in parentheses.

***p significant at 0.001, **0.01, *0.05.

Appendix 4.3 Predicting the Partisan Vote Choice, All U.S. Counties

	Incumbent Administration			
	Republican		Democrat	
	1948–2004	1972–2004	1948–2004	1972–2004
Constant	0.525***	1.285***	0.542***	0.517***
	(.009)	(.066)	(.010)	(.014)
Turnout	−0.071***	0.037***	−0.052***	−0.192***
	(.007)	(.009)	(.009)	(.013)
Southern	−0.131***	−0.120***	−0.161***	−0.066***
	(.008)	(.009)	(.010)	(.011)
Urban	0.097***	0.069***	0.093***	0.101***
	(.008)	(.008)	(.009)	(.010)
Rural	0.010***	0.019***	0.001	0.002
	(.002)	(.002)	(.002)	(.002)
% Black	0.285***	0.324***	0.214***	0.377***
	(.007)	(.008)	(.009)	(.009)
% Foreign Born	−0.106*	0.411***	0.089	−0.078
	(.046)	(.051)	(.054)	(.062)
Real GDP (in millions of dollars)	−2.999***	−0.345***	−3.799***	−0.011***
	(.000)	(.000)	(.000)	(.000)
Statewide dummy variables	Yes	Yes	Yes	Yes
Election Year dummy variables	Yes	Yes	Yes	Yes
N	21,999	15,724	21,987	9,436
SE	0.102	0.090	0.128	0.088
Adjusted R-square	0.415	0.488	0.314	0.466

Notes: These estimates are unstandardized regression coefficients. Standard errors in parentheses.

***p significant at 0.001, **0.01, *0.05.

Appendix 5.1 Predicting the Party Vote in U.S. House Districts, 2002–2010

	2002 Simple	2002 Full	2004 Simple	2004 Full	2006 Simple	2006 Full	2008 Simple	2008 Full	2010 Simple	2010 Full
Constant	0.750***	0.481*	0.816***	0.456*	0.691***	0.482*	0.902***	0.762**	0.748***	0.718***
	(.043)	(.220)	(.047)	(.205)	(.036)	(.193)	(.053)	(.234)	(.033)	(.142)
Turnout	−0.721***	−0.277	−0.579***	−0.382	−0.417	−0.455	−0.586***	−0.625*	−0.662***	−0.797***
	(.121)	(0.366)	(.088)	(.260)	(.092)	(.296)	(.093)	(.251)	(.083)	(.199)
% Black	—	0.778***	—	0.669***	—	0.613***	—	0.785***	—	0.507***
		(.165)		(.162)		(.154)		(.168)		(.109)
% Hispanic	—	0.300	—	0.103	—	0.087	—	0.171	—	−0.050
		(.188)		(.193)		(.182)		(.205)		(.129)
% Under age 30	—	−0.344	—	0.401	—	0.306	—	0.012	—	0.263
		(.649)		(.642)		(.610)		(.746)		(.436)
Income, in $10,000	—	−0.002	—	−0.002	—	−0.002	—	0.000	—	0.000
		(.004)		(.004)		(.003)		(.005)		(.003)
Statewide dummy (OR is the baseline)	No	Yes	No	Yes	No	Yes	No	Yes	No	Yes
N	355	100	369	91	375	90	429	107	405	99
SE	0.184	0.179	0.175	0.168	0.170	0.154	0.221	0.206	0.158	0.120
Adjusted R-square	0.089	0.277	0.103	0.235	0.049	0.275	0.082	0.323	0.133	0.481

Notes: These estimates are unstandardized regression coefficients. Standard errors in parentheses.

***p significant at 0.001, **0.01, *0.05.

Appendix 5.2 Predicting Party Vote in U.S. House Districts, 2012–2016

	2012		2014		2016	
	Simple	Full	Simple	Full	Simple	Full
Constant	0.518***	−0.355**	0.522***	−0.334**	0.682***	−0.447***
	(.063)	(.106)	(.039)	(.119)	(.068)	(.106)
Turnout	−0.003	0.276	−0.134	0.106	−0.315**	0.109
	(.112)	(.142)	(.013)	(.174)	(.114)	(.157)
% Black	—	0.713***	—	0.746***	—	0.828***
		(.053)		(.064)		(.058)
% Hispanic	—	0.366***	—	0.310***	—	0.407***
		(.056)		(.068)		(.058)
% Under age 30	—	1.765***	—	1.746***	—	1.743***
		(.222)		(.256)		(.234)
Income, in $10,000	—	0.002	—	0.005*	—	0.020**
		(.002)		(.003)		(.007)
Statewide dummy variables (OR is the baseline)	No	Yes	No	Yes	No	Yes
N	387	365	356	336	368	341
SE	0.172	0.101	0.166	0.109	0.174	0.101
Adjusted R-square	−0.003	0.665	0.002	0.576	0.018	0.676

Notes: These estimates are unstandardized regression coefficients. Standard errors in parentheses.

***p significant at 0.001, **0.01, *0.05.

Appendix 5.3 Surge and Decline: Interelection Turnout Change and the Democratic Vote

	Surge		
Change in Democratic share of the two-party vote	2002 to 2004	2006 to 2008	2014 to 2016
Constant	0.169***	−0.010	−0.025*
	(.039)	(.024)	(0.011)
Change in turnout	−0.820***	0.075	0.181***
	(.209)	(.119)	(0.045)
N	366	412	318
SE	0.271	0.167	0.051
Adjusted R-square	0.038	−0.001	0.045

	"Decline"		
Change in Democratic share of the two-party vote	2004 to 2006	2008 to 2010	2012 to 2014
Constant	−0.100*	−0.092***	0.014
	(0.040)	(.026)	(0.008)
Change in turnout	−0.867***	−0.079	0.116**
	(.248)	(.144)	(0.042)
N	385	402	327
SE	0.264	0.174	0.043
Adjusted R-square	0.028	−0.002	0.020

Notes: These estimates are unstandardized regression coefficients. Standard errors in parentheses.

***p significant at 0.001, **0.01, *0.05.

Appendix 6.1 Predicting the Party Vote in U.S. House Districts, 2002–2010

	2002		2004		2006		2008		2010	
	Simple	Full	Simple	Full	Simple	Full	Simple	Full	Simple	Full
Constant	0.750*** (.043)	0.481* (.220)	0.816*** (.047)	0.456* (.205)	0.691*** (.036)	0.482* (.193)	0.902*** (.053)	0.762** (.234)	0.748*** (.033)	0.718*** (.142)
Turnout	−0.721*** (.121)	−0.277 (.366)	−0.579*** (.088)	−0.382 (.260)	−0.417 (.092)	−0.455 (.296)	−0.586*** (.093)	−0.625* (.251)	−0.662*** (.083)	−0.797*** (.199)
% Black	—	0.778*** (.165)	—	0.669*** (.162)	—	0.613*** (.154)	—	0.785*** (.168)	—	0.507*** (.109)
% Hispanic	—	0.300 (.188)	—	0.103 (.193)	—	0.087 (.182)	—	0.171 (.205)	—	−0.050 (.129)
% Under age 30	—	−0.344 (.649)	—	0.401 (.642)	—	0.306 (.610)	—	0.012 (.746)	—	0.263 (.436)
Income, in $10,000	—	−0.002 (.004)	—	−0.002 (.004)	—	−0.002 (.003)	—	0.000 (.005)	—	0.000 (.003)
Statewide dummy (OR is the baseline)	No	Yes	No	Yes	No	Yes	No	Yes	No	Yes
N	355	100	369	91	375	90	429	107	405	99
SE	0.184	0.179	0.175	0.168	0.170	0.154	0.221	0.206	0.158	0.120
Adjusted R-square	0.089	0.277	0.103	0.235	0.049	0.275	0.082	0.323	0.133	0.481

Notes: These estimates are unstandardized regression coefficients. Standard errors in parentheses.

*** p significant at 0.001, **0.01, *0.05.

Appendix 6.2 Predicting Party Vote in U.S. House Districts, 2012–2016

	2012		2014		2016	
	Simple	Full	Simple	Full	Simple	Full
Constant	0.518***	−0.355**	0.522***	−0.334**	0.682***	−0.447***
	(.063)	(.106)	(.039)	(.119)	(.068)	(.106)
Turnout	−0.003	0.276	−0.134	0.106	−0.315**	0.109
	(.112)	(.142)	(.013)	(.174)	(.114)	(.157)
% Black	—	0.713***	—	0.746***	—	0.828***
		(.053)		(.064)		(.058)
% Hispanic	—	0.366***	—	0.310***	—	0.407***
		(.056)		(.068)		(.058)
% Under age 30	—	1.765***	—	1.746***	—	1.743***
		(.222)		(.256)		(.234)
Income, in $10,000	—	0.002	—	0.005*	—	0.020**
		(.002)		(.003)		(.007)
Statewide dummy variables (OR is the baseline)	No	Yes	No	Yes	No	Yes
N	387	365	356	336	368	341
SE	0.172	0.101	0.166	0.109	0.174	0.101
Adjusted R-square	−0.003	0.665	0.002	0.576	0.018	0.676

Notes: These estimates are unstandardized regression coefficients. Standard errors in parentheses.

***p significant at 0.001, **0.01, *0.05.

Appendix 6.3 Surge and Decline: Interelection Turnout Change and the Democratic Vote

Change in Democratic share of the two-party vote	Surge		
	2002 to 2004	2006 to 2008	2014 to 2016
Constant	0.169***	−0.010	−0.025*
	(.039)	(.024)	(0.011)
Change in turnout	−0.820***	0.075	0.181***
	(.209)	(.119)	(0.045)
N	366	412	318
SE	0.271	0.167	0.051
Adjusted R-square	0.038	−0.001	0.045
Change in Democratic share of the two-party vote	"Decline"		
	2004 to 2006	2008 to 2010	2012 to 2014
Constant	−0.100*	−0.092***	0.014
	(0.040)	(.026)	(0.008)
Change in turnout	−0.867***	−0.079	0.116**
	(.248)	(.144)	(0.042)
N	385	402	327
SE	0.264	0 .174	0.043
Adjusted R-square	0.028	−0.002	0.020

Notes: These estimates are unstandardized regression coefficients. Standard errors in parentheses.

***p significant at 0.001, **0.01, *0.05.

Appendix 7.1 The 2016 Turnout Equation: Predicting Turnout in 2016

	Unstandardized regression coefficient	Standard error	Wald Statistic	Statistical significance	Log odds ratio: Exp(B)
Religious observance	.291	.064	20.381	.000	1.338
Education	.603	.061	97.002	.000	1.827
Age	.237	.068	12.081	.001	1.268
Married	.407	.102	15.846	.000	1.502
Time resident in community	.537	.101	28.376	.000	1.712
Campaign interest	.502	.070	51.811	.000	1.652
Strength of partisanship	.681	.072	89.621	.000	1.976
Strength of candidate preference	.096	.046	4.335	.037	1.100
Care about election outcome	.790	.104	57.349	.000	2.202
Contacted by campaign	.368	.101	13.375	.000	1.445
Constant	−7.028	.351	400.082	.000	.001

Model Summary: -2 Log Likelihood 2986.9. Nagelkerke R Square = .333.

Data are from the 2016 ANES survey. The dependent variable is self-reported turnout. These results can be compared to those in Table 7.4.

Notes

1. According to the American National Election Studies (ANES), those who were at least somewhat interested exceeded 86 percent in 2016, with over 50 percent describing themselves as very interested.
2. The ANES figures for 1998 and 2002 (the most recent midterm elections for which we have data) are 69 percent and 73 percent, respectively.
3. According to the 2016 ANES survey, 75 percent said they cared "a great deal" or "a lot" about the presidential election outcome. Concern about the outcome of the off-year elections is lower simply because they receive less attention in the news, but they too elicit expressions of interest and concern. According to the 1990 American Citizen Participation Survey, 78 percent said that their "duty as a citizen" was a "very important" reason prompting them to cast a ballot
4. Certainly numerous public officials brought this belief to the 2016 contest. In a May 2017 interview with *New York* magazine, Hillary Clinton blamed her loss in the 2016 presidential election on low turnout due to "voter suppression" (Traister 2017). Meanwhile Clinton's supporters homed in on low turnout rates in Milwaukee County, Wisconsin, and Wayne County, Michigan as a critical reason why she lost the Electoral College: both are key counties in battleground states; both have significant black populations that vote heavily Democratic; both experienced a significant drop in turnout from 2012 to 2016. There was no consideration or mention in the article of the possibility that the absence of a black candidate in 2016 – a significant short-term force – depressed interest and turnout among potential black voters.
5. If it is not yet clear, we refer to asymmetric turnout rates between partisan identifiers as turnout bias.

CHAPTER 2

1. All of these changes, and others not mentioned, reduced electoral mobilization and generally eroded turnout levels from their nineteenth-century highs. However, the ability of party organizations to assure their vote was tallied on Election Day was not completely undone by Progressive reforms, as has been detailed by many books on nineteenth- and early twentieth-century party organizations and their activities. These methods survived well into the twentieth century, as *Fortune* magazine documented in an August 1936 article titled "The Kelly-Nash Political Machine." That article has a box insert at the end (126) with the caption "Thirteen Ways of Getting the Right Answer from the Ballot Box." The insert detailed methods by which the vaunted Chicago machine would get the votes needed to ensure a winning margin, no matter what the voters did.

2. The institutionalized population includes those who are legally committed for disorders and those who are in prison or otherwise disqualified from voting because of their criminal record. The prison and parole population constitutes most of the institutionalized population that adjusts the denominator. This is a large number, and efforts are being made in many states, especially Florida as this is being written, to return voting rights to those disfranchised because of a criminal record, particularly when their sentence has been completed. Estimates of the VEP are from the United States Election Project (http://www.electproject.org/national-1789-present, last accessed on August 19, 2019). Estimates of the VAP are from the American Presidency Project at UCSB (https://www.presidency.ucsb.edu/statistics/data/voter-turnout-in-presidential-elections, last accessed on August 19, 2019).

3. Figure 2.2 might have provided a third turnout estimate: turnout as a fraction of registered voters. This percentage yields the highest estimate of turnout—often at or above 80 percent—but because it fails to count citizens who might have voted if they had registered it is an artificially high number. The election law in many states requires registration prior to Election Day, which makes voting a two-step process of registration and then voting. Calculating turnout as a fraction of the registered ignores that fact and without substantive justification deflates the size of the potential electorate, creating a too small denominator.

4. All turnout estimates are based on either the VEP or the VAP. The VEP is used except for long historical periods, such as Figure 2.1. As explained earlier, we do not calculate turnout as a fraction of registered voters.

5. However, as Figure 2.6 indicates, black turnout seems to have been stimulated by Barack Obama's candidacy in 2008 and (especially) 2012, a year in which blacks reported (in the 2012 ANES survey) voting at a higher rate than whites.

6. This description is based upon an analysis of a merge of ANES for the years from 2000 through 2016, with the samples weighted to an equal size to eliminate sample size differences among the studies.

7. There is useful research to be done on the topic of denomination, religiosity, and political activity. For now, we are content to leave with the observation that voting (as well as candidate and party preference) is tied to the religious associations of Americans, no matter what the conventional intuition might be on the matter in our increasingly secular culture.

8. Recent work by Inbody (2015) demonstrates that there is variance in the turnout rates for active military compared to those of veteran status, making any single generalization about "military turnout" problematic. He also observes that the votes of military deployed overseas are subject to an array of institutional hurdles that make calculating an accurate turnout rate difficult.

9. Figures 2.6 through 2.8 plot data from Current Population Survey (CPS) estimates of voter turnout. The substantive conclusions one would proffer based on these and more common survey data would not differ. However, the CPS data are corrected for nonresponse and other biases that are endemic in survey data.

10. Educational attainment is correlated with many aspects of political belief and behavior in mass publics throughout the world, so the U.S. is not unique in that regard. However, as we note in the next section, few countries seem to exhibit such a strong relationship between education and voting participation. It is not a completely American phenomenon, but the strength of the relationship sets the U.S. apart from most electoral democracies.

11. Traditional in-person voting precincts are not available in these mail-balloting states.

12. Although turnout in the U.S. is low, it is (historically) far from the lowest in comparison with other developed democracies. Switzerland has always enjoyed that distinction.

13. The heterogeneous coalitional structure of the Democrats and Republicans in 2018 is measurably less so than it was in decades past, and there is good evidence that it has diminished further in more recent years. This, at least potentially, has consequences for many aspect of our politics; policy polarization and turnout are certainly two things to consider.

CHAPTER 3

1. For a detailed and important elaboration of this basic setup, see Riker and Ordeshook (1968).

2. Some have questioned the durability of these attachments, arguing that voters update their party identification based on a "running tally" of political assessments (Fiorina 1981).

3. It is important to distinguish between rational choice (or strategic) voting, which refers to the mindset and calculus of the voter, and economic voting, which refers to the explicit criteria for evaluation used by the voter.

4. For example, analyses of vote choice in the 2004 presidential election show that higher levels of fearfulness and anxiety in the wake of the 9/11 attacks correlate with higher support for the incumbent president, George W. Bush (Albertson and Gadarian 2015).

5. As of 2017, twenty-two countries have compulsory voting, among them Argentina, Australia, Belgium, Brazil, Congo, Egypt, Greece, Mexico, Peru, and Uruguay.

6. Of course, there is a vivid public debate today about the need to issue voter identification cards with pictures, a change that critics insist would depress turnout and proponents argue is necessary to limit illegal voting.

7. We measure internal efficacy by asking people whether they agree or disagree with the following statement: "Politics are too complicated for people like me." People who disagree strongly are rated high on internal efficacy. We measure external efficacy by asking people whether they agree or disagree with the following statement: "Public officials don't care what people like me think." People who disagree strongly are rated high on external efficacy.

8. The strong link between the intensity of one's partisanship and the likelihood of voting makes intuitive sense. Turnout depends on the costs of voting (which are unconnected with party preference) compared with the benefits of voting (which relate to the strength of your party preference but not its direction). As a practical matter, is it possible that the direction of party preference—Republican or Democratic—is systematically correlated with either the costs or benefits of voting (and thus with turnout)? Many scholars have strong opinions about this, and we take up this question shortly.

9. Calling it the "Piven-Cloward thesis" is a convenience that is not meant to diminish the contributions of so many others to this proposition. As of 2017, the twenty-two countries with mandatory voting laws include (1) several chaotic and unstable democratic regimes, which are mostly run by small cliques (Congo and Egypt come to mind); (2) a few countries that have functionally abandoned such laws; and (3) a few countries that retain them without any enforcement.

10. This argument, that turnout effects have diminished due to changes in the nature of party attachments, especially in the South, is common.

11. While DeNardo's (1980) work is the recent benchmark for this issue, Campbell (1960) first showed that support oscillated as one moved from consistent to peripheral voters. Subsequently Burnham (1970) used the idea of the peripheral electorate in his examinations of historical realignments. Andersen (1979) and Petrocik (1981) adopted his insight in their examinations of realignments in American history, especially (for Andersen) in studying the emergence of the New Deal. And earlier still Roberto Michels (1962), studying election-to-election changes, proposed that peripheral voters were at least as likely to support the minority as the majority party regardless of their respective left/right orientation.

12. The purported weather effect noted by Hansford and Gomez (2010), among others, is controversial. For example, Knack (1994) examines the relationship between

individual-level turnout data from the ANES and weather and demonstrates that weather has no effect on turnout after controlling for civic duty. Moreover he finds no differential partisan impact from inclement weather because Democrats are *not* disproportionately reliant on peripheral voters.

13. We are not claiming that bandwagon effects do not exist. Bandwagons, however, refer to vote choice rather than turnout. We explicitly discuss this phenomenon, and endogeneity more generally, in chapter 8.

14. It is also the case that survey evidence consistently shows that competitiveness has the greatest effect on voters with the *weakest* preference intensity (Campbell et al. 1960; Lewis-Beck et al. 2008: chapter 5). In other words, peripheral voters are more likely to vote when the race is close.

CHAPTER 4

1. By comparison, approximately two-thirds of the candidates of the challenging party won when the incumbent did not seek reelection.

2. These totals can be reviewed in Table 1.1 of chapter 1.

3. There is no substantive effect of looking at the turnout-vote relationship without separating on- and off-years, as a reader of these plots will notice. The relation is completely flat.

4. The Democratic percentages in Figures 4.1 and 4.2 are not directly comparable to those in Figure 4.5. Figures 4.1 and 4.2 report the recorded vote for the Democratic candidate(s) as a percentage of the total vote. This simple percentage is not useful for Senate races because of the differing size of the state electorates and the effect this would have on the yearly Democratic vote totals. The shifting combination of states of different-size electorates among the elections also precludes using the simple percentage calculation. To maximize comparability, Figure 4.5 therefore reports the Democratic vote in the states holding Senate elections and the turnout rate in these states in that election year.

5. To construct this data set, we rely on data from the relevant editions of *The Almanac of American Politics*, which contains district-level data on the voting-age population, turnout, and general election results, along with information on the district's race and ethnicity, age, and median income (see Barone and Cohen 2003, 2005, 2007, 2009, 2011; Barone and McCutcheon 2013; Cohen and Barnes, 2015; Cohen 2017).

6. Complete results for the models are presented in Appendix Tables 4.1–4.3.

7. The coefficient is halved from –0.16 to –0.07, eroding the finding that increased turnout helps the Republican vote to a finding that reports that turnout does not help either.

8. Estimates of real GDP come from the federal government's Bureau of Economic Analysis, 1948–2004 (https://www.bea.gov/data/gdp/gross-domestic-product, last accessed August 19, 2019).

CHAPTER 5

1. This comment does not apply to the presidential elections presented in Figures 4.1 and 4.2 or the congressional elections presented in Figure 4.3 because they examine changes in turnout and the vote share from election to election within a constant political unit.

2. For the congressional analysis, the assessment was done within redistricting regimes to hold constant as many unknown factors as possible. That is, the analysis of the turnout–vote share connection for House elections is replicated four times: for the periods from 1972 through 1980, 1982 through 1990, 1992 through 2000, and 2002 through 2010. The districts are unchanged, except in a few cases, within these decades, reducing confounding influences.

3. This discrepancy is a reminder to always look at the data and not just the coefficient. Regressions always estimate a slope, however poorly that slope describes the data upon which the calculation is based. If one election had not produced such a low Democratic vote, the calculated slope would have been zero.

4. Gubernatorial elections are further complicated by the fact that some states hold these in off-years (Louisiana, Kentucky, Mississippi, Virginia, and New Jersey), some in midterm years (the clear majority), and some in presidential years.

5. We chose these states because they were the states of residence of the authors at the time this project began.

6. An election was regarded as uncontested if there was only one candidate or the winner received 75 percent or more of the vote. The missing seat had too few contested elections to make the calculation of the slope reasonable.

7. Angus Campbell (1960) first offered a theory of "surge and decline" to explain vote loss for the president's party in midterm elections. It was posited as an alternative to the coattail theory, offered originally by Bean (1948).

8. Ninety-six districts are lost because the analysis was limited to districts that had competitive contests for all five of the elections during the period.

CHAPTER 6

1. Results for the full models are presented in Appendix Table 6.1.

2. Results for th e full models are presented in Appendix Table 6.2.

3. Results for the full models are presented in Appendix Table 6.3.

CHAPTER 7

1. As we noted earlier, we do not claim that turnout never matters. For example, the votes in the 2017 Alabama special election between Republican Roy Moore and Democrat Doug Jones were being cast as we drafted this chapter. The news media's political commentariat observed that high black turnout would be essential for a Democratic victory. We agreed. African Americans constitute about 25 percent

of the eligible electorate in Alabama. About 95 percent can be expected to vote Democratic, which required that Jones pull about 38 percent of the white vote to win. Thirty-eight percent is not a lot, but the conservative whites of Alabama offer very little support for Democrats, and 38 percent is near the limit. In the event, the black turnout rate seems to have exceeded white turnout—blacks constituted 29 percent of the electorate—and they gave 96 percent of their votes (according to the published exit polls) to Jones. This high support and turnout required fewer white votes for Jones to win; the 30 percent white support for Jones was enough for the victory. We do not have access to a survey that permits a detailed analysis of the Alabama vote. However, we are confident that the major determinant of Jones's victory was not turnout but the accusations directed at Moore that probably discouraged potential supporters from voting or voting for him. The issue environment of the election, not turnout itself, elected Jones in a special election in which only about 40 percent of registered voters (35 percent of age-eligible voters) participated.

2. Democrats and Republicans in this analysis include strong, weak, and leaning identifiers. Only those who insist they have no preference are categorized as independent. The similarity of the voting choices of weak and leaning identifiers justifies this treatment.

3. Self-reported turnout has consistently exceeded the official numbers throughout the specified period. Some of the gap reflects respondents who misremember their behavior; some of it reflects an unwillingness to confess not engaging in a civic behavior that is normatively expected (more on that later); and some of it reflects the effect of the interview. All presidential election studies in the ANES series are panels for which respondents are interviewed before and after the election. The pre-election interview stimulates voting for some fraction of the respondents. Essentially the ANES interviews are a get-out-the-vote contact that increases the turnout rate for the sample over the general population (e.g., Clausen 1968).

4. Campbell (1960) developed the notions of the core and the periphery of the electorate as a simple model to explain the twin observations that in midterm elections turnout declines and the president's party loses votes and seats. Numerous studies of turnout—conducted by scholars and practitioners—have relied on these concepts ever since.

5. These figures are from ANES data from the early 1950s through 1980. The question about whether Americans have a right not to vote is from the 2014 General Social Survey (GSS). Attitudes toward other civic obligations also correlate with turning out at the polls. For example, about 60 percent of the 2004 ANES sample, when asked how they would feel about being selected for jury duty, indicated that they would be quite happy to serve, while the remainder reported they would prefer not to. The answer correlated with voting in that presidential year. About 61 percent of the reluctant selectees reported voting, but 80 percent of those who said they would be happy to serve turned out at the polls. Data such as these help us to explain the strength of so many demographic correlates of turnout. The similarity of

the effect over the years suggests that there has not been a significant change in the underlying orientation about voting obligations in recent decades.

6. Republicans who support these norms are a couple of percentage points more likely than similarly disposed Democrats to report voting in the extant election. The differences are trivially small. But their persistence may indicate that Republicans are a bit more likely than Democrats to act on the norms.

7. The 2012 ANES attempted to validate self-reported turnout using three different voter list vendors. Unfortunately discrepancies plagued the effort, and 1988 remains the last election for which we have a reliable validated vote measure.

8. The difference between the sum of these values and 100 percent is the share of the electorate who describe themselves as independents who lean toward neither party.

9. Campbell (1960) suggested this presidential to midterm difference might exist, but mostly rejected it (a fact often overlooked in later applications of the "surge and decline" theory). It was more clearly refuted by Kernell (1977) and later work on congressional elections (Campbell 1987).

10. Turnout probability is modeled on the logistic regression results in Table 7.4.

11. As always, leaning, weak, and strong identifiers are treated as partisans of the party with which they identify. Only those who insist that they have no partisan leanings are classified as independents.

12. Independents, with their lower likelihood of voting, become increasingly numerous as turnout increases.

13. The notion of short-term forces was first articulated in *The American Voter.* More recent research has drawn on, clarified, and confirmed the central notion that short-term forces—in the form of candidate evaluations, party images, issue appraisals, and retrospective evaluations—can affect vote choice (Campbell 1997).

14. This measure is based on self-reported interest in politics and public affairs ("How interested are you in politics and public affairs?") and self-reported emotional investment in the election outcome ("How much do you care about who wins the election?"). The resultant scale is divided into deciles, arrayed from low to high interest/engagement. Data are from ANES surveys.

15. Turnout increased between the two elections, although not as much as our memories seem to celebrate the fact that the 1960 election was a twentieth-century turnout high point. Slightly more than 60 percent of the eligible electorate turned out in 1956, and 63.8 percent of eligible voted in 1960—a 3.6-percentage-point increase.

CHAPTER 8

1. There is some evidence that blame is weightier than credit. That is, good times do not seem to be as helpful as hard times are hurtful (Kramer 1971; Fair 1978).

2. There are models that include more than economic variables, but the economic dimension has received the bulk of the attention among academics and the commentariat.

3. Note that although the coattail effect is visible well down the ballot, our examination of it is limited to its expression in House elections. The House completely populates both the presidential and the off-year midterms, which is not true for gubernatorial elections, most of which occur in the off-years, and Senate elections, which have a cycle that does not correspond to the presidential cycle.

4. The reader will recall that we considered some elements of surge and decline in chapter 6.

5. We examine this relationship later in this chapter, after a further elaboration of the surge and decline dynamic that pairs elections.

6. This failure to decline in 1962 was the event that produced Campbell's (1966) initial ruminations about the on-/off-year cycle of surge and decline.

7. At one point in late 1974 national polls were reporting a near-collapse of the Republican Party when only 18 percent in a national sample expressed an identification with the party.

8. It has the same finding, of course, although 1960 does not appear as anomalous.

9. The 1994 declines were probably exaggerated by redistricting that destabilized many Democratic incumbents, particularly in the South, as a result of court-mandated majority-minority districts that removed Democratic-supporting minority voters from districts of Democratic incumbents and generally moved voters such that many Democratic incumbents lost large numbers of constituents with whom they enjoyed the bond of a familiar incumbency. See Desposato and Petrocik (2003).

10. Losses in the House and Senate were only part of the decline in these years. There were losses at all levels across the country for the Republicans in 1974 and 2006, and the Democrats in 1994.

11. There is a 99 percent probability they are influencing congressional seat shifts.

12. This loss was unusually large and probably reflects the big Democratic surge in 2006 as well as 2008. In 2010 an unusually large number of Democrats were incumbents in districts in which they were not a good fit.

13. These data include several independent candidates, such as Angus King (ME) and Bernie Sanders (VT). King and Sanders are treated as Democrats for purposes of analysis. Elections not contested by one of the major parties (e.g., the U.S. Senate race for California in 2016 featured two Democratic candidates, Kamala Harris and Loretta Sanchez) are excluded from the analysis.

14. Despite the fact that presidential approval data reference chief executives from different political parties (Bush in 2008 and Obama in 2014), positive shifts in the presidential approval numbers should still correlate with relatively better Democratic performances. For instance, a shift in approval of 20 percentage points (from 20 percent approval of Bush to 40 percent for Obama) should correlate with a relatively smaller decline in Democratic vote share.

CHAPTER 9

1. While Michigan, Pennsylvania, and Minnesota have a clear Democratic tilt, they—unlike the states in the lower cell—are potentially competitive venues for the Republican Party. Trump's wins in Michigan and Pennsylvania and his close loss in Minnesota in 2016 may be additional evidence for that reading.

2. Oregon's PDI value indicates more competitiveness in the state than it probably should because it does not display the sharp Democratic shift we've observed in the past few years. The twenty-year average suppresses the change. Arguably, Oregon, by fiat if not the data, belongs in the cell below.

3. There is only a 13 percent change in significance to the presidential results, while the other two are at a probability level at or above 94 percent.

4. Just to cite a recent example, in New York's 2018 Democratic primary elections, Alexandria Ocasio-Cortez shocked the ten-term incumbent congressman, Joe Crowley, on the strength of surprisingly high turnout. This is consistent with methodological arguments offered by Przeworski and Sprague (1971, 1988), who conclude that socialist parties do worse when turnout drops considerably. The literature on the emergence of the second and fifth party systems in the U.S. also demonstrates the power of turnout surges to create long-term partisan change (see Burnham 1970).

5. That is, a person needs to like one candidate sufficiently more than the other(s) to motivate a trip to the polls or a search for the mail-in ballot and the time to make a choice and carry the marked ballot to the postbox for the mail carrier.

References

Abramowitz, Alan I. (2012). *The Polarized Public: Why American Government Is So Dysfunctional*. New York: Pearson.

Abramowitz, Alan I. (2016). What Will Time for a Change Mean for Trump? *PS: Political Science and Politics*, 49(4), 659–660.

Albertson, Bethany, and Shana Kushner Gadarian. (2015). *Anxious Politics: Democratic Citizenship in a Threatening World*. New York: Cambridge University Press.

Aldrich, John. (1993). *Why Parties?* Chicago: University of Chicago Press.

Althaus, Scott L. (1998). Information Effects in Collective Preferences. *American Political Science Review*, 92(3), 545–558.

American Political Science Association. (1950). Toward a More Responsible Two-Party System: A Report of the Committee on Political Parties. *American Political Science Review*, 44(3). Supplement.

Andersen, Kristi. (1979). *The Creation of the Democratic Majority, 1928–1936*. Chicago: University of Chicago Press.

Ansolabehere, Stephen. (2009). Effects of Identification Requirements on Voting: Evidence from the Experiences of Voters on Election Day. *PS: Political Science and Politics*, 42(1), 127–130.

Barone, Michael, and Richard E. Cohen. (2003). *The Almanac of American Politics, 2004*. Washington, D.C.: National Journal Group.

Barone, Michael, and Richard E. Cohen. (2005). *The Almanac of American Politics, 2006*. Washington, D.C.: National Journal Group.

Barone, Michael, and Richard E. Cohen. (2007). *The Almanac of American Politics, 2008*. Washington, D.C.: National Journal Group.

Barone, Michael, and Richard E. Cohen. (2009). *The Almanac of American Politics, 2010*. Washington, D.C.: National Journal Group.

Barone, Michael, and Richard E. Cohen. (2011). *The Almanac of American Politics, 2012*. Washington, D.C.: National Journal Group.

Barone, Michael, and Chuck McCutcheon. (2013). *The Almanac of American Politics, 2014*. Chicago: University of Chicago Press.

Bartels, Larry. (2002). Uninformed Voters: Information Effects in Presidential Elections. *American Journal of Political Science*, 40(1), 194–230.

Bean, Louis H. (1948). *How to Predict Elections*. New York: Knopf.

Berelson, Bernard, Paul Lazarsfeld, and William McPhee. (1954). *Voting: A Study of Opinion Formation in a Presidential Campaign*. Chicago: University of Chicago Press.

Blais, André. (2000). *To Vote or Not to Vote*. Pittsburgh: University of Pittsburgh Press.

Blake, Aaron. (2014). Obama Blames Lack of African American, Latino Turnout for Democrats' Midterm Woes. *Washington Post*, April 10. Retrieved from https://www.washingtonpost.com/news/post-politics/wp/2014/04/10/obama-democrats-lose-in-midterms-because-african-americans-latinos-young-people-dont-turn-out-to-vote/?utm_term=.c62c1de40f3c.

Brader, Ted. (2006). *Campaigning for Hearts and Minds: How Emotional Appeals in Political Ads Work*. Chicago: University of Chicago Press.

Burnham, Walter Dean. (1970). *Critical Elections and the Mainsprings of Electoral Politics*. New York: Norton.

Calvert, J., and J. Gilchrist. (1991). The Social and Issue Dimensions of Voting and Nonvoting in the United States. Paper presented at the 1991 annual meeting of the American Political Science Association, Washington, D.C.

Campbell, Angus. (1960). Surge and Decline: A Study of Electoral Change. *Public Opinion Quarterly*, 24(3), 397–418.

Campbell, Angus. (1966). Surge and Decline: A Study of Electoral Change. In A. Campbell, P. Converse, W. Miller, and D. Stokes (eds.), *Elections and the Political Order*. New York: Wiley & Sons.

Campbell, Angus, Philip Converse, Warren Miller, and Donald Stokes. (1960). *The American Voter*. New York: Wiley & Sons.

Campbell, James E. (1987). The Revised Theory of Surge and Decline. *American Journal of Political Science*, 31(4), 965–979.

Campbell, James E. (1991). The Presidential Surge and Its Midterm Decline in Congressional Elections, 1868–1988. *Journal of Politics*, 53(2), 477–487.

Campbell, James E. (1997). *The Presidential Pulse of Congressional Elections*. Lexington: University of Kentucky Press.

Campbell, James E. (2016). The Trial-Heat and Seats-in-Trouble Forecasts of the 2016 Presidential and Congressional Elections. *PS: Political Science and Politics*, 49(4), 664–668.

Citrin, Jack, Eric Schickler, and John Sides. (2003). What If Everyone Voted? Simulating the Impact of Increased Turnout in Senate Elections. *American Journal of Political Science*, 47(1), 75–90.

Clausen, Aage R. (1968). Response Validity in Surveys. *Public Opinion Quarterly*, 32(3), 588–606.

Cohen, Richard E. (2017). *The Almanac of American Politics*. New York: Columbia Books.

Cohen, Richard E., and James A. Barnes. (2015). *The Almanac of American Politics, 2016*. New York: Columbia Books.

Cohn, Nate. (2014). Turnout, a Scapegoat, Wasn't Always the Difference This Time. *New York Times*, November 6. Retrieved from https://www.nytimes.com/2014/11/06/us/turnout-a-scapegoat-wasnt-always-the-difference-this-time.html.

Cohn, Nate. (2017). A 2016 Review: Turnout Wasn't the Driver of Clinton's Defeat. *New York Times*, March 28. Retrieved from https://www.nytimes.com/2017/03/28/upshot/a-2016-review-turnout-wasnt-the-driver-of-clintons-defeat.html.

Dahlgaard, Jens Olav, Jonas H. Hansen, Kasper M. Hansen, and Martin V. Larsen. (2017). How Election Polls Shape Voting Behaviour. *Scandinavian Political Studies*, 40(3), 330–343.

Delli Carpini, Michael X., and Scott Keeter. (1996). *What Americans Know about Politics and Why It Matters*. New Haven, CT: Yale University Press.

DeNardo, James. (1980). Turnout and the Vote: The Joke's on the Democrats. *American Political Science Review*, 74(4), 406–420.

Desposato, Scott W., and John R. Petrocik. (2003). The Variable Incumbency Advantage: New Voters, Redistricting, and the Personal Vote. *American Journal of Political Science*, 47(1), 18–32.

Downs, Anthony. (1957). *An Economic Theory of Democracy*. New York: Harper and Row.

Enelow, James, and Melvin Hinich. (1984). *The Spatial Theory of Voting: An Introduction*. New York: Cambridge University Press.

Enten, Harry. (2017). Registered Voters Who Stayed Home Probably Cost Clinton the Election. *FiveThirtyEight*, January 5. Retrieved from https://fivethirtyeight.com/features/registered-voters-who-stayed-home-probably-cost-clinton-the-election/.

Erikson, Robert S. (1995). State Turnout and Presidential Voting: A Closer Look. *American Politics Quarterly*, 23(4), 387–396.

Fair, Ray C. (1978). The Effect of Economic Events on Votes for President. *Review of Economics and Statistics*, 60, 159–173.

Finnegan, Michael. (2014). Low Turnout in California in November Could Lift Prospects for GOP. *Los Angeles Times*, September 2. Retrieved from http://www.latimes.com/local/politics/la-me-pol-california-election-20140903-story.html.

Fiorina, Morris P. (1981). *Retrospective Voting in American National Elections*. New Haven, CT: Yale University Press.

Fortune Magazine. "The Kelly-Nash Political Machine." 14 (August, 1936). 47-52, 114-126.

Fowler, Anthony. (2015). Regular Voters, Marginal Voters, and the Electoral Effects of Turnout. *Political Science Research and Methods*, 3(2), 205–219.

Fraga, Bernard. (2018). *The Turnout Gap: Race, Ethnicity, and Political Equality in a Diversifying America*. New York: Cambridge University Press.

Gant, M., and W. Lyons. (1993). Democratic Theory, Nonvoting, and Public Policy: The 1972–1988 Presidential Elections. *American Politics Quarterly*, 21(3), 185–204.

Gerber, Alan S., Donald P. Green, and Ron Shachar. (2003). Voting May Be Habit Forming: Evidence from a Randomized Field Experiment. *American Journal of Political Science*, 47(3), 540–550.

Haidt, Jonathan. (2013). *The Righteous Mind: Why Good People Are Divided by Politics and Religion.* New York: Vintage.

Hansford, Thomas G., and Brad T. Gomez. (2010). Estimating the Electoral Effects of Voter Turnout. *American Political Science Review*, 104(May), 268–288.

Hart, Austin. (2017). *Economic Voting: A Campaign-Centered Theory.* New York: Cambridge University Press.

Hood, M. V., III, and Charles S. Bullock III. (2012). Much Ado about Nothing? An Empirical Assessment of the Georgia Voter Identification Statute. *State Politics & Policy Quarterly*, 12(4), 394–414.

Hotelling, Harold. (1929). Stability in Competition. *Economic Journal*, 39, 41–57.

Inbody, Donald. (2015). *The Soldier Vote.* New York: Palgrave.

Jacobson, Gary C. (1978). Strategic Politicians and the Dynamics of U.S. House Elections, 1946–86. *American Political Science Review*, 83(3), 773–793.

Jacobson, Gary C., and Samuel Kernell. (1982). Strategy and Choice in the 1982 Congressional Elections. *PS: Political Science and Politics*, 15(Fall), 423–430.

Joesten, Danielle A., and Walter J. Stone. (2014). Reassessing Proximity Voting: Expertise, Party, and Choice in Congressional Elections. *Journal of Politics*, 76(3), 740–753.

Judis, John. (2014). Here's Why the Democrats Got Crushed—and Why 2016 Won't Be a Cakewalk. *New Republic*, November 5. Retrieved from https://newrepublic. com/article/120138/2014-election-results-heres-why-democrats-lost-senate-gop.

Kernell, Samuel. (1977). Presidential Popularity and Negative Voting: An Alternative Explanation of the Midterm Congressional Decline of the President's Party. *American Journal of Political Science*, 71(1), 44–66.

Key, Vladimir Orlando. (1966). *The Responsible Electorate: Rationality in Presidential Voting, 1936–1960.* Cambridge, MA: Harvard University Press.

Kilgore, Ed. (2012). Turnout Disparities and the Democratic Dilemma for 2014. *Washington Monthly*, November 9. Retrieved from http://washingtonmonthly. com/2012/11/09/turnout-disparities-and-the-democratic-dilemma-for-2014/.

Kinder, Donald R., and D. Roderick Kiewiet. (1981). Sociotropic Politics. *British Journal of Political Science*, 11, 129–161.

Knack, Steve. (1994). Does Rain Help Republicans? Theory and Evidence on Turnout and the Vote. *Public Choice*, 79(1–2), 187–209.

Kramer, Gerald H. (1971). Short-term Fluctuations in U.S. Voting Behavior, 1896–1964. *American Political Science Review*, 71, 131–143.

Ledyard, J. (1984). The Pure Theory of Large Two-Candidate Elections. *Public Choice*, 44(1), 7–43.

Lewis-Beck, Michael S., William G. Jacoby, Helmut Norpoth, and Herbert F. Weisberg. (2008). *The American Voter Revisited.* Ann Arbor: University of Michigan Press.

Lewis-Beck, Michael S., and Charles Tien. (2016). The Political Economy Model: 2016 U.S. Election Forecasts. *PS: Political Science and Politics*, 49(4), 661–663.

Lijphart, Arend. (1997). Unequal Participation: Democracy's Unresolved Dilemma. *American Political Science Review*, 91(1), 1–14.

Lillis, Mike. (2014). Pelosi Delivers Postmortem to Her Troops. *The Hill*, November 6. Retrieved from http://thehill.com/homenews/house/223281-pelosi-delivers-postmortem.

Lipset, Seymour Martin, and Stein Rokkan. (1967). *Party Systems and Voter Alignments: Cross-National Perspectives.* New York: Free Press.

Martinez, Michael D., and Jeff Gill. (2005). The Effects of Turnout on Partisan Outcomes in U.S. Presidential Elections, 1960–2000. *Journal of Politics*, 67(4), 1248–1274.

Michels, Roberto. (1962). *Political Parties: A Sociological Study of the Oligarchical Tendencies of Modern Democracy.* New York: Free Press.

Nagel, Jack H., and John E. McNulty. (1996). Partisan Effects of Voter Turnout in Senatorial and Gubernatorial Elections. *American Political Science Review*, 90(4), 780–793.

Nagel, Jack H., and John E. McNulty. (2000). Partisan Effects of Voter Turnout in Presidential Elections. *American Politics Research*, 28(3), 408–429.

Nardulli, Peter. (2007). *Popular Efficacy in the Democratic Era: A Reexamination of Electoral Accountability in the United States, 1828–2000.* Princeton, NJ: Princeton University Press.

Niemi, Richard G., and M. Kent Jennings. (1991). Issues and Inheritance in the Formation of Party Identification. *American Political Science Research*, 35(4), 970–988.

Palfrey, Thomas R., and Howard Rosenthal. (1985). Voter Participation and Strategic Uncertainty. *American Political Science Review*, 79(1), 62–78.

Petrocik, John R. (1981). *Party Coalitions: Realignment and the Decline of the New Deal Party System.* Chicago: University of Chicago Press.

Petrocik, John. (1987). Voter Turnout and Electoral Preference: The Anomalous Reagan Election. In K. Schlozman (ed.), *Elections in America.* New York: Allen and Unwin.

Piven, Frances Fox, and Richard A. Cloward. (1988). *Why Americans Don't Vote.* New York: Pantheon Books.

Plutzer, Eric. (2002). Becoming a Habitual Voter: Inertia, Resources, and Growth in Young Adulthood. *American Political Science Review*, 96(1), 41–56.

Powell, G. Bingham. (1986). American Voter Turnout in Comparative Perspective. *American Political Science Review*, 80(1), 17–43.

Przeworski, Adam, and John Sprague. (1971). Concepts in Search of Explicit Formation: A Study in Measurement. *Midwest Journal of Political Science*, 15(2), 183–218.

Przeworski, Adam, and John Sprague. (1988). *Paper Stones: A History of Electoral Socialism.* Chicago: University of Chicago Press.

Radcliff, Benjamin. (1994). Turnout and the Democratic Vote. *American Politics Research*, 22(3), 259–276.

Riker, William H., and Peter C. Ordeshook. (1968). A Theory of the Calculus of Voting. *American Political Science Review*, 62(1), 25–42.

Robinson, William S. (1950). Ecological Correlations and the Behavior of Individuals. *American Sociological Review*, 15(3), 351–357.

Rosenstone, Steven J., and John Mark Hansen. (1993). *Mobilization, Participation, and Democracy in America*. New York: Macmillan.

Shanks, J. Merrill, and Warren E. Miller. (1996). *The New American Voter*. Cambridge, MA: Harvard University Press.

Shaw, Daron R., Robert C. Luskin, Marc Hetherington, and Kelsey Swindle. (2019). Macro-Partisanship and Realignment in the American States: Estimating Statewide Party Identification from 1990–2016. Unpublished manuscript. University of Texas at Austin.

Sigelman, Lee, and Malcolm E. Jewell. (1986). From Core to Periphery: A Note on the Imagery of Concentric Electorates. *Journal of Politics*, 48(4), 440–449.

Stokes, Donald E. 1966. "Spatial Models of Party Competition." In Angus Campbell, Philip E. Converse, Warren E. Miller, and Donald E. Stokes (eds.), *Elections and the Political Order*. New York: John Wiley and Sons.

Stolwijk, Sjoerd, Andreas R. T. Schuck, and Claes H. de Vreese. (2016). How Anxiety and Enthusiasm Help Explain the Bandwagon Effect. *International Journal of Public Opinion*, 29(4), 554–574.

Teixeira, Ruy. (1987). *Why Americans Don't Vote*. New York: Greenwood Press.

Traister, Rebecca. (2017). Hillary Clinton Is Furious. And Resigned. And Funny. And Worried. *New York*, May 29. Retrieved from http://nymag.com/daily/intelligencer/2017/05/hillary-clinton-life-after-election.html.

Tucker, Harvey J., Arnold Vedlitz, and James DeNardo. (1986). Does Heavy Turnout Help Democrats in Presidential Elections? *American Political Science Review*, 80(4), 1291–1304.

Tufte, Edward. (1978). *Political Control of the Economy*. Princeton, NJ: Princeton University Press.

Valentino, Nicholas A., Ted Brader, Eric W. Groenendyk, Krysha Gregorowicz, and Vincent L. Hutchings. (2011). Election Night's Alright for Fighting: The Role of Emotions in Political Participation. *Journal of Politics*, 73(1), 156–170.

Verba, Sidney, Norman H. Nie, and Jae-on Kim. (1978). *Participation and Political Equality: A Seven-Nation Comparison*. New York: Cambridge University Press.

Verba, Sidney, Kay Lehman Schlozman, and Henry Brady. (1995). *Voice and Equality: Civic Voluntarism in American Politics*. Cambridge, MA: Harvard University Press.

Wolfinger, Raymond E., and Steven J. Rosenstone. (1980). *Who Votes?* New Haven, CT: Yale University Press.

Wolfinger, Raymond E., Steven J. Rosenstone, and Richard A. McIntosh. (1978). *Voter Turnout in Midterm Elections*. Berkeley: Institute of Governmental Studies, University of California.

Index

For the benefit of digital users, indexed terms that span two pages (e.g., 52–53) may, on occasion, appear on only one of those pages.

absentee ballots, x, 22, 29–30

African American voters
civil rights movement and voting
rights of, 23
Democratic Party and, 8–9, 36, 69, 71,
158–59t, 161–62t, 164–65t
disenfranchisement throughout US
history of, 15–16, 17
education levels among, 23–25
election of 1988 and, 26f
election of 1992 and, 26f
election of 1996 and, 26f
election of 2000 and, 7t, 26f
election of 2004 and, 7t, 26f
election of 2008 and, 2, 7t, 26f, 26–27,
31, 151
election of 2012 and, 7t, 26f, 26–27,
31, 151
election of 2016 and, 10, 26f, 26–27, 31
midterm congressional elections
and, 8–9
Obama and, 31, 151
in Southern states, 23–25
turnout rates among, 2, 7t, 25,
26–27, 31
US House districts and, 95, 96, 97f, 97–98

aggregation fallacy, 55, 65–66
Alabama, 22f, 142–43, 143t, 153, 174–75n1
Alaska, 22f, 143t
Arizona, 22f, 143t, 144
Arkansas, 22f, 143t, 144
Asian American voters, 2, 12, 26, 36
Australia, 30f, 49
Austria, 30f, 31

ballot formatting, 124–27
Barone, Michael, 10–11
Belgium, 30f, 31, 49
Bentsen, Lloyd, 83f
Boxer, Barbara, 82f, 84
Brady, Henry, 44–45
Bush, George H.W., 115
Bush, George W., 91, 133–34, 135–36,
137, 154

California
Democratic Party performance in, 5–6,
81–84, 82f
elections of 2014 in, 5–6
nonpartisan voters in, 144–46
party identification imbalance in,
143t, 144

California (*Cont.*)
    registration laws in, 43
    Republican Party voters in, 144–46
    turnout rates in, 22*f*, 43
    US Senate elections in, 81–84, 82*f*
campaign spending, 13, 138–40, 138*t*
Campbell, Angus, 13, 52, 121
Canada, 30*f*
Carter, Jimmy, 54, 115, 131
Catholics, 25
Chile, 30*f*
Cincinnatus, 137
civil rights movement, 23, 114–15
Clark, Tim, 5–6
Clinton, Bill, 90, 114–15, 118, 133–34
Clinton, Hillary
    African American voters and, 10, 31
    Midwestern states and, 153
    nonpartisan voters and, 6–7
    probabilistic calculations regarding
        turnout in election of 2016 and,
        110*f*, 110
Cloward, Richard, 9, 48, 49
coattail voting
    elections of 1960 and, 130*f*, 130, 131
    elections of 1964, 130–32*f*, 131
    elections of 1972 and, 133*f*
    elections of 1976 and, 130–32*f*, 130–31
    elections of 1992 and, 90, 133*f*
    elections of 2000 and, 132*f*, 154
    elections of 2004 and, 132–33*f*
    elections of 2008 and, 89, 130–33*f*,
        130, 151
    elections of 2012 and, 132–33*f*, 151
    elections of 2016 and, 89, 130–33*f*, 154
    incumbency and partisan
        identification as potential
        countervailing forces and,
        126–29, 127*t*
    landslide elections and, 128–29, 131–32
    proportion to margin of presidential
        victory and, 131–34, 133*f*

    subsequent midterm congressional
        elections and the reversal of, 129,
        130–36, 133*f*, 140
    turnout-driven explanations of
        electoral outcomes and, 129
    US House elections and, 89–90, 126–
        27, 126–27*t*, 128–30
Cohn, Nate, 9–11
Colorado, 22*f*, 22, 29–30, 56, 81, 143*t*
congressional elections. *See also* midterm
    congressional elections; US House
    elections; US Senate elections
    in 2000, 3*t*, 62*f*, 154
    in 2002, 3*t*, 62*f*, 62–63, 96*f*, 96,
        134–35, 154
    in 2004, 3*t*, 4, 62*f*, 96*f*, 96, 98–99, 99*f*
    in 2006, 3–4, 3*t*, 9, 62*f*, 62–63, 65, 91,
        96*f*, 96, 99–100, 100*f*, 130–31, 135–36
    in 2008, 2, 3*t*, 62*f*, 89, 91, 138*t*, 139–40
    in 2010, 2–4, 3*t*, 62*f*, 62–63, 91, 96*f*, 96,
        99–100, 100*f*, 138–39, 138*t*
    in 2012, 3–4, 3*t*, 59, 64*f*, 97*f*, 97–98, 99*f*
    in 2014, 3–4, 3*t*, 5–6, 8–11, 62*f*,
        64*f*, 97*f*, 97–98, 99–100, 100*f*,
        138*t*, 139–40
    in 2016, 3–4, 3*t*, 62*f*, 64*f*, 89, 97*f*, 97–
        99, 99*f*, 138–39, 138*t*, 154
    in 2018, 3*t*, 59, 62*f*, 153
Connecticut, 22*f*, 143*t*, 144
conservative voters, 7*t*, 8, 11
Constitution of the United States
    congressional districts
        established in, 15
    Electoral College established in, 15
    federalism regarding electoral
        eligibility and, 15–16
    The Federalist Papers and, 15–16
    Fifteenth Amendment and, 17
    Nineteenth Amendment and, 17*f*, 18
    Twenty-Sixth amendment and, 18–19
    US Senate election provisions and, 15
Cornyn, John, 81–84, 83*f*

Cranston, Alan, 82f, 84
cross-sectional inference fallacy,
  55, 65–66
Cruz, Ted, 81–84, 83f
Czech Republic, 30f

Delaware, 22f, 143t
Democratic Party. *See also specific*
  politicians
  African American voters and, 8–9, 36,
    69, 71, 158–59t, 161–62t, 164–65t
  Asian American voters and, 36
  defection rates among voters in,
    10–11, 103
  demographic profile of voters in, 8,
    105–6, 105t
  expanded voter registration and poll
    access as priorities for, 148, 149
  foreign-born voters and, 69, 158–60t
  Latino voters and, 8–9, 36, 56, 81, 161–
    62t, 164–65t
  midterm congressional elections and,
    3–5, 8–9, 109–10
  rural voters and, 69, 158–60t
  Southern states and, 23, 69, 71, 158–60t
  state-by-state measures of registration
    strength of, 142–44, 143t
  turnout and the electoral performance
    of, 2–5, 8–9, 10–11, 12, 36, 41–42,
    48–50, 51, 53–54, 55–57, 59, 60,
    61–62f, 62–63, 63–67f, 64–65, 66,
    68–70, 70–72f, 71–73, 76–80, 79–
    83f, 81–84, 85–88, 89–93, 95–97, 96f,
    98–100, 101–2, 108f, 108, 109–10,
    124, 140, 141, 144, 148, 150, 158–62t,
    164–65t
  turnout rate among voters in, 7t,
    8, 11, 65–66, 102–3, 102t, 106,
    108f, 109–10
  urban voters and, 66, 159–60t
  voters' age and, 105t
  voters' education levels and, 105t
  voters' length of residence in a
    community and, 105t
  voters' marital status and, 105t
  voters' political interest levels and,
    105–6, 105t
  voters' religiosity levels and, 105, 105t
  voters' strength of partisan
    identification in, 105–6, 105t
  white working class voters and, 10–11
  women voters and, 8–9
  younger voters and, 8–9, 161–62t,
    164–65t
DeNardo, James, 51–53, 56–57, 80, 144
Denmark, 30f
District of Columbia, 22f
Dole, Bob, 115
Downey, Thomas, 80
Downs, Anthony, 37, 46, 53–54, 149–51

early voting, 22, 29–30
economic performance factors
  alternative explanations for electoral
    outcomes and, 122–24
  election of 1956 and, 122–23, 123f
  election of 1958 and, 130–31
  election of 1960 and, 130–31
  election of 1964 and, 122–23, 123f
  election of 1972 and, 122–23, 123f
  election of 1980 and, 123f
  election of 2008 and, 123f, 131, 152–53
  election of 2016 and, 123f
  electoral predictions based on
    statistical modeling of, 122–23, 123f
  incumbents' ability to influence, 122
economic theory of democracy, 37
Eisenhower, Dwight D., 50–51,
  116–17, 125
elections of 1934, 134–35
elections of 1944, 19f, 21f, 24f
elections of 1946, 21f
elections of 1948, 19–21f, 24f, 114f
elections of 1950, 21f, 24f

elections of 1952
  Korean War and, 72–73
  nonvoters' candidate preferences in,
    50f, 51
  turnout in, 3–4, 19–21f, 24f
  voters' partisan choice switches from
    1948 election and, 114f
elections of 1954, 21f, 24f
elections of 1956
  economic performance factors and,
    122–23, 123f
  nonvoters' candidate preference in,
    50f, 50–51
  turnout in, 19–21f, 24f
  US House elections and, 116–17
  voters' partisan choice switches in
    1960 election and, 113–15, 114f, 116–
    17, 116–17t, 118
  voters' partisan vote switches in 1958
    election and, 117–18, 117t
elections of 1958, 21f, 24f, 117–18,
    117t, 130–31
elections of 1960
  close margin of presidential election
    in, 54, 131
  coattail voting and, 130f, 130, 131
  economic performance factors
    and, 130–31
  fraud in Illinois and, 54
  nonvoters' candidate preference in, 50f
  turnout rate in, 2, 3–4, 19–21f, 19,
    24f, 60f
  US House elections and,
    116–17, 130–31
  voters' partisan choice switches from
    1956 election and, 113–15, 114f, 116–
    17, 116–17t, 118
  voters partisan vote switches from 1958
    election and, 117t, 118
elections of 1962, 21f, 24f
elections of 1964
  coattail voting, 130–32f, 131

Democratic Party landslide victory in,
    60, 65, 128–29, 131, 151
economic performance factors and,
    122–23, 123f
nonvoters' candidate preference in,
    50f, 50–51
turnout rate in, 19–21f, 24f, 60f, 60, 65
voters' partisan vote choice switches in
    1968 election and, 114f
elections of 1966, 21f, 24f
elections of 1968, 19–21f, 24f, 50f,
    72–73, 114f
elections of 1970, 21f, 24f, 65
elections of 1972
  coattail voting and, 133f
  economic factors and, 122–23, 123f
  nonvoters' candidate preference in, 50f
  Republicans' large margin of victory
    in, 90, 128–29, 151
  turnout levels in, 19–21f, 24f
  US House elections and, 90
  voters' partisan choice switches in 1974
    election and, 117t, 118
  voters' partisan choice switches in
    1976 election and, 113–15, 114f,
    116–17t, 118
elections of 1974
  candidates' decision to run in, 137
  Democrats' large margin of victory in,
    65, 90, 114–15, 130–31, 133f, 133–34
  reversal of coattail voting effects in,
    133f, 133–34
  turnout rates in, 21f, 24f, 90, 135
  US House elections in, 90
  US Senate elections and, 65
  voters' partisan choice switches from
    1972 election and, 117t, 118
  voters' partisan vote switches in 1976
    election and, 117t, 118
  Watergate scandal and, 118, 130–31
elections of 1976
  coattail voting and, 130–32f, 130–31

nonvoters' candidate preferences
and, 50*f*
turnout levels in, 3–4, 19*f*, 21*f*, 24*f*, 90
voters' partisan choice switches from
1972 election and, 113–15, 114*f*, 116*t*
voters' partisan choice switches from
1974 election and, 117*t*, 118
elections of 1978, 21*f*, 24*f*
elections of 1980
Carter's concession in, 54
economic performance factors
and, 123*f*
nonvoters' candidate preference in,
50*f*, 50–51
Reagan's large margin of victory
in, 128–29
turnout in, 19–21*f*, 24*f*
US House elections and, 90
elections of 1982, 21*f*, 24*f*, 65, 90
elections of 1984, 19–21*f*, 24*f*, 50*f*, 90, 151
elections of 1986, 21*f*, 24*f*, 90, 125
elections of 1988, 19–21*f*, 24–29*f*, 50*f*,
107, 109
elections of 1990, 21*f*, 24*f*
elections of 1992
coattail voting and, 90, 133*f*
nonvoters' candidate preference in,
50*f*, 50–51
turnout and, 19–21*f*, 24–27*f*, 114–15
voters' partisan choice switches in 1994
election and, 113–15, 117*t*, 118
voters' partisan choice switches in 1996
election and, 113–15, 116–17*t*, 118
elections of 1994
candidates' decision to run in, 137
reversal of coattail voting effects in, 90,
133*f*, 133–34
turnout rates in, 21*f*, 24*f*, 62–63
US House elections and, 62–63, 90
US Senate elections and, 49–50
voters' partisan choice switches from
1992 election and, 113–15, 117*t*, 118

voters' partisan choice switches in 1996
election and, 113–14, 117*t*, 118
elections of 1996
nonvoters' candidate preference and,
50*f*, 50–51
turnout rate in, 19–21*f*, 24–27*f*, 62–63,
109, 114–15
US House elections and, 62–63, 90
voters' partisan choice switches
from 1992 election and, 113–15,
116–17*t*, 118
voters' partisan choice switches from
1994 election and, 113–14, 117*t*, 118
voters partisan vote switches in 2000
elections and, 114*f*
elections of 1998, 21*f*, 24*f*, 49–50, 90
elections of 2000
African American voters and, 7*t*, 26*f*
coattail voting and, 132*f*, 154
congressional elections and, 3*t*,
62*f*, 154
gubernatorial elections and, 3*t*
Latino voters and, 7*t*, 26*f*
nonpartisan voters and, 7*t*
presidential election and, 3*t*, 4, 19*f*, 24*f*,
50*f*, 60–61*f*
state legislature elections and, 3*t*
turnout rate in, 3*t*, 4, 7*t*, 19*f*, 21*f*,
24–27*f*, 60–62*f*
voters' partisan vote switches from
1996 election and, 114*f*
voters partisan vote switches in 2004
elections and, 114*f*
white voters and, 7*t*, 26*f*
elections of 2002
congressional elections and, 3*t*, 62*f*,
62–63, 96*f*, 96, 134–35, 154
gubernatorial elections and, 3*t*
presidential approval rating in, 134–35
state legislature elections and, 3*t*
turnout rate in, 3*t*, 21*f*, 24*f*, 62*f*, 62–63,
96*f*, 163*t*, 166*t*

elections of 2004
  African American voters and, 7*t*, 26*f*
  coattail voting and, 132–33*f*
  congressional elections and, 3*t*, 4, 62*f*,
    96*f*, 96, 98–99, 99*f*
  gubernatorial elections and, 3*t*, 4
  Latino voters and, 7*t*, 26*f*
  nonpartisan voters and, 7*t*
  presidential election and, 3*t*, 4, 19*f*,
    24–26*f*, 50*f*, 60–61*f*
  state legislature elections and, 3*t*, 4
  turnout rate in, 3*t*, 4, 7*t*, 19*f*, 21*f*, 24–27*f*,
    60–62*f*, 96*f*, 98–99, 99*f*, 163*t*, 166*t*
  voters' partisan vote switchers from
    2000 election and, 114*f*
  voters' partisan vote switches in 2008
    election and, 114*f*
  white voters and, 7*t*, 26*f*
elections of 2006
  candidates' decision to run
    in, 136–37
  congressional elections and, 3–4, 3*t*, 9,
    62*f*, 62–63, 65, 91, 96*f*, 96, 99–100,
    100*f*, 130–31, 135–36
  Democratic Party performance in, 3–
    4, 3*t*, 9, 62–63, 111, 130–31
  gubernatorial elections and, 3*t*, 91
  Hurricane Katrina and Iraq War as
    short-term forces influencing, 131,
    136, 152–53
  presidential approval rating in, 135–36
  reversal of coattail voting effects in,
    133*f*, 133–34, 135–36
  state legislature elections and, 3*t*, 91
  turnout rate in, 3–4, 3*t*, 9, 21*f*, 24*f*, 62*f*,
    62–63, 96*f*, 99–100, 100*f*, 163*t*, 166*t*
elections of 2008
  African American voters and, 2, 7*t*,
    26*f*, 26–27, 31, 151
  Asian American voters and, 2
  coattail voting and, 89, 130–33*f*, 130, 151
  congressional elections and, 2, 3*t*, 62*f*,
    89, 91, 138*t*, 139–40

Democratic Party performance in, 2,
  7*t*, 111, 151
economic performance factors and,
  123*f*, 131, 152–53
GOTV efforts in, 2
gubernatorial elections and, 2, 3*t*
Latino voters and, 2, 7*t*, 26*f*
nonpartisan voters and, 7*t*
Obama's large margin of victory
  in, 128–29
presidential election and, 2, 3*t*, 19*f*, 19,
  24*f*, 50*f*, 54, 60–61*f*, 97
representativeness of voters in, 2–5
state legislature elections and, 3*t*
turnout rate in, 2, 3*t*, 7*t*, 9, 19*f*, 19, 20,
  21*f*, 24–27*f*, 60–62*f*, 91–92, 96*f*, 97,
  98–99, 99*f*, 109, 163*t*, 166*t*
US Senate elections and, 91,
  138*t*, 139–40
voters' partisan vote switches from
  2004 election and, 114*f*
white voters and, 7*t*, 26*f*, 31
younger voters and, 2
elections of 2010
  congressional elections and, 2–4, 3*t*,
    62*f*, 62–63, 91, 96*f*, 96, 99–100, 100*f*,
    138–39, 138*t*
  gubernatorial elections and, 3*t*
  Republican Party performance in,
    2–4, 111
  reversal of coattail voting effects in,
    133*f*, 135–36
  state legislature elections and, 3*t*
  turnout rate in, 2–4, 3*t*, 9, 21*f*, 24*f*, 62*f*,
    62–63, 96*f*, 97, 99–100, 100*f*, 121,
    163*t*, 166*t*
  US House elections and, 91, 96*f*, 96,
    99–100, 100*f*
  US Senate elections in, 91, 138–39, 138*t*
elections of 2012
  African American voters and, 7*t*, 26*f*,
    26–27, 31, 151
  coattail voting and, 132–33*f*, 151

congressional elections and, 3–4, 3*t*, 59,
64*f*, 97*f*, 97–98, 99*f*
gubernatorial elections and, 3*t*
Latino voters and, 7*t*, 26*f*
nonpartisan voters and, 7*t*
presidential election and, 3–4, 3*t*, 10,
19*f*, 19, 24–26*f*, 50*f*, 54, 60–61*f*
state legislature elections and, 3–4, 3*t*
turnout rate in, 3–4, 3*t*, 7*t*, 9, 19*f*, 19,
20, 21*f*, 24–27*f*, 60–62*f*, 97*f*, 97–98,
109, 151, 163*t*, 166*t*
US House elections and, 97*f*,
97–98, 99*f*
US Senate elections and, 64*f*
voters' partisan vote switches in 2016
election and, 114*f*
voters' recall errors regarding, 115
white voters and, 7*t*, 10, 26*f*, 31
elections of 2014
congressional elections and, 3–4, 3*t*,
5–6, 8–11, 62*f*, 64*f*, 97*f*, 97–98, 99–
100, 100*f*, 138*t*, 139–40
Democratic Party performance in, 3*t*,
5–6, 8–10
gubernatorial elections and, 3*t*
presidential incumbent approval rates
and, 124*f*
Republican Party performance in, 3–4
reversal of coattail voting effects
in, 133*f*
state legislature elections and, 3*t*
turnout rate in, 3–4, 3*t*, 8–11, 21*f*, 24*f*,
62*f*, 97*f*, 97–98, 99–100, 100*f*, 121,
163*t*, 166*t*
US House elections and, 97*f*, 97–98,
99–100, 100*f*
US Senate elections and, 64*f*,
138*t*, 139–40
white voters and, 10–11
younger voters and, 9–10
elections of 2016
African American voters and, 10, 26*f*,
26–27, 31

coattail voting and, 89, 130–33*f*, 154
congressional elections and, 3–4, 3*t*,
62*f*, 64*f*, 89, 97*f*, 97–99, 99*f*, 138–39,
138*t*, 154
Democratic Party voters and,
6–7, 6*t*, 10
economic performance factors
and, 123*f*
gubernatorial elections and, 3*t*
Latino voters and, 26*f*
nonpartisan voters and, 6–7, 6*t*
polarizations evident in the outcome
of, 153
presidential election and, 3–4, 3*t*, 6–7,
10, 19*f*, 19, 24–27*f*, 50*f*, 60–61*f*
probabilistic calculations regarding
turnout and, 110*f*, 110, 167*t*
Republican Party voters and, 6–7, 6*t*
state legislature elections and, 3–4, 3*t*
turnout rate in, 3–4, 3*t*, 6–7, 10, 19*f*, 19,
21*f*, 24–26*f*, 60–62*f*, 97*f*, 97–99, 99*f*,
109, 162*t*, 166*t*
US House elections and, 97*f*,
97–99, 99*f*
US Senate elections and, 64*f*,
138–39, 138*t*
voters' partisan vote switches from
2012 election and, 114*f*
white voters and, 10–11, 26*f*
elections of 2018
congressional elections and, 3*t*, 59,
62*f*, 153
Democratic Party performance in, 3*t*, 4
gubernatorial elections and, 3*t*, 63*f*
presidential incumbent approval rates
and, 124*f*, 154
Republican incumbents' retirements
prior to, 136
reversal of coattail voting effects in, 133*f*
state legislature elections and, 3*t*
turnout rate in, 3*t*, 4, 21*f*, 24*f*,
62–63*f*, 154
US Senate elections and, 64*f*

Electoral College, 15, 16–17, 63–64
eligibility requirements for voting
   African Americans and, 15–16, 17
   federalism regarding, 15–16
   Jacksonian Era expansion of voting
     rights and, 16
   literacy tests and, 17
   Native Americans and, 15–16
   Nineteenth Amendment and, 17f, 18
   poll taxes and, 17
   Progressive Era ballot reforms and, 18
   property ownership requirements
     and, 16
   Twenty-Sixth Amendment and,
     17f, 18–19
Enten, Harry, 6–8
Erikson, Robert, 52
Estonia, 30f

The Federalist Papers, 15–16
Feinstein, Diane, 81–84, 82f
Fifteenth Amendment, 17
Finland, 30f
Florida, 10, 22f, 143t
Ford, Gerald, 130–31, 133–34
Fowler, Anthony, 52
France, 30f

Georgia, 22f, 143t, 153
Germany, 30f
Gilmore, Paul, 78–79
Gomez, Brad, 9, 52, 53, 65–66
GOTV (get out the vote) campaigns, x,
   2, 61, 77, 93
Gramm, Phil, 83f
Greece, 30f
gubernatorial elections
   in 2000-2018, 3t
   in 2004, 3t, 4
   in 2006, 3t, 91
   in 2010, 2–3
   in 2018, 3t, 63f
   candidates' decisions to run in, 137

competitiveness of electorate and, 144
Democratic Party electoral
   performance and, 63f, 64, 77, 80,
     87f, 87, 92–93, 101
"odd-year elections" and, 20
"off-year cycles" and, 146, 147f, 174n4
"on-year cycles" and, 146, 147f
party identification balance among
   voters and, 144
short-term forces and, 146, 147f
turnout rates and, 22, 63f, 63–64,
   76–77, 80–81, 87f, 87, 92–93, 101,
   144, 146

Hansen, John Mark, 43–44
Hansford, Thomas, 9, 52, 53, 65–66
Harris, Kamala, 81–84, 82f
Hawaii, 22f, 22, 143t
Hayakawa, S.I., 82f
high-income voters, 7t, 8, 11
Hispanic voters. *See* Latino voters
Hotelling, Harold, 37
Hungary, 30f
Hurricane Katrina (2005), 131, 136, 152–53
Hutchison, Kay Bailey, 83f, 84

Iceland, 30f
Idaho, 22f, 143t
Illinois, 22f, 54, 125, 143t
incumbent approval rates
   coattail voting and, 127–28
   election of 2002 and, 134–35
   election of 2006 and, 135–36
   election of 2014 and, 124f
   election of 2018 and, 124f, 154
   electoral outcomes influenced by, 13,
     61f, 61, 123–24
   measures of, 123–24
   presidential approval rating's
     correlation with US House election
     outcomes and, 124f, 127t, 134–36
Indiana, 22f, 143t
infrequent voters. *See* peripheral voters

Iowa
  Congressional District 1 in, 78–80, 79*f*
  Democratic Party performance in,
    79*f*, 79–80
  elections of 1992 in, 79–80
  party identification levels in, 143*t*
  turnout rates in, 22*f*, 79*f*, 79–80
Iraq War (2003-12), 131, 136, 152–53
Ireland, 30*f*
Israel, 30*f*
Italy, 30*f*

Jacksonian Era, 16–17, 17*f*
Japan, 30*f*
Jews, 25
Johnson, Lyndon B., 50–51, 131
Jones, Doug, 174–75n1
Judis, John, 10–11

Kansas, 22*f*, 143*t*
Kennedy, John F., 2, 115, 116–17, 131
Kentucky, 22*f*, 143*t*, 174n4
Key, V.O., 151–52, 153
Kim, Jae-on, 30–31
Korean War, 72–73
Krueger, Bob, 83*f*

Latino voters
  Democratic Party and, 8–9, 36, 56, 81,
    161–62*t*, 164–65*t*
  elections of 1992-2016 and, 26*f*
  elections of 2000 and, 7*t*, 26*f*
  elections of 2004 and, 7*t*, 26*f*
  elections of 2008 and, 2, 7*t*, 26*f*
  elections of 2012 and, 7*t*, 26*f*
  midterm congressional elections
    and, 8–9
  Obama and, 12
  turnout rates among, 2, 7*t*, 26
  US House districts and, 95, 96,
    97*f*, 97–98
Latta, Del, 78–79
Latvia, 30*f*

Leach, Jim, 79–80
liberal voters, 7*t*, 8
Lijphart, Arend, 48, 49
Lipset, Seymour Martin, 152
Louisiana, 22*f*, 125, 143*t*, 174n4
low-income voters, 7*t*, 8, 48–49
Luxembourg, 30*f*

mail-in voting states, 22, 29–30, 56, 81. *See
    also* absentee ballots
Maine, 22*f*, 22, 143*t*
mandatory voting countries, x, 32–33,
    49, 172n5
Maryland, 22*f*, 143*t*
Massachusetts, 22*f*, 75–76, 143*t*
McCain, John, 9, 152–53
McGovern, George, 90
McNulty, John E., 52
Mexico, 30*f*, 172n5
Michels, Roberto, 52, 141, 144–46
Michigan, 22*f*, 142–43, 143*t*, 153, 178n1
middle-income voters, 7*t*, 102
midterm congressional elections. *See also
    specific elections*
  Democratic Party performance in, 3–5,
    8–9, 109–10
  demography of electorate in, 5–6, 8–9
  incumbency advantage in, 21
  magnitude of surge in congressional
    seats in previous election and,
    134, 135*t*
  potential candidates' decisions to run
    in, 136–37
  presidential approval rating and,
    134–36, 135*t*
  reversal of coattail voting effects in,
    129, 130–36, 133*f*, 140
  short-term forces and, 111
  turnout rates in, 3–4, 5–6, 8–9, 12, 20,
    21*f*, 22, 24*f*, 62*f*, 62–63, 89, 101, 108,
    109–10, 124, 135–36, 135*t*
  voter enthusiasm regarding, 1, 8–9, 21
  younger voters and, 8–10

Minnesota, 22f, 22, 143t, 153, 178n1
Mississippi, 22f, 143t, 174n4
Missouri, 22f, 143t
moderate voters, 7t
Montana, 22f, 143t
Moore, Roy, 174–75n1

Nagel, Jack H., 52
Nardulli, Peter, 67
Native Americans, 15–16
Nebraska, 22f, 142–43, 143t
The Netherlands, 30f, 31, 32, 49
Nevada, 22f, 143t
New Hampshire, 22f, 22, 143t
New Jersey, 20, 22f, 125, 143t, 174n4
New Mexico, 22f, 143t
New York
    Congressional District 2 in, 78–79,
        79f, 80
    Democratic Party performance in,
        79f, 80
    party identification levels in, 143t
    turnout rates in, 22f, 79f, 80
New Zealand, 30f
Nie, Norman, 30–31
Nineteenth Amendment, 17f, 18
Nixon, Richard M., 2, 54, 90,
    116–17, 130–31
nonpartisan voters
    demographic characteristics of,
        105–6, 105t
    elections of 2000-2016 and, 7t
    elections of 2016 and, 6–7, 6t
    short-term forces and, 103
    turnout rates among, 7t, 25, 102–3,
        102t, 105, 109
nonvoters
    assumptions regarding the political
        inclinations of, 48–50, 118–19
    demographic profile of, 48–49
    preference for winning candidates
        among, 50–51

presidential elections of 1952-2012 and,
    49–51, 50f
US Senate elections of 1994-98
    and, 49–50
North Carolina, 10, 22f, 143t
North Dakota, 22f, 143t
Norway, 30f

Obama, Barack
    African American voters and, 31, 151
    approval ratings of, 135–36, 138–39
    Asian American voters and, 12
    on Democratic Party voters in
        midterm elections, 8–9
    election of 2012 and, 10, 54
    GOTV efforts by campaign of, 2
    Latino voters and, 12
    mandate claimed (2008) by, 2
    white working class voters and, 10
    younger voters and, 12
off-year elections. *See* midterm
    congressional elections
Ohio
    Congressional District 5 in, 78–79, 79f
    Democratic Party performance in,
        78–79, 79f
    party identification levels in, 143t
    turnout rates in, 22f, 78–79, 79f
Oklahoma, 22f, 75–76, 143t
older voters
    community engagement among, 28
    exposure to public policy costs
        among, 28
    party identification among, 105t
    party identification and, 39–40
    turnout rates among, 26, 28–29, 29f,
        36, 45, 104, 104t, 107t, 167t
Oregon, 22f, 29–30, 143t, 178n2

partisan vote choice
    competitiveness of electorates
        and, 142–44

confounding influences and, 65–68

cost-benefit analysis in, 39, 43, 53–54

information collection and, 39, 41

intensity of partisan preference and, 39, 46–47, 53–54, 104*t*, 167*t*

opinion leaders and, 40–41

party identification balance among voters and, 39–40, 142–44

rational choice theory explanations of, 35, 37–39, 46, 53–54

social media and, 40–41

turnout and, 35, 36, 41–42, 47–48, 66, 141–44, 149

universal turnout scenario and, 48

voters' retrospective evaluations of national conditions and, 40, 71

Pelosi, Nancy, 8–9

Pennsylvania, 10, 22*f*, 143*t*, 153, 154, 178n1

peripheral voters

    bandwagon effects among, 13, 53–54, 151

    demographic characteristics of, 69–70

    latent party identification among, 51, 52, 102

    minority party and, 144–46

    partisan vote choice switches and, 113–14, 114*f*

    Republican Party candidates and, 8

    short-term forces and, 8, 13, 51–52, 103, 110–11, 112–14*f*, 112–14, 118–19, 121, 149, 151–52

Perot, Ross, 116*t*

Piven, Frances Fox, 48, 49

Poland, 30*f*

polarized party systems, 152

Portugal, 30*f*

presidential elections. *See also specific election years*

    coattail voting and, 89, 126–27, 126–27*t*, 128–30

    Democratic incumbent elections and, 71, 72*f*, 72–73

demography of electorate in, 5–6

economic performance factors and, 71–73, 72*f*

incumbency effects and, 61*f*, 61, 71–73

nonvoters preferences (1952–2016) and, 49–51, 50*f*

Republican incumbent elections and, 71–72, 72*f*

rural *versus* urban voters and, 70*f*, 70–71

short-term forces and, 92, 111, 146, 147*f*

turnout rates during, ix–x, 3*t*, 5–6, 19, 20, 21*f*, 22, 24*f*, 60–62*f*, 60–63, 68–69, 75, 85*f*, 85–93, 97, 98–99, 99*f*, 101, 108, 109, 124, 144, 146

US House elections influenced by, 89–91, 98–99, 99*f*

voter enthusiasm regarding, 1, 21, 89

Progressive Era, 17–18

Protestants, 25

provisional ballots, 22, 43

purging of electoral rolls, 43–44

Radcliff, Benjamin, 52

rational choice theory explanations of voting, 35, 37–39, 46, 53–54

Reagan, Ronald, 90

referendum elections, ix–x, 148

registration of voters

    Democratic Party's efforts to expand, 148, 149

    Election Day options for, 29–30, 43, 56, 81

    Republican Party's attempts to limit, 148, 149

    state variations regarding, 22

    turnout rates and, 29–30, 42–44, 51, 56, 81

Republican Party. *See also specific politicians*

    defection rates among voters in, 10–11, 103

Republican Party (*Cont.*)
  demographic profile of voters in, 8,
    102, 105–6, 105*t*
  election of 2012 and, 151
  election of 2016 and, 6–7, 6*t*
  elections of 1994 and, 62–63
  elections of 2004 and, 4, 111
  elections of 2010 and, 2–4, 111
  elections of 2014 and, 3–4
  expanded voter registration and poll
    access viewed as threats by, 148, 149
  Southern states and, 23
  state-by-state measures of registration
    strength of, 142–44, 143*t*
  turnout rate among voters in, 7*t*, 8, 11,
    46–47, 65–66, 97–98, 102–3, 102*t*,
    106, 108*f*, 109–10, 151
  voters' age and, 105, 105*t*
  voters' education levels and, 105, 105*t*
  voters' length of residence in a
    community and, 105, 105*t*
  voters' marital status and, 105, 105*t*
  voters' political interest levels and,
    105–6, 105*t*
  voters' religiosity levels and, 105, 105*t*
  voters' strength of partisan
    identification in, 105–6, 105*t*
Rhode Island, 22*f*, 143*t*
Rokkan, Stein, 152
Romney, Mitt, 9, 54
Roosevelt, Franklin D., 125,
    131–32, 134–35
Rosenstone, Steven J., 43–44

Schlozman, Kay, 44–45
"Second Party System" (Jacksonian
    Era), 16
September 11 terrorist attacks
    (2001), 154
Seymour, John, 82*f*, 84
short-term forces
  election of 1958 and, 117–18

Global Financial Crisis of 2008 as
    example of, 123*f*, 131, 152–53
Hurricane Katrina and Iraq War as
    examples of, 131, 136, 152–53
  issue debates and, 111–12
  landslide elections and, 113
  media coverage and, 111–12
  nonpartisan impact of, 110–11
  nonpartisan voters and, 103
  partisan vote choice switches and,
    113–14, 118–19
  peripheral voters and, 8, 13, 51–52, 103,
    110–11, 112–14*f*, 112–14, 118–19, 121,
    149, 151–52
Slovakia, 30*f*
Slovenia, 30*f*
Smith, Al, 23
South Carolina, 22*f*, 143*t*
South Dakota, 22*f*, 143*t*
South Korea, 30*f*
Spain, 30*f*
state legislature elections, 2–4, 3*t*, 91
Stevenson, Adlai, 23, 116–17
Stokes, Donald, 13
Sweden, 30*f*
Switzerland, 30*f*

Tennessee, 22*f*, 143*t*
Texas
  Democratic Party performance in,
    81–84, 83*f*, 86
  party identification levels in, 143*t*
  turnout in, 24*f*, 83*f*
  US Senate elections in, 81–84, 83*f*, 86
Tower, John, 83*f*
Trump, Donald
  lack of coattail effects for, 89
  lack of previous experience in public
    office of, 137
  nonpartisan voters and, 6–7
  probabilistic calculations regarding
    turnout in election of 2016 and, 110*f*, 110

resistance movement against the presidency of, 153

white working class voters and, 10–11

Tucker, Harvey J., 52, 56–57

Tunney, John, 82*f*

turnout

African American voters and, 2, 7*t*, 25, 26–27, 31

aggregation fallacy regarding, 55, 65–66

Asian American voters and, 2, 26

bandwagon effects and, 151

candidate support among voters and, 53, 55–56, 149–51

Catholics' rates of, 25

citizenship norms and, x, 1–2

civic duty sentiments among voters and, 46, 54, 103–4, 112

civic education and, 1–2

civic skills among voters and, 44–45

coattail voting and, 129

college-educated voters and, 27*f*, 27–28

conservative voters' rates of, 7*t*, 8, 11

contacts by political campaign and, 43–44, 44*f*, 106–7, 107*t*, 167*t*

conventional wisdom regarding, 4, 5–7, 9–10, 11, 12, 36, 52–53, 75, 76, 78*f*, 92–93, 121, 124, 140, 148–49, 154, 155

cross-sectional correlations, 76

defection rates among voters compared to, 10–11

Democratic Party electoral performance and, 2–5, 8–9, 10–11, 12, 36, 41–42, 48–50, 51, 53–54, 55–57, 59, 60, 61–62*f*, 62–63, 63–67*f*, 64–65, 66, 68–70, 70–72*f*, 71–73, 76–80, 79–83*f*, 81–84, 85–88, 89–93, 95–97, 96*f*, 98–100, 101–2, 108*f*, 108, 109–10, 124, 140, 141, 144, 148, 150, 158–62*t*, 164–65*t*

Democratic Party voters rates of, 7*t*, 8, 11, 65–66, 102–3, 102*t*, 106, 108*f*, 109–10

education levels among voters and, 27–28, 44–45, 104, 104*t*, 107*t*, 167*t*

Election Day national holidays and, 32

election scheduling and, 32, 148

elections of 1952 and, 3–4

elections of 1960 and, 2, 3–4, 19–21*f*, 19, 24*f*, 60*f*

elections of 1964 and, 19–21*f*, 24*f*, 60*f*, 60, 65

elections of 1976 and, 3–4

elections of 1980 and, 19–21*f*, 24*f*

elections of 1992 and, 19–21*f*, 24–27*f*, 114–15

elections of 1994 and, 21*f*, 24*f*, 62–63

elections of 1996 and, 19–21*f*, 24–27*f*, 62–63, 109, 114–15

elections of 2000 and, 3*t*, 4, 7*t*, 19*f*, 21*f*, 24–27*f*, 60–62*f*

elections of 2002 and, 3*t*, 21*f*, 24*f*, 62*f*, 62–63, 96*f*, 163*t*, 166*t*

elections of 2004 and, 3*t*, 4, 7*t*, 19*f*, 21*f*, 24–27*f*, 60–62*f*, 96*f*, 98–99, 99*f*, 163*t*, 166*t*

elections of 2006 and, 3–4, 3*t*, 9, 21*f*, 24*f*, 62*f*, 62–63, 96*f*, 99–100, 100*f*, 163*t*, 166*t*

elections of 2008 and, 2, 3*t*, 7*t*, 9, 19*f*, 19, 20, 21*f*, 24–27*f*, 60–62*f*, 91–92, 96*f*, 97, 98–99, 99*f*, 109, 163*t*, 166*t*

elections of 2010 and, 2–4, 3*t*, 9, 21*f*, 24*f*, 62*f*, 62–63, 96*f*, 97, 99–100, 100*f*, 121, 163*t*, 166*t*

elections of 2012 and, 3–4, 3*t*, 7*t*, 9, 19*f*, 19, 20, 21*f*, 24–27*f*, 60–62*f*, 97*f*, 97–98, 109, 151, 163*t*, 166*t*

elections of 2014 and, 3–4, 3*t*, 8–11, 21*f*, 24*f*, 62*f*, 97*f*, 97–98, 99–100, 100*f*, 121, 163*t*, 166*t*

turnout (*Cont.*)
 elections of 2016 and, 3–4, 3*t*, 6–7, 10, 19*f*, 19, 21*f*, 24–26*f*, 60–62*f*, 97*f*, 97–99, 99*f*, 109, 162*t*, 166*t*
 elections of 2018 and, 3*t*, 4, 21*f*, 24*f*, 62–63*f*, 154
 emotional reactions among voters and, 41, 47
 endogeneity concerns regarding analysis of electoral outcomes and, 149
 expected electoral outcome and, 104*t*
 federalism in electoral system and, 42–43
 government employees' rates of, 25
 gubernatorial elections and, 22, 63*f*, 63–64, 76–77, 80–81, 87*f*, 87, 92–93, 101, 144, 146
 high-income voters' rates of, 7*t*, 8, 11
 high school-educated voters and, 27*f*, 27–28
 incumbency effects and, 18, 61*f*
 interest in politics among voters and, 46, 104, 104*t*, 107*t*, 167*t*
 international comparisons regarding, 30*f*, 30–31, 32
 Jacksonian Era and, 16–17, 17*f*
 Jews' rates of, 25
 labor union members and, 25
 Latino voters and, 2, 7*t*, 26
 legitimacy of electoral outcomes and, x, 2, 11
 LGBT voters' rates of, 26
 liberal voters' rates of, 7*t*, 8
 low-income voters' rates of, 7*t*, 8
 mandatory voting countries and, x, 32–33, 49
 married people's rates of, 25, 102, 104, 104*t*, 167*t*
 middle-income voters' rates of, 7*t*, 102
 midterm Congressional elections and, 3–4, 5–6, 8–9, 12, 20, 21*f*, 22, 24*f*, 62*f*, 62–63, 89, 101, 108, 109–10, 124, 135–36, 135*t*
 military veterans' rates of, 26, 171n8
 minority party benefited by, 144
 moderate voters' rates of, 7*t*
 Nineteenth Amendment's impact on, 18
 nineteenth century rates of, 16–18, 17*f*, 29
 non-high school diploma voters and, 27*f*, 27–28
 nonpartisan voters' rates of, 7*t*, 25, 102–3, 102*t*, 105, 109
 older voters' rates of, 26, 28–29, 29*f*, 36, 45, 104, 104*t*, 107*t*, 167*t*
 partisan vote choice and, 35, 36, 41–42, 47–48, 66, 141–44, 149
 party identification distributions and, 13, 46–47, 52
 political efficacy sentiments among voters and, 46, 103–4
 polling hours and, 42–43
 postgraduate-educated voters and, 27*f*, 27–28
 presidential elections and, ix–x, 3*t*, 5–6, 19, 20, 21*f*, 22, 24*f*, 60–62*f*, 60–63, 68–69, 75, 85*f*, 85–93, 97, 98–99, 99*f*, 101, 108, 109, 124, 144, 146
 probabilistic calculations regarding, 106–10, 107*t*, 108–10*f*
 Progressive Era and, 17–18
 proportional representation systems and, 32–33
 Protestants' rates of, 25
 proximity models of vote choice and, 38–39
 purging of electoral rolls and, 43–44
 regional variation in, 23, 24*f*
 registration regulations and, 29–30, 42–44, 51, 56, 81
 religiously observant individuals' rates of, 25, 102, 104, 104*t*, 107*t*
 Republican Party electoral performance and, 5–6, 9, 48–49, 106, 108*f*

Republican Party voters' rates of, 7*t*,
  8, 11, 46–47, 65–66, 97–98, 102–3,
  102*t*, 106, 108*f*, 109–10, 151
rural *versus* urban voters and, 26, 66
short-term forces and, 13, 51–52, 103,
  110–14, 112*f*, 146, 147*f*
statewide electoral competitiveness
  and, 13, 43
surge-and-decline model of, 121, 129–
  31, 140, 163*t*
Twenty-Sixth Amendment's impact
  on, 18–19
uncompetitive districts and, 32, 69
US House elections and, 12, 61, 62*f*, 75,
  76–77, 78–79, 80, 81, 88*f*, 88, 89–93,
  92*f*, 95–100, 96–97*f*, 101
US Senate elections and, 63–64, 64*f*,
  65, 75, 76–77, 80–84, 82–83*f*, 86*f*,
  86, 91, 92–93, 101, 138*t*, 139–40,
  144, 146
voters' assumptions regarding certainty
  of electoral outcome and, 54
voter's length of residence in a
  community and, 104, 104*t*,
  107*t*, 167*t*
voters' strength of partisan
  identification, 105–7*t*
voting-age population *versus* voting-
  eligible population measures of,
  19*f*, 19–20
weather effects and, 52
white voters' rates of, 7*t*, 8, 11, 26–27,
  31, 36, 102
women's rates of, 25
younger voters and, 2, 18–19, 26,
  28–29, 29*f*, 48–49, 104, 104*t*,
  107*t*, 167*t*
Twenty-Sixth Amendment, 17*f*, 18–19

United Kingdom, 30*f*
US House elections. *See also*
  congressional elections
  in 1956, 116–17

in 1958, 117–18
in 1960, 116–17, 130–31
in 1972, 90
in 1974, 90
in 1980, 90
in 1982, 90
in 1984, 90
in 1986, 90
in 1990, 90
in 1992, 90, 133*f*
in 1994, 62–63, 90
in 1996, 62–63, 90
in 1998, 90
in 2002, 96*f*, 96, 134–35
in 2004, 96*f*, 96, 98–99, 99*f*
in 2006, 91, 96*f*, 96, 99–100, 100*f*
in 2008, 91, 96*f*, 96, 98–99, 99*f*, 131
in 2010, 91, 96*f*, 96, 99–100, 100*f*
in 2012, 97*f*, 97–98, 99*f*
in 2014, 97*f*, 97–98, 99–100, 100*f*
in 2016, 97*f*, 97–99, 99*f*
African American presence in districts
  and, 95, 96, 97*f*, 97–98
coattail voting and, 89–90, 126–27,
  126–27*t*, 128–30
Democratic electoral performance in,
  77, 78–79, 80, 81, 88*f*, 88, 89–93, 92*f*,
  95–97*f*, 98–100, 101
incumbency effects and, 127–29
Latino presence in districts and, 95, 96,
  97*f*, 97–98
median household income levels in
  districts and, 95, 96, 97*f*, 97–98
presidential elections' effects on, 89–
  91, 98–99, 99*f*
redistricting and, 67–68, 76–77,
  95, 177n9
turnout rates in, 12, 61, 62*f*,
  75, 76–77, 78–79, 80, 81,
  88*f*, 88, 89–93, 92*f*, 95–100,
  96–97*f*, 101
younger voters' presence in districts
  and, 95, 96, 97*f*, 97–98

US Senate elections. *See also*
　　congressional elections
　　in 1966, 65
　　in 1970, 65
　　in 1974, 65
　　in 1982, 65
　　in 2006, 65, 91
　　in 2008, 91, 138*t*, 139–40
　　in 2010, 91, 138–39, 138*t*
　　in 2012, 64*f*
　　in 2014, 64*f*, 138*t*, 139–40
　　in 2016, 64*f*, 138–39, 138*t*
　　in 2018, 64*f*
　　campaign spending in, 138–40, 138*t*
　　candidates' decisions to run in,
　　　137, 139–40
　　competitiveness of electorate and, 144
　　constitutional rules regarding, 15
　　Democratic Party performance in, 64*f*,
　　　65, 77, 80, 81–84, 82–83*f*, 86*f*, 86, 91,
　　　92–93, 101
　　economic conditions and, 138–39
　　models of full turnout scenarios in
　　　elections of 1994-98 and, 49–50
　　party identification balance among
　　　voters and, 144
　　presidential approval ratings and,
　　　138–39, 138*t*
　　short-term forces and, 146
　　turnout levels in, 63–64, 64*f*, 65, 75,
　　　76–77, 80–84, 82–83*f*, 86*f*, 86, 91,
　　　92–93, 101, 138*t*, 139–40, 144, 146
　　unemployment rates and, 138*t*, 139
Utah, 22*f*, 142–43, 143*t*

Vedlitz, Arnold, 52, 56–57
Verba, Sidney, 30–31, 44–45
Vermont, 22*f*, 143*t*
Vietnam War, 23, 72–73
Virginia, 20, 22*f*, 125, 143*t*, 174n4

voter turnout. *See* turnout
Voting Rights Act of 1965, 52

Washington State, 22*f*, 29–30, 143*t*
Watergate scandal, 118, 130–31
West Virginia, 22*f*, 143*t*
white voters
　　election of 1988 and, 26*f*
　　election of 1992 and, 26*f*
　　election of 1996 and, 26*f*
　　election of 2000 and, 7*t*, 26*f*
　　election of 2004 and, 7*t*, 26*f*
　　election of 2008 and, 7*t*, 26*f*, 31
　　election of 2012 and, 7*t*, 10, 26*f*, 31
　　election of 2014 and, 10–11
　　election of 2016 and, 10–11, 26*f*
　　Trump and, 10–11
　　turnout rates among, 7*t*, 8, 11, 26–27,
　　　31, 36, 102
　　in working class, 10–11
Wilson, Pete, 82*f*, 84
Wisconsin, 22*f*, 143*t*, 153
women voters, 8–9, 17*f*, 18, 25
Wyoming, 22*f*, 142–43, 143*t*

Yarborough, Ralph, 83*f*
younger voters
　　Democratic Party and, 8–9, 161–62*t*,
　　　164–65*t*
　　election of 2008 and, 2
　　election of 2014 and, 9–10
　　midterm congressional elections
　　　and, 8–10
　　Obama and, 12
　　party identification among, 105*t*
　　turnout rates among, 2, 18–19, 26,
　　　28–29, 29*f*, 48–49, 104, 104*t*,
　　　107*t*, 167*t*
　　Twenty-Sixth Amendment and, 17*f*,
　　　18–19